# Hegel's Rational Religion

# Hegel's Rational Religion

The Validity of Hegel's Argument
for the Identity in Content
of Absolute Religion
and Absolute Philosophy

Stephen Rocker

Madison • Teaneck
Fairleigh Dickinson University Press
London: Associated University Presses

© 1995 by Associated University Presses, Inc.

All rights reserved. Authorization to photocopy items for internal or personal use, or the internal or personal use of specific clients, is granted by the copyright owner, provided that a base fee of $10.00, plus eight cents per page, per copy is paid directly to the copyright Clearance Center, 222 Rosewood Drive, Danvers, Massachusetts 01923.
[0–8386–3637–3/95 $10.00 + 8¢ pp, pc.]

Associated University Presses
440 Forsgate Drive
Cranbury, NJ 08512

Associated University Presses
25 Sicilian Avenue
London WC1A 2QH, England

Associated University Presses
P.O. Box 338, Port Credit
Mississauga, Ontario
Canada L5G 4L8

The paper used in this publication meets the requirements
of the American National Standard for Permanence of Paper
for Printed Library Materials Z39.48–1984.

**Library of Congress Cataloging-in-Publication Data**

Rocker, Stephen, 1953-
　　Hegel's rational religion : the validity of Hegel's argument for the identity in content of absolute religion and absolute philosophy / Stephen Rocker.
　　　　p. cm.
　　Includes bibliographical references and index.
　　ISBN 0–8386–3637–3 (alk. paper)
　　1. Hegel, Georg Wilhelm Friedrich, 1770–1831--Contributions in philosophy of religion. 2. Religion--Philosophy--History--19th century. 3. Philosophy and religion--History--19th century. 4. Absolute, The--History--19th century. I. Title.
　　B2949.R3R55　1995
　　210'.92--dc20　　　　　　　　　　　　　　　　　　　　　　　　　　　　95-16686
　　　　　　　　　　　　　　　　　　　　　　　　　　　　　　　　　　　　　　　　　CIP

PRINTED IN THE UNITED STATES OF AMERICA

# Contents

| | | |
|---|---|---|
| Acknowledgments | | 7 |
| Introduction | | 9 |
| 1. | The Religious-Philosophical Context of the Problem | 17 |
| 2. | The Argument for the Identity in Content of Religion and Philosophy | 38 |
| 3. | Representation | 62 |
| 4. | Philosophy's Sublation of Religion | 112 |
| 5. | Truth | 137 |
| 6. | Hegel's Rational Religion: The Perdurance of Religion in Philosophy and the Actualization of Philosophy in Religion | 164 |
| List of Abbreviations | | 191 |
| Notes | | 193 |
| Selected Bibliography | | 213 |
| Index | | 221 |

# Acknowledgments

I owe a debt of thanks to professors Theodore Geraets and Dale Schlitt, O.M.I., for their advice throughout the course of writing this work, to Christine Morkovsky, C.D.P., for her advice on segments of chapter 3, and to James Crowley for his technical assistance in putting the manuscript together. I wish also to thank Wadhams Hall Seminary-College for the financial backing and leisure to pursue this study. I gratefully acknowledge the permission of the State University of New York Press to include material within chapter 5 that appeared in slightly rearranged form as "The Integral Relation of Religion and Philosophy" in *New Perspectives on Hegel's Philosophy of Religion*, edited by David Kolb (Albany: SUNY Press, 1992).

# Introduction

When the news media deal with religion, it is not uncommon to find religion associated with the irrational. The case is similar in works of psychology, sociology, and history. Often enough it is stated or implied that a religion has adherents because it appeals to imagination, hope, mystery; because it provides consolation; because it bolsters public morality and social order; and because it gives direction to the uncertain and confused. Seldom does the public mind additionally consider religion to make claims to truth available to universal reason. If not opposed to science, religion, in the minds of adherents and detractors alike, dwells alongside science as an uncommunicative neighbor. While sometimes looked upon with respect, religion is often viewed as a private matter based on feelings. Seldom in the public eye is religion viewed as rational, or dignified with the name of "knowledge." So much is religion thought to be separated from reason that it must seem unusual to many to encounter a philosophy that argues on rational grounds that actual religion is rational, and that the Christian religion in particular is the highest expression of the absolute truth available to all people. It must seem more unusual yet when such argument is made not so as to defend religion from the attacks of science but for the sake of knowledge, because religion, it is philosophically argued, is an indispensable means of the human spirit's coming to the truth.

The course of the history of human thought, however, has many apparent ironies. Though the philosophy of Hegel claims to express the absolute truth of Christianity, Hegel's thought has not found wide welcome or approbation among the adherents of Christianity. McTaggart thought that with "friends" like Hegel, Christianity has no need of enemies. Certainly the atheistic developments of Hegel's thinking would not lead one to perceive Hegel as a "Christian philosopher."

The popular perception of religion, the self-understanding of science, the self-understanding of Christianity, and the fact of one or another interpretive development of Hegel's thought are not immediately germane to the study of Hegel's philosophy, although these attitudes and developments create a context in and for which Hegel's thought on religion has present-day interest and importance. By contrast with the present cultural and intellectual context, Hegel's thought, as philosophy, must be investigated and evaluated on its own principles and inner coherence.

This study investigates Hegel's exposition of the relation of religion and philosophy — more specifically, Hegel's argument that the absolute, or Christian, religion and the absolute, or speculative, philosophy are identical in content, though different in form. The central conclusion of this study is that Hegel's claim for the identity in content of absolute religion and absolute philosophy is valid, though this identity must be conceived dialectically in such a way that the content of the Christian religion is recognized to have been reformulated in speculative philosophy. In regard to the meaning and implications of the claim that absolute religion and absolute philosophy have the same content, Hegel's own exposition is found to be underdeveloped such that, upon scrutiny, questions as to the meaning and validity of Hegel's argument may legitimately arise. The fact that there are an ambiguity and a lacuna within a most extensive and brilliant philosophical treatment of religion is not cause for criticism but an invitation for clarification and exposition.

In order to carry through this exposition of the relation of absolute religion and absolute philosophy, this study entails a general explanation of Hegel's philosophy of religion, a development of Hegel's argument for the identity in content of the Christian religion and philosophy according to the principles of Hegel's system of thought, and an interpretation of Hegel's philosophy vis-à-vis the present and future status of religion. In principle this writer accepts Hegel's philosophy, but in an interpretation that clarifies and nuances his thinking. This presentation has necessarily a somewhat different phraseology than Hegel's but lies within the ambit of his thought. Where I differ with a few texts of Hegel I do so on the grounds of his own system. With regard to the content of Hegel's philosophy of religion, my study lies at the more formal level of treatment and focuses upon the relation of religion and philosophy and the implications of this relation for religion. The precise meaning of the sublation of religion in philosophy is ambiguous in Hegel's philosophy, and I attempt to make precise philosophy's sublation of religion in the light of the Hegelian system.

By way of delimitation of the subject, my approach is systematic rather than genetic. The study of the history of the development of Hegel's philosophy and the situating of his thought in its historical context, as well as the study of the reactions to Hegel's philosophy, are of enormous value in sharpening the understanding and discussion of his thought. A philosophical question arises, however, concerning the relevance of such historical-genetic study. A historicist approach would tend to argue that in some way the philosophical and theological concerns of Hegel's time, as well as the subsequent history of critical reaction to his philosophy, relativize or qualify his philosophical claims. A rationalist approach would tend to investigate the arguments in their own right. A Hegelian approach would tend to view the development of Hegel's philosophy and its adoption or adaptation in later thought, not simply as the activity of finite subjects but as the activity of reason itself toward the truth. It seems to me that historical factors cannot be absolutized without leading to contradiction and, in some way, returning to a Hegelian reading of history, so that a historical-genetic reading of Hegel's philosophy must ultimately return to a systematic reading that confronts the arguments in themselves. For this reason I limit myself to a systematic reading.

This study also limits its treatment to religion in general, and to the Christian religion in particular, because its focus is Hegel's claim to identify the content of the absolute religion and the absolute philosophy. It may be that a reader of Hegel's philosophy is offended by his seemingly cavalier presentations of non-Christian religions and his finding Christianity to be the "consummate" religion, but, for philosophical reasons, one should openly approach Hegel's claims and carefully distinguish Hegel's less-than-rigorous comments from his systematically reasoned presentations. The first can be dismissed as unphilosophical: the second must be philosophically confronted and rationally appraised. Further study of Hegel's claim with regard to other religions must be undertaken to appraise fully Hegel's philosophy of religion. In a way this study is a mere beginning for further investigation.

Chapter 1 briefly contextualizes the problem of the relation of religion and philosophy in the history of thought of the Christian West and presents in broad outline Hegel's grounds for the reconciliation of faith and reason. This chapter has the purpose of showing that many elements of Hegel's thought have an integral place in the Christian theological tradition and helps to set in relief Hegel's own answer to the problem of the relation of religious faith and reason.

Chapter 2 presents the argument for the identity in content, and difference in form, of religion and philosophy by a logical exposition of the Hegelian meaning of identity, content, and form and by an application of the logical meaning of these terms to the argument. Chapter 2 demonstrates that the identity of religion's and philosophy's content cannot be conceived straightforwardly but as a complex, dialectical movement from one form-content unity to another form-content unity in which the outer form of religion relinquishes itself to the inner form of thought. The fact of the identity in content is only recognized and grounded in philosophy. While chapter 2 contains the kernel of thought necessary to understand the relation of the Christian religion to philosophy in Hegel's philosophy, the fuller meaning and implications of this relation would hardly be apparent without the elaboration in subsequent chapters of the meaning of *Vorstellung*, or representation, as religion's proper form of expression, the meaning of philosophy's *Aufhebung*, or sublation, of religion, and the Hegelian exposition of truth as the agreement of concept and actuality.

Because religion and philosophy differ in the form by which they express the same content, it is necessary to explicate representation as religion's form of expression. Within our presentation we note a change in tone in the philosophical evaluation of representation from Hegel's *Phenomenology of Spirit* of his Jena period to the thought of his last years in Berlin. This explication entails his discussion of philosophy's own linguistic expression and its achievement in the realm of thought. Chapter 3 argues that Hegel's philosophy transcends the formal limitations of representational language and expresses the basic structures of the order of reality. It is argued, however, that the full historical achievement of the dialectical process is not yet accomplished but is a goal at work in the world drawing the world toward its definitive achievement. The argument is presented that the goal of the dialectic is already achieved in thought to the extent that this goal is available to thought as goal, but the goal is only provisionally achieved with regard to the world.

Chapter 4 treats the meaning of religion's sublation in philosophy. Philosophy is religion's higher moment in the dialectical movement of absolute spirit by which spirit fully reveals itself without admixture of externality or alienation. By responding to certain criticisms of the Hegelian meaning of sublation, it is argued that religion is not eclipsed, or subsumed, in its philosophical elucidation but is preserved in its truth as the concrete means by which humanity is related to God, and religion is stripped only of its irrational accoutrements that hinder the process of concretion of the infinite spirit in and by finite spirit. As sublated in philosophy, religion receives its justification and is preserved as rational religion.

Chapter 5 explicates the Hegelian meaning of truth as the actualization of the concept, the correspondence of the real and ideal, which is the goal of the entire dialectic. It is shown that Hegel's explanation of truth implies that religion and philosophy unite in the goal of reconciling the world with God by bringing the human spirit into self-conscious unity with absolute spirit. In this view, religion, as integrally joined with philosophy in the overarching goal of the truth, has the indispensable role of embodying reason within the concrete life of humanity.

Chapter 6 draws together the conclusions of the previous chapters by an analysis and interpretation of Hegel's reflections at the close of the four series of his *Lectures on the Philosophy of Religion* on the realization of the spiritual community and his argument that "religion takes flight in the concept." By carrying out the implications of Hegel's thinking, it is argued that religion, as justified and sustained by its philosophical elucidation, perdures as the concrete means of the transforming presence of the spirit in the world. This argument is further buttressed by a brief consideration of Herman Hinrichs's philosophy of religion, which draws from Hegel's thought the argument that knowledge and religion unite as the self-manifestation of absolute spirit. Response is then made to claims of the incompatibility of Christianity and Hegel's philosophy. Chapter 6 concludes that religion is related to philosophy as the concrete means by which philosophy's highest revelation of absolute spirit has its indwelling presence in the world. This chapter also briefly considers some concrete implications of this relation for religion.

As regards the editorial method employed in the text, all references to Hegel's works are placed in brackets within the text according to the abbreviations found in the "List of Abbreviations." Standard academic works are referred to parenthetically. Quotations from non-English secondary sources have been translated into English.

# Hegel's Rational Religion

# 1
# The Religious-Philosophical Context of the Problem

## Faith and Reason in the Western Intellectual Tradition before Hegel

It will be of some benefit at the beginning briefly to situate Hegel's understanding of the relation of faith and reason within the wider intellectual history of this relation and to refer back to certain of these ideas in appropriate places as they aid in the exposition of this theme. This presentation of the relation of faith and reason in the Christian West is, of necessity, brief and selective. However, the lines of development that emerge should help to set in relief the precise nature of the Hegelian reconciliation of faith and reason.

Christianity had its early growth in the Hellenistic world and thus came into contact with Greek philosophy. Some of the early church fathers were pagan philosophers before their conversion to Christianity. In general the church fathers were divided in two major groupings in their attitude toward the use and place of philosophy in relation to the Christian faith. One group found the relation of faith to reason, in some fashion, to be congruent and ancillary; the other found the relation antagonistic. Justin Martyr (ca. 100–165) and Athenagoras (second century) belong to the first group, while Tatian (b. ca. 120) and Hippolytus (ca. 170–235) belong to the second. Tertullian (ca. 160–230), an opponent of any reconciliation, posed the famous question What has Athens to do with Jerusalem? and gave us fideism's tersest motto, *Credibile est, quia ineptum est*. Clement of Alexandria (ca. 150–215), on the other hand, sought to transform simple faith into reasoned faith by the use of Platonic, Aristotelian, and Stoic philosophy. Gregory of Nyssa (ca. 331–95) attempted to give rational arguments for all the doctrines of the church.

Among the church fathers who were sympathetic to Greek learning, the attitude was apologetic, i.e., philosophic arguments were used to support the truth that had been revealed in the Christ event. Those Christian thinkers with a favorable attitude toward philosophy considered purely rational argumentation to have an auxiliary, though not a determinative, role in the formulation of Christian doctrine.

St. Augustine (354–430) continued the attitude of looking upon philosophy as a means for understanding Christianity's intelligible content. Augustine's attitude toward the natural human capacity to know in relation to what is revealed is expressed in his famous formula, "Understand, so that you may believe; believe, so that you may understand" (*Sermo* 43, 9; Migne's *Patrologia Latina Sancti Aurelii Augustini Sermones De Vetere Testamento*). According to Augustine, human reason by itself cannot attain the highest truth, which has been given by God in Christ. Human reason is useful in the measure that it leads one to the understanding of the Christian faith; that faith, in turn, guides the mind in uncovering greater truths. By themselves, human beings can know some truth, but the full and unchangeable truth is God, who graciously reveals himself for human salvation. There is a distinction for Augustine between knowledge and wisdom, that is, between knowledge for its own sake and knowledge that leads to salvation. For Augustine, mere intellectual knowledge of God is empty unless there is love of God, the movement of the will toward the greatest good. In other words, knowledge alone is not enough for salvation unless there is divine grace that infuses the human soul with love. The soul must already desire God if it is to be disposed to divine wisdom. Reason, faith, and love must be joined if the human soul is to be healed of the inherent weakness in intellect and will. For Augustine, reason has not an independent role in coming to the truth but rather serves in the self-interpretation of Christian wisdom.

The Augustinian synthesis of faith and reason exerted an enormous influence over the thousand-year course of what is called the medieval period. Though the development of philosophy and its relation to faith in the Middle Ages is a large and intricately woven history, philosophy had always a close, and often subordinate, connection to theology. The Christian outlook was pervasive.

The introduction of the Aristotelian corpus and Islamic philosophy in the twelfth and thirteenth centuries had a stimulating and challenging effect on Christian thinkers who encountered a rich and brilliant body of knowledge that had developed independently of Christian revelation. Throughout the Middle Ages, philosophy would largely continue its auxiliary role to faith, but partly as a result of this influx of non-Christian philosophy, it would more and more come to acquire a status of its own within the Christian milieu.

St. Thomas Aquinas (1225–74) encountered the philosophy of Aristotle and of the great Muslim and Jewish thinkers as a natural light of truth alongside the light of the Christian revelation. The making congruent of these two lights formed Aquinas's intellectual task.

The whole of Aquinas's thought can be looked upon as the attempt to formulate a consistent and systematic relationship between faith and reason. Aquinas belongs integrally to the Augustinian-Anselmian tradition. In this view, faith — i.e., assent to what has been revealed — has priority over human knowledge because the source of faith is God and human learning by itself is prone to go astray. As will be seen, Aquinas adapted this position by placing a greater emphasis on the natural human capacity to know divine truths, while yet maintaining reason's dependence upon revelation for its direction and scope.

While Aquinas found a fideistic attitude mistaken, he also thought a rationalistic attitude misguided. In the Middle Ages, Averroës, for example, represents this latter attitude. Under the influence of Aristotelian epistemology, he had argued that one discerns the truth of revelation (in Averroës's case, Islam) through a rational adjudication of the Qur'an and religious tradition which express truths by means of stories and images (cf. Averroës's *The Decisive Treatise Determining the Nature of the Connection between Religion and Philosophy*). Aquinas's attitude was humbler in that he accepted the living faith-tradition of the church as his supreme guide. He was not blind to the difficulties that the figurative expression of the tradition presents, but he was rationally convinced that reason and the church's faith cannot be opposed. Some points in the Thomistic tradition should be briefly considered.

Because truth has its foundation properly and primarily in the divine intellect, there is in God a unity of thought and reality. Further, creation has its perfection in intellect. Aquinas argued that because it is the nature of good to diffuse itself into other goods, God, the perfect goodness, creates (*Summa Contra Gentiles* I, 37, 5). Moreover, perfect goodness must[1] communicate itself by bringing into being effects that are perfect in their proper order as effects; and because the effect most resembles the divine cause through knowledge,

> it was necessary that the divine goodness be communicated to things by likeness not only in existing, but also in knowing. But only an intellect is capable of knowing the divine goodness. Accordingly, it was necessary that there should be intellectual creatures. (*Summa Contra Gentiles* II, 46, 6)

Furthermore, all things tend toward what is good, and God as the highest good is the highest end, thus all things are ordered to God and tend to become like God (*Summa Contra Gentiles* III, 17–19), and because an intellectual creature "chiefly becomes like [*assimilatur*] God by the fact that it is intellectual, ... to understand [*intelligere*] God is the ultimate end of every intellectual substance" (*Summa Contra Gentiles* III, 25, 8),

While Aquinas's amalgam of faith and reason differs significantly from Hegel's, there are profound similarities. Because of the unity of truth and the intelligibility of reality, one can discern in the order of the world, according to Aquinas, the intelligible motive of its creation and the intellectual nature of the creator. In the order of truths open to the human intellect, Aquinas placed Scripture quotations alongside Aristotle and other philosophers in support of purely rational arguments, and revealed that truths that exceed the grasp of the human intellect, e.g., the Trinity, were shown not to be contrary to human reason. While the tenor of his work was at every moment deferential to the accepted data of the faith tradition, his supposition of the harmony of revealed and natural truth allowed him to bring forth the rational content of the faith tradition even though the Scripture writers could not have intended, or perhaps even have understood, some of his interpretations. Matters of faith that exceed the human intellect were set forth as in principle completely in harmony with reason. Any apparent absurdities in these matters were resolved by rationally making precise what is claimed on divine authority. Excepting these suprarational matters, all other truths were set forth as necessary conclusions of rational demonstration. In all cases, the procedure was rational and ontologically founded upon the unity and intelligibility of reality.

> Since natural reason ascends to a knowledge of God through creatures and, conversely, the knowledge of faith descends from God to us by a divine revelation — since the way of ascent and descent is still the same — we must proceed in the same way in the things above reason which are believed as we proceeded in the foregoing with the investigation of God by reason. (*Summa Contra Gentiles* IV, 11)

Not until Hegel will rational argumentation be as closely tied to Christian revelation in a systematic way.

Hegel's own appraisal of the church fathers and Scholastics is noteworthy. He comments that in the transition from Greek philosophy to Christianity, the church fathers "applied that philosophical profundity of spirit to the teachings of Christianity" (LPR I, 153; V3, 65). In the Middle Ages, Hegel says philosophy and theology were identified. Instead of regarding conceptual thought as hostile to theology, the medievals regarded philosophy "as necessary, as essential to theology itself" (LPR I, 154; V3, 65). Hegel mentions Anselm and Abelard by name and quotes Anselm (in *Cur Deus Homo*) to the effect that a faith is negligent that does not seek to understand what is believed (LPR I, 154; V3, 65).

Except for Anselm, Hegel seems to have had little direct knowledge of medieval thought.

The Thomistic synthesis was a critical acceptance of Aristotle in the cause of Christianity within an integration of the Platonically influenced, Christian theological tradition. Philosophy gained a certain autonomy in that its premises and methods were not drawn from revelation, though philosophy could draw from theology external directions so as to avoid a false course. In this way of thinking, if a philosopher reached conclusions at variance with revealed doctrine, then he felt it incumbent to reassess his premises and/or reasoning or to show how his conclusions were congruent with revealed doctrine. The widespread study of Aristotle's philosophy, however, had the effect of distinguishing theology and philosophy so that the tendency was set in motion for philosophy to develop as an independent discipline and inevitably, at times, to find church teaching no longer a guide but a restriction on free inquiry.

William of Ockham's (1280–1349) philosophy represented, and in turn further contributed to, the late medieval weakening of the bond between faith and reason. His study of Aristotelian logic led him to criticize the natural theology and metaphysics of his predecessors. Ockham argued that rational arguments for God's existence and the soul's immortality were at best probable. Truths that formerly had belonged to the "preambles of faith" were relegated to faith alone, and philosophy came increasingly to have a secular character.

Another factor in the late medieval divorce of philosophy from religion, related in complex ways to the intellectual currents of its time, was the rise of mysticism. The thirteenth-century synthesis of faith and reason seemed to some a rationalistic contamination of the Christian faith so that mystical experience in comparison with rational inquiry was seen as the surer approach to God. Furthermore, the arguments and academic approach of the Scholastics turned some mystical writers away from philosophy toward an emphasis on purely religious experience. Some spiritualities, as that of Thomas à Kempis (1380–1471), were anti-intellectual. Also, the Ockhamist tendency to relegate suprasensible matters to faith contributed to an experiential emphasis in religious life. Of course the lines of this intellectual and religious movement only became clear in the light of its subsequent development in modern times, with the religious and political division of Europe and the rise of secularism.

The rationalism of Descartes (1596–1650) brought to philosophy a new phase, with its epistemological starting point in the subject and its complete confidence in the natural light of reason. Descartes saw no conflict between his philosophy and the teachings of the church. The existence of God and the divine order of the world are integral to the Cartesian system, and Descartes made efforts to undo any apparent opposition between his philosophy and Catholic doctrine, as, for example, his rational justification of the church's teaching on the Eucharist. On the surface, he retained the medieval view that matters that belong solely to faith are best left beyond human reasoning — "the revealed truths which ... are beyond our understanding, I would not have dared submit them to my weak powers of reasoning" (*Discourse on Method*, Discourse 1). Notwithstanding his sincere intentions, the rationalistic spirit of Descartes's philosophy had either to make religious faith a matter of nonrational conviction or to reduce actual religion to a body of rationalistic doctrines.

The latter development is found in Spinoza (1632–77), who regarded religion (Christianity in particular) as superstition because neither could its claims be deduced nor could the idea of a personal and gracious God be made compatible with his metaphysics.

In many ways, Pascal (1623–62) had a far deeper realization of the effects of the scientific-rationalistic spirit of his age on religion, and he had far greater reservations about the power of reason to resolve humanity's deepest questions than did his contemporary, Descartes. By contrast with Descartes, Pascal took ethical and religious concerns as the starting point of reflection. While not opposing faith and reason, Pascal found philosophy inadequate to grasp religious truth. Pascal asserted that the revealed truths of Christianity when accepted and lived provide light to human life. He distinguished two complementary attitudes of mind — the *esprit de géometrie* and the *esprit de finesse* — an analytic and an intuitive form of knowing, respectively. Rationalist logic in its "spirit of geometry" is crude and inadequate to know ultimate reality. For Pascal, it is rather the "heart" that knows religious truth — "the heart has its reasons which the reason does not know" (*Pensées* #277 Brunschvicq/#814 Krailsheimer).

As the inheritors of the Cartesian legacy, the philosophers of the French Enlightenment of the eighteenth century tended to look upon religion as an impediment to intellectual progress, while they looked upon reason as the means to human and social progress. In general, the

Enlightenment had the effect of extending the scientific outlook to the fields of morality, society, and religion.

Hegel sees in the Enlightenment the birth of philosophic autonomy and the intellectual freedom proper to spirit. However his positive regard for the Enlightenment is qualified by the fact that its rationality is that of the finite understanding. Thus, he finds negatively that the Enlightenment has engendered a divorce of knowledge and religious content — the former reserved for the empirical world and the latter assigned to private feelings.

In the *Phenomenology of Spirit,* Hegel points out the one-sidedness of (1) simple belief and (2) what he typifies as Enlightenment thought: insight (*Einsicht*). For him they are opposing moments, which when viewed together show the pathway of spirit's advance. The believer is oriented to God without self-consciousness of his belief. Belief, then is inherently alienated, for it is directed outside itself. Insight, on the other hand, means intellectual penetration by which a spirit sounds its own depths. Pure insight is "the spirit that calls to *every* consciousness: *be for yourselves* what you are *in yourselves* — *rational*" (PS, 328; W3, 398). Insight alone negates everything beside itself and exists for itself alone and hence is contentless, while belief has the content without the self-penetration of insight (PS, 324; W3, 394). Quentin Lauer sums up Hegel's thinking on this point in a paraphrase of Kant's well-known dictum, "Insight without belief is empty; belief without insight is blind."[2]

Because the Enlightenment attitude could not comprehend the ground of faith which is God or spirit, it failed to recognize the true content of faith and attacked the external, contingent elements of faith as though those were the ground of faith. Enlightenment thinking turned the content of faith — namely, "eternal life and holy spirit" — "into an actual, *transient thing*" [*einem wirklichen vergänglichen Dinge*] (PS, 337; W3, 409). The point is that while faith is based on the subject's relation to its absolute object, the rationalistic attitude was incapable of setting the conditions by which faith can justify itself because faith concerns the relation to the infinite or absolute. By contrast with faith, the Enlightenment attitude negated the absolute so as to turn inward on contentless pure insight. The Enlightenment was based on the principle of the understanding which gave a finite meaning to the entire content of religion and *eo ipso* destroyed the proper character of the divine, viz., its infinite character (F-M, 231–33; F-L, 249–50; W11, 48–51). This rationalistic spirit exerted a great influence, even in the teaching of theology in the universities, so that Hegel forcefully criticizes the "rational theologians" of his time who in adopting the spirit of the Enlightenment reduce the content of religion to exegesis and history but no longer possess the knowledge of God: "We would have to compare such theologians with countinghouse clerks, who keep the ledgers and accounts of other people's wealth" (LPR I, 128; V3, 44).

> If faith wants to appeal to historical data in order to get that kind of foundation [i.e., in historical fact], or at least confirmation, of its content that the Enlightenment talks about, and seriously intends [*meint*] and acts as if that were a matter of importance, then it has already let itself be corrupted [or "led astray," *verführen lassen*] by the Enlightenment; and its efforts to establish and consolidate itself in such a way are merely evidences it gives of its corruption [*Ansteckung*] [by the Enlightenment]. (PS, 338; W3, 411)

Because Enlightenment thinking has closed itself to the knowledge of God even in the academic field of the theology of his time, Hegel characterizes the Enlightenment as the "vanity of the understanding" and hence "the most vehement opponent of philosophy" (LPR III, 246–47; V5, 175); and by philosophy Hegel means, literally, "theology," or knowledge of God.

These intellectual currents of the eighteenth century preceding Hegel, which emphasize the empirical elements of religion while lessening the metaphysical dimension of religion's content, provide the background of the problems to which the philosophy of Immanuel Kant (1724–1804) responds. From one perspective it can be said that Kant sought to resolve the conflicting insights of empiricism and rationalism; but Kant recognized a deeper and more significant problem, namely, that the scientific worldview — more precisely, the universal application of the Newtonian method — brought into question the foundations of religious and moral claims. The aim of Kant's philosophy was to rectify the deficiency of empiricism in failing to give theoretical justification to science, as well as the deficiency of science in failing to allow for the validity of religious faith and moral experience. His solution was the distinction of the phenomenal — the realm of experience, of that which appears to consciousness, and the noumenal — the realm of reality that does not appear to consciousness, that is beyond our finite faculties of apprehension, but can be thought. In regard to religion, this distinction of phenomenal and noumenal allowed Kant to reconcile science and religion as they apply to separate realms without interaction, and therefore without conflict.

In order to understand Kant's philosophy of religion and thus the background of Hegel's philosophy, we need to look more closely at Kant's theory of knowledge. In the attempt to give a better account of the order of experience, Kant reversed the assumption that the mind conforms to the objects of experience. He classified the faculties of the mind and the respective scope of each: (1) Sensibility has as its scope the synthetic *a priori* truths of mathematics that state the necessary conditions for the occurrence of perception and the application of mathematics to space and time; (2) understanding produces the synthetic *a priori* truths of natural science that state the necessary conditions for the occurrence of understanding, and; (3) reason produces metaphysical statements that express beliefs and ideals necessary for the employment of reason.

(1) Under the heading of "transcendental aesthetic," Kant argued that space and time are forms of intuition, i.e., they are modes by which we perceive. We recognize that all sense experience occurs in time, in a unidirectional succession, and that all external experience occurs in three dimensions. Perception cannot occur otherwise. All the contents of sense experiences (*Anschauungen*) are in time and space, which are *a priori* forms, or molds that configure the *a posteriori* matter of experience.

(2) In the "transcendental analytic," Kant argued that the modes by which we know and judge are the *a priori* categories of the understanding. These organizing principles of the understanding — as, for example, the categories of substance and causal relation — are the conditions of possibility for the experience of an orderly interrelation of objects.

(3) In the "transcendental dialectic," Kant argued that it is reasonable to think, though impossible to prove, matters which concern the soul, the world as a whole, and God. It is our inclination as rational beings, however, to attempt to know everything, but because the categories by which we synthesize experience apply only to the phenomenal realm and cannot properly be applied to the metaphysical realm, soul, world, and God then are limit concepts, or regulative concepts, of reason — unachievable goals of our desire to know. While we cannot prove metaphysical ideas, we cannot disprove them, and it is reasonable to believe them.

Kant's theory of knowledge resulted in establishing science on the *a priori*, universal structures of the understanding, while the contents of religion and morality lie beyond science, so that we can supply only practical and moral reasons for believing in the soul, the cosmos, and God. Because the understanding extends only to objects of possible experience, Kant said he found it necessary "to deny knowledge, in order to make room for faith" (*Critique of Pure Reason*, preface to the second edition).

Kant's philosophy can be viewed as a blending of the Protestant principle of subjective faith and the Enlightenment thought of empirical, finite reasoning. Philosophy in this view can no longer be the "handmaid of faith" but can only supply the justification for finite, empirical experience. Because the absolute lies forever beyond the attainments of knowledge, faith must be a private, subjective matter.

Kant's "reconciliation" of science and faith was in effect a dichotomous compartmentalization that assigns knowledge to the empirical realm and faith to the subjective realm. Hegel criticizes this supposed reconciliation for failing to do justice to either faith or reason. "The new born peace that hovers triumphantly over the corpse of reason and faith, uniting them as the child of both, has as little of reason in it as it has of authentic faith [*echtem Glauben*]" (FK, 55; W2, 288).

The ground of the problem of Kant's philosophy is the dualism of phenomenon and noumenon and his failure to account for the uniting of the subjective forms of experience with the matter of experience. Hegel points out that in Kant's theoretical philosophy there is the opposition of (A) the formal, *a priori* element (viz., the pure ego-concept) on the side of the subject and (B) the manifold content of experience (which derives from the noumena in an incomprehensible way). In any act of knowing, these two elements, according to Kant, are brought together (A+B). But Hegel points out that this "+" is incomprehensible. If this act of synthesis, the "+", derives from the subject, then it is not a middle, which is what it must be if knowledge is to be possible. In parallel fashion, in Kant's practical philosophy there is the opposition between the *a priori*, formal practical reason (freedom and law) on the one hand, and its opposite (nature, necessity, inclination) on the other. Reason and nature are in absolute antithesis. Reason and nature can be united only on the supposition of a middle which Kant posits as a matter of belief in God. Yet, as Hegel points out, the content of that belief is an "uncomprehensible beyond" [*unbegreifliches Jenseits*] (FK, 91–92; W2, 330). In the Hegelian critique, Kant's philosophy empties thought of spiritual content and leaves the human spirit yearning for truth, the knowledge of God.

This brief and flagrantly incomplete exposition of the relation of faith and reason in the Western intellectual tradition serves only to clarify the peculiar relation between Christianity and reason in Hegel's philosophy and to indicate something of Hegel's own reading of the intellectual past. Obviously many more thinkers — Luther, Böhme, Jacobi, Fichte, Schleiermacher, and Schelling, for example — would need to be considered to understand different approaches to the problem and Hegel's own position. However, our purpose is not to trace the many influences on Hegel's thought but to set forth the problem and to provide a clarification of how it may be answered by way of Hegel's philosophy. Having set forth this background, we can proceed with Hegel's conception of philosophy and of religion.

## The Hegelian Reconciliation of Faith and Reason

*Hegel's Conception of Philosophy*

To define philosophy is not to "define" in the usual meaning of the term — i.e., to set limits to something — since for Hegel philosophy is infinite and eternal, the process of thought grasping itself. Even less so should we think of defining philosophy so as to provide an abstract idea for a multiplicity of singulars, for in Hegelian fashion, philosophy must define itself from within itself in its concrete manifestations. Philosophy is the scientific system of the truth (PS, 3; W3, 14); it is the science of "conceptual cognizing" [*begreifendes Erkennen*] in contrast with opinion (ILHP, 17; H, 27). Hegel's famous statement that identifies the rational and the actual (*wirklich*) (PR, 10; W7, 24) means that philosophy's task is to find in the show (*Schein*) of passing phenomena the immanent, eternal substance (PR, 10; W7, 25). Thus for Hegel, philosophy makes explicit the implicit rationality of the world, or in religious terms, it shows forth the divine order and providence of the world. There is no reality unrelated to thought. Rather, the whole of reality opens itself to "the courage of knowing" [*dem Mute des Erkennens*] (ILHP, 3; H, 6) because "the rational is actual," which is to say that when reality is actualized in thought it is reason's own actualization.

The object of philosophy is the absolute, which is a united, comprehensive movement that operates in, and contains, all its aspects as they express and concretize the absolute. The absolute is reason that unites all the moments of reality as their principle and end. This totally inclusive process and result of absolute reason Hegel calls spirit (*Geist*).

Of course, this truth does not reveal itself to human consciousness until a certain stage in the development of the human spirit has occurred. In the *Phenomenology of Spirit*, Hegel sets out the pathway of spirit in its appearance to human consciousness. But logically and ontologically, reason does not wait upon the slow awakening of the human spirit because what reveals itself to consciousness is the eternal identification of the categories of thought with the order of reality. The *Science of Logic* is Hegel's attempt to articulate the order of reality in its ontological priority to human thought, or, what is the same, to discover in human thought the principle of thought and to set forth its "necessary forms and self-determinations" (SL, 50; W5, 44).

Although there is a history of thought, thought itself is eternal, and although there are many philosophies, there is only one philosophy because the truth is one. In studying Hegel, one must keep in mind the convolution that is present at every moment. Every philosophical articulation has its meaning only in relation to the whole, and the whole is articulating itself in each particular articulation. There is no outside standpoint from which to investigate reason. Philosophy is the investigation of reason and as such is its own ground. No one can learn to swim except by entering the water, and "one cannot make cognition [*Erkennen*] into one's object without thereby behaving cognitively [*erkennend*] at the same time" (LPR I, 139; V3, 53; also LPR I, 169; V3, 78–79; cf. Enc § 10, R).

Philosophy begins the investigation of reason already "in the water." With other sciences, philosophy shares the concern of finding what is universal and constant within the diversity and seeming disorder of the world (cf. Enc § 7). Unlike the other sciences, however, philosophy does not remain at the empirical level but subsumes this level and its laws into the scope of the infinite (cf. Enc § 8) and seeks to comprehend the whole according to the form of necessity (cf. Enc § 9). All other sciences, save philosophy, have their beginning in what is immediate, given, and supposed (Enc § 9). Physics studies nature, history studies the course of human affairs, economics studies the management of wealth: not one of these sciences is absolute — each begins from some defined field of interest. But unlike these sciences, philosophy has as its task the cognition and justification of what is absolute. Philosophy must prove its objects and "indicate the *necessity* of its content" (Enc §1).

Philosophy, then, really has no beginning because any point of departure for philosophic reflection — e.g., art, religion, consciousness, history — must implicitly contain its end. So philosophy is likened to a circle in which its end result is a return to its beginning point, and this circular movement is the life of absolute spirit, the self-demonstration of the unity, necessity, and relation of all things.

For Hegel, the proper beginning of philosophy is the avoidance of falsely thinking that one's beginning is a true beginning, when, in fact, one's beginning has many assumptions. Hegel's insight in this matter is to see that a true beginning implies a process through which one moves toward a result. "The beginning is itself also becoming, it already yet expresses the look back to the further advance [*Fortgehen*]" (Enc § 88, R, pp. 190–91).

Logically speaking, though, philosophy does have a beginning, by which is meant the absolute or the first, within which is contained the whole of reality and the ground of all knowledge (cf. SL, 70; W5, 68–69). This beginning, to be truly the beginning, must contain within itself everything that will come to be, so "that the whole of the science be within itself a circle [*Kreislauf*] in which the first is also the last and the last is also the first" (SL, 71; W5, 70). Once having become a fully articulated unity, the whole of philosophy finds itself where it began. Nothing can be extraneous to the process of its own becoming. The reason (*Grund*) for the beginning of the science of logic must be directly (*unmittelbar*) given in the science itself (SL, 72; W5, 72).

As should be evident, every statement of Hegel's philosophy must be considered in relation to the goal of thought: absolute spirit, which is at once thought's principle. Thus, at the end of the *Science of Logic*, Hegel says that the true beginning is the absolute, which paradoxically is not the beginning but the consummation (*Vollendung*) of the process. This consummation is the concept — the *concipere*, the *begreifen*, the "grasping together" of all the elements in their finality. But the absolute is in the beginning as its implicit goal and is "endowed with the urge [*Triebe*] to carry itself further" (SL, 829; W6, 555). The immanent goal of this process of cognition is the stage that is most concrete and most subjective, which is "pure personality" that "embraces [*befasst*] and holds everything within itself" (SL, 841; W6, 570).

Hegel's philosophy is a system, and the core of this system is his logic, which attempts to delineate reality in the form of pure thought.[3] When Hegel begins his logic with the thought of what is most general and most abstract, what he calls "being,"[4] this thought forces the mind in thinking it to move — to move from what is abstract and empty to the concrete[5] whole. Hence, Hegel calls the beginning becoming, since the beginning expresses its own further development.

> In its beginning, the thing [*Sache*] is not yet, but it is not merely nothing, rather its being is already in the beginning. The beginning is itself becoming, though the look back to the beginning expresses the further advance. (Enc § 88, R, pp. 190–91)

One can see that thought is characterized, defined, by its own movement of negation or dialectic. Because all fixed forms reveal themselves as limited, they dissolve themselves in a process of mediation by thought. Reason is the process of overcoming the negativity in what is immediately given to consciousness. Thus Hegel can say, "Inasmuch as we know something as a restriction [*Schranke*], we are already beyond it" (LPR I, 425; V3, 317). Thinking by its internal workings is thrust outward and upward as it seeks to know reality because each mode of experience and knowledge is found wanting, and the human spirit from within is pushed on to higher modes of knowing. At each level of thought the mind encounters contradiction or opposition (*Widerspruch*), which it must subsume and explain if the human spirit is to move on. An element of the former position is denied so that a new position may emerge. The negation is an incipient recognition of the new, more inclusive position.

While logic is the architectonic of reality as a whole, *"the exposition [Darstellung] of God as he is in his eternal essence before the creation of nature and a finite spirit"* (SL, 50; W5, 44), human consciousness can only become aware of the identity of thought and reality within a historical process which the human spirit in its "look back" can recognize as the concretion of God's eternal essence. Here a question must be presented though it receives only sparse treatment, viz., what is the relation of logic and phenomenology in Hegel's philosophy? According to Hegel in his 1812 preface to the *Science of Logic,* the content of logic is the *"pure essentialities"* [*reinen Wesenheiten*], which in their inner self-movement are the same content of pure knowing (*reinen Wissen*) as achieved by the external movement of consciousness, which is the history of the appearance of spirit (SL, 28; W5, 17). This history of the appearance of spirit — i.e., the *Phenomenology of Spirit* — is the history of spirit in coming to self-consciousness, which at the level of absolute knowledge is the concept (PS, 490; W3, 588). Once having appeared in consciousness, the concept can be given exposition purely as the determinations of thought, i.e., as a purely inner, logical movement (cf. PS, 491; W3, 589).[6]

In one way, logic and phenomenology are related in that spirit's unification of radical self-division is logically complete from eternity yet is in the phenomenological process of its own completion.[7] From the human standpoint, thought has a history by which its eternal logical structure takes concrete form and unites the whole of reality as thought in the process of spirit. "The spirit has time enough ... [and] that it lays out a prodigious expenditure [*ungeheuren Aufwand*] of coming-to-be and passing-away [*des Entstehens und Vergehens*], matters nothing to it" (ILHP, 43; H, 62).

Any phenomenon — of nature, history, art, or religion — can be grasped in its eternal *logos*. The history of philosophy, for instance, when looked upon as a succession of externally and accidentally related ways of thinking fails to grasp the core of the history of philosophy, which is the realization of the concept of philosophy in the concrete history of thought. It is spirit aware of itself as the truth, that is to say, aware of itself as the process of agreement between concept and reality. Though tortuous and laborious, Hegel asserts that the history of philosophy is the awakening of consciousness in the course of time (ILHP, 42; H, 61). But philosophy's temporal course is subsumed within the eternal process that is spirit — not a static eternity but an epochal movement that is "roundabout" [*Umweg*], mediated through the temporal course of natural and human events but transcending every finite event, which is to say, in Hegel's words, that spirit "paints with a large brush" [*treibt sein Werk im Grossen*] (ILHP, 43; H, 62).

*Hegel's Conception of Religion*

It has been necessary to indicate briefly Hegel's conception of philosophy and to refer to the relation of phenomenology and logic within his philosophy in order to proceed to Hegel's philosophy of religion and to an extensive treatment of the exact relation between reason and religion.

Religion for Hegel was a matter of intense and lifelong interest. Moreover, Hegel was a Lutheran by conviction (cf. ILHP, 133; H, 178). To say these things, however, gives little indication of the importance of religion, especially Christianity, in the formation of Hegel's system. Hegel identifies philosophy's content with religion's, and his whole philosophy is a systematic and scientific demonstration of Christian revelation. His terminology and ideas would hardly be thinkable without the religious doctrines of Creation, Revelation, Trinity, and Incarnation and their theological development. Though explanation would be needed, it would not be incorrect to call Hegel a "Christian philosopher."[8] Hegel argues that, when conceptualized, Christianity is speculative philosophy.

In relation to the philosophical tradition of the Christian West, briefly presented above, Hegel is not a Christian apologist who attempts to give rational justification to the Christian faith. Nor is he a philosopher who once having worked out his thought subsequently looks for harmony and contact points with some elements of the Christian faith. Nor is he a "Christian Averroës" who translates the apparent meaning of Scriptural statements and their figurative interpretation into their inner, rational form. Certainly Hegel does the last, but his philosophy is not simply, or primarily, the rational explanation of the Christian faith tradition. In one sense, Hegel does not philosophize *out of* Christianity because his philosophy is a scientific and systematic whole that must be evaluated on its own grounds. In another sense, however, he does philosophize *out of* Christianity in that Christianity is a certain stage in the life of absolute spirit that expresses concretely the inner order of reality, and, because spirit is essentially revelatory, religion is essential in the life of spirit. It is only from the concrete fact of the Christ story and the history of the church that we can look back and think out rationally the inner order of reality. Hence, Hegel says, the story of Jesus cannot be approached in the same way as can the Greek myths.

> There is also something historical [*Geschichtliches*] that is a divine history [*Geschichte*], and indeed so, that is supposed to be history [*Geschichte*] in the proper sense, namely the story [*Geschichte*] of Jesus. This does not merely count as a myth, in the mode of images. Instead it involves sensible occurrences; the nativity, passion, death of Christ count as something completely historical [*Geschichtliches*]. Of course it therefore exists for representation [*Vorstellung*] and in the mode of representation, but it also has another, intrinsic [*an sich*] aspect. The story [*Geschichte*] of Jesus is something twofold, a divine history [*Geschichte*], which should only be taken as the ordinary story [*Geschichte*] of a man, but also it has the divine as its content, a divine happening [*Geschehen*]. (LPR I, 399; V3, 294)

The datum of the Christ event is not incidental to speculative truth. On the contrary, the Christ event is essential, but its truth is not in the show of empirical happenings but in the spiritual meaning of the story of Jesus. Within the history of the relation of philosophy and religion, Hegel's thought cannot be easily categorized. Its uniqueness demands a rethinking of the precise relation between philosophy and religion.

Whatever may be said in criticism, Hegel does not intend to remake religion but to comprehend actual religion according to its concept, according to what it really is. Hegel states quite clearly that religion is not a human invention (*Erfindung*) but the work of God within humanity. Actual religion is begotten by reason — that is to say, by spirit (LPR I, 130; V3, 46) — and for Hegel reason, spirit, and God are synonymous. Because religion is already the product of spirit, Hegel argues that the rational comprehension of religion does not change religion's content but gives it appropriate form by bringing forth what it is implicitly, viz., rational. "The essential content of religion is rational" (ILHP, 30; H, 45) because in its essence religion rises above its ephemeral modes and focuses upon the spiritual — the infinite and eternal truth (ILHP, 29; H, 43).

Religion "is the relation of human consciousness to God" (LPR I, 150; V3, 61). This relationship is not passive but rather an inward movement of elevation (*Erhebung*) or passing over (*Übergehen*) of the human spirit to God (LPR I, 414; V3, 308) by which human persons seek to know and love God and to be known and loved by God. We see in religion, then, two aspects of one movement: the inward movement of the human spirit toward God, which is at once God's own movement within the human spirit. Religion expresses most fully, except as conceptually grasped in philosophy, the Hegelian notion of spirit as unity-in-difference in which absolute spirit and finite spirit are one yet remain different.

While religion can be defined in general, actual religion is concrete and historical and belongs essentially to a cultural-social context because it contains a people's thoughts about the absolute and the human spirit's relation to it (ILHP, 123–24; H, 167). The criterion by which Hegel evaluates concrete, historical religions is the level of the human spirit's awareness of the divine as spirit. Hence, revealed religion is the highest form of religion because its content is spirit or absolute subjectivity as the self-determining movement of diremption and return. By this movement, spirit constitutes itself. "What moves itself is spirit; it is the subject of the movement and is equally *the moving* itself" (PS, 477; W3, 572).

On first encounter, Hegel's philosophy may seem to force the data to fit his scheme, and some critics read Hegel's philosophy as a bed of Procrustes, but Hegel is clear that philosophy's task is "to cognize and comprehend" [*zu erkennen und zu begreifen*] actual religion (*die Religion, die IST*) (LPR I, 91; V3, 10), not to bring forth the foundation (*Grundlage*) of religion but to comprehend the *Sache* that is already *vorhanden* (LPR I, 89; V3, 8). Religion, then, must determine itself according to its concept and not be determined according to one or another subjective way of thinking. Speculatively, the history of religion must be grasped as the *Bestimmung* (determination, definition, and vocation) of the concept of religion. "Determination [*Bestimmung*] [generally is] only a positing of what the concept already is implicitly [*an sich*]" (LPR I, 111; V3, 28). The religion which most fully actualizes the implicit concept of religion is Christianity because in it God is revealed as spirit, the absolute unity-in-difference manifesting itself to and by finite spirit. Therefore, Hegel terms Christianity "the consummate [*vollendete*] religion."

The concept of the Christian religion is the concept of religion *par excellence* because its content is wholly its concept. This content is the divine subjectivity that has itself for its object. Because this content is the absolute subjectivity, Hegel also calls this content "infinite form, the infinite elasticity of substance that enables it to dirempt itself inwardly [*in sich*]" (LPR III, 169; V5, 105). Because the content of the Christian religion is infinite subjectivity, it is essentially revelatory and true. It is revelatory because God is cognized as spirit, as being eternally the process of being for another. Equally, it is true because the object is not foreign to the subject: subject and object are fully adequate to each other (LPR III, 170–71; V5, 105–6).

It is evident that Hegel's concept of the content of the Christian religion when expressed speculatively as philosophical thought is pure, infinite form. "In its pure form it is what is logical" (LPR III, 172; V5, 107). What Hegel says of the content of the Christian religion is identical with what he says in the *Science of Logic* of the logical idea, "whose determinateness does not have the shape [*Gestalt*] of a *content*, but exists wholly [*schlechthin*] as *form*" (SL, 825; W6, 550). Here we see the basis for Hegel's claim that the speculative content of the Christian religion is identical with the content of absolute knowledge. Because the Christian religion is essentially revelatory — having God as spirit, as relational — Hegel can argue that its content is already infinite form but not yet in the appropriate form. Philosophy then does not properly add this infinite form to the religion's content since this form is interior to the content of absolute religion. From the Hegelian standpoint there is no destruction of religion's true content; rather, its content is preserved by the removal of the representational form that is exterior to the infinite form-content. The difficult and complex relation of form and content will be treated in detail below; for now it is enough that we begin to see the manner in which Hegel relates religion and philosophy.

Religion and philosophy share the same subject matter, namely, what is absolutely true. Philosophy differentiates itself from religion by virtue of its grasping the spiritual content in its pure form as absolute spirit. In religion, the objective, spiritual content initially appears as external to subjective spirit; then, through devotion (*Andacht*), subjective spirit is joined to this objective content. Even when religion bases itself wholly upon the knowledge of God and "the witness of the spirit," that knowledge in its religious form is unmediated, or only partly mediated, by thought; by contrast, in philosophy this same knowledge of God (and witness of the spirit) is fully concrete and mediated in the form of spirit (LPR III, 255–56; V5, 182–83).[9] In philosophy, the unity of the objective, spiritual content with subjective spirit occurs in thought (*Gedanke*), wherein subjective spirit "finds itself" in the radical unity of spirit (cf. ILHP, 137–38; H, 185). Philosophy, then, perfects the inner truth of religion, which is the witness of the spirit, by founding this truth without reference to anything outside spirit itself, wholly in the form of spirit. "The witness of spirit in its highest form is that of philosophy, according to which the concept develops the truth purely as such from itself without presuppositions" (LPR III, 256; V5, 183).

Religion apprehends the divine in the mode of *Vorstellung*.[10] While *Vorstellung* lies between *Anschauung* (intuition, or sense perception) and *Denken* (thinking), it is misleading to define *Vorstellung* in general as a pictorial or figurative mode of thought because *Vorstellung* may not always involve a presentation derived from sense experience. Some religious *Vorstellungen* are not essentially linked with the figurative (*bildlich*) or sensible (*sinnlich*), as, for example, historical accounts (LPR I, 399; V3, 294). Furthermore, some *Vorstellungen* are "nonsensible configurations" [*nichtsinnliche Gestaltungen*], such as the creation of the world (LPR I, 400; V3, 295). The essential characteristic of *Vorstellung*, then, is its expression of a spiritual content in a form external to that content. The word *Vorstellung* — which, of course, literally means a "setting before" — suggests this externality of expression to the matter expressed.

When religious representation is viewed in relation to thought, Hegel tends to emphasize the deficiency and misleading nature of what is represented since the object of consciousness "relates itself to it [consciousness] only in an external manner; it is revealed to it as something alien" (PS, 466; W3, 560). As a result, the understanding is prone to retain "the purely external element in faith" and to lose its inner content (PS, 466; W3, 560). In brief, the religious mode of expression is foreign to the content that it expresses.

However, Hegel's criticisms more directly pertain to the understanding in the way it misrepresents religion by interpreting it in the understanding's finite categories of thought, because religion does not veil its truths in myths and images as the understanding superficially supposes. On the contrary, religious representations unveil spirit by showing God to be the answer to the riddles that confront human experience, and they bring the human spirit into the realm of eternal peace where the finite spirit is joined to the infinite (cf. ILHP, 39–40; H, 56–57; LPR I, 83; V3, 3). Moreover, the consummate religion in particular is essentially revelatory: it explicitly reveals God as spirit.

Even though religion and philosophy have the same content and goal — viz., the knowledge of God — religion cannot grasp this content according to its internal necessity but must apprehend the truth in a partly external manner (cf. PS, 466; W3, 560). Religion veils its truth. Philosophy, by contrast, has its object in purely inward form so that the human spirit is inwardly joined to absolute spirit freely, i.e., on its own as spirit rather than by a means partly outside its own spirit. Philosophy, then, is "superior" to religion in knowing the divine since the human spirit has broken through the shell of representations and grasps the essence of spirit in truth and freedom. Religious faith does not know the nature of its own relation to the divine, whereas philosophy comprehends itself and faith (cf. Enc § 573, R).

Many religious people find a philosophical conception of God inferior to the religious awareness of God because, they say, philosophy does not involve the whole person in his or her depths (in the "heart," in Pascal's meaning), in a fully engaged manner. The God of the philosophers is merely an abstract conception that has not the deeply personal character of the God of religious faith, as Pascal asserted. Certainly this objection has weight and must be faced. But Hegel's claim is that the rational conception of the divine breaks through the abstract, finite, inadequate categories of reflective thought. Because spirit is one, and religion is most genuinely itself when it follows the inherent thrust of the human spirit toward absolute truth, purely rational knowledge is the perfection of the concept of religion. Philosophy shows the necessity of religion, and in so doing, philosophy is the destiny and truth of spirit that has been advancing in the religious mode of expression (LPR I, 90; V3, 8–9). Rational comprehension is the destiny and the ground of religion. Truth is one, and thus there cannot be religious truth that is somehow different from philosophical truth. "There cannot be two kinds of reason and two kinds of spirit," but only divine reason in human reason (LPR I, 130; V3, 46).

It belongs to philosophy to demonstrate how the same spirit is at work in religion and philosophy and so to overcome any apparent opposition between religion and philosophy. The church and theologians may disdain the insights of philosophy, but in fact "philosophy wants to ground the truth of religion," and Hegel calls the reconciliation of religion and philosophy the "triumph of *Erkenntnis*" (LPR I, 131; V3, 47).

The differing claims of religion and philosophy cannot be held in abeyance by a kind of treaty of noninterference because the human spirit cannot be satisfied with less than absolute truth. If religious claims cannot be supported by rational investigation, then religion has no claim to truth and hence no grounding. "There is no ground for supposing that faith in the content or in the doctrine of positive religion can still persist when reason has convinced itself of the contrary" (LPR I, 134; V3, 49–50).

The precise meaning of Hegel's reconciliation of religion and philosophy and his transfiguration of religion's content into rational form have to be taken up in greater detail later. For now it is enough to state his basic arguments and to recognize that there is an apparent ambiguity in the Hegelian treatment of the content of religion that we must investigate and clarify, namely, that the content changes and that the content does not change when expressed in the pure form of thought. This ambiguity arises because the meaning of the content of religion is complex and requires a making precise of the relation of the determination of form and content within the content itself.

## *Hegel's Conception of the Philosophy of Religion*

Lastly by way of introduction, something should be said of Hegel's conception of the philosophy of religion. Whether or not Hotho's statement is trustworthy that Hegel claimed to be the first to make religion the object of philosophical consideration (LPR I, 33; V3, 33), it is true that Hegel treated religion as such from a philosophical standpoint unlike any of his predecessors. Kant, for instance, largely reduced religion to ethics, while Hegel investigates the concrete forms of religious experience, faith, and worship with utter seriousness as a philosopher. The reason for investigating religion is integral to Hegel's entire philosophy because God as spirit can only be known as he reveals himself. A rational consideration of God apart from God's concrete manifestation in religion yields only a sterile, abstract conception of God (LPR I, 116; V3, 33). Hence, philosophy of religion takes as its object God, not simply in an abstract form of thought "but also in the form of his manifestation" (LPR I, 119; V3, 36), as he actively relates a community of believers to himself (LPR I, 116; V3, 33). In the other branches of philosophy, the appearance of God is the result of their investigations, but the philosophy of religion begins with the appearance of God in concrete religions. Thus it begins with the representation of God and seeks the meaning of this representation not only as God is *an sich*, as the logical idea, but also as God is *für sich*, in his appearing (LPR I, 119; V3, 35), because it is of the essence of spirit to appear.

# 2
# The Argument for the Identity in Content of Religion and Philosophy

### The Setting Forth of the Argument

As indicated above, the problematic nature of the relation of religion and philosophy is as old as the history of philosophy in the Western world. Hegel's reconciliation of religion and philosophy, however, takes its specific form in answer to the religious and philosophical thought of his time. We can add that these attitudes and forms of thought are in the main present today as well.

In the 1807 preface to the *Phenomenology of Spirit* and in the 1812 preface to the *Science of Logic*, Hegel notes with regret the loss of "the heaven-ward gaze" of science. There was a time, he says, when "the eye of the spirit had to be forcibly turned and held fast to the things of this world," whereas now "sense is so fast rooted in earthly things that it requires just as much force to raise it" (PS, 5; W3, 16–17). The Enlightenment had wrought a great change in thought by applying in universal fashion the thought of the natural sciences. It attacked actual religions as superstition that blinded humanity to its power of free thought and its latent capacities to know the world and shape it in rational form. The result of this intellectual outlook was a greater concern with this world and its empirical phenomena. In philosophy this attitude removed metaphysics from "the ranks of the sciences." Kant's philosophy in particular, by confining the understanding to experience (*Erfahrung*), justified in general education "the renunciation of speculative thought" and an exclusive emphasis on practical matters. Hegel finds the lack of metaphysical concerns within the science of philosophy comparable to "a temple richly ornamented in other respects but without a holy of holies" (SL, 25; W5, 13–14). Philosophy and the other sciences then had become increasingly less concerned with the knowledge of the divine. The concomitant development was religion's finding its satisfaction in feeling. Theology, the science which once safeguarded metaphysics, had become largely engaged with feelings and historicity (SL, 25–26; W5, 14). In place of the science of metaphysics, religious thinkers sought the divine spirit in feelings and intuitions — "the absolute is not supposed to be comprehended [*begriffen*], it is to be felt and intuited" (PS, 4; W3, 15). Hegel has in mind such thinkers as Jacobi and Schlegel and would later apply the same criticism to Schleiermacher. In Hegel's estimation both the philosophy and the theology of his time had cut themselves off from the knowledge of God, and Hegel views his own work as laying a new foundation for philosophy's proper task — the knowledge of God.

The common goal of religion and philosophy to unite the human spirit with God is the basis for Hegel's reconciliation of religion and philosophy. Spirit is one, and it is of the nature of spirit to reveal itself to finite spirit. Thus philosophy's intellectual quest for the truth is part of the same spiritual process that guides the religious quest for the truth in its representational and cultic modes. "Philosophy is only explicating [*expliziert*] itself when it explicates religion, and when it explicates itself it is explicating religion" (LPR I, 152–53; V3, 63). Hegel goes so far as to say philosophy is *Gottesdienst* (LPR I, 153; V3, 63–64) because like religious worship, it too is the "service of God," though in the form of thought. Philosophy does conceptually what religion does cultically and ethically, viz., join the human spirit to the divine.[1]

Because religion is the consciousness (*Bewusstsein*) of God, religion is integral to the process of *Wissenschaft*.[2] This *Bewusstsein* of God, literally "being conscious" of God, is the being of the activity of consciousness that is at once the being that is given to consciousness. Philosophical knowledge in its goal is absolute knowledge wherein the separation of God and the human spirit is overcome so that the content of consciousness is consciousness itself as absolute spirit and beyond the distinction constitutive of consciousness.

Hegel's claim, then, that religion and philosophy are identical in content rests upon the claim that he explicates throughout his entire philosophy: that absolute spirit is multiform but one in activity, and that activity is its self-revelation. The historical antithesis of religion and philosophy results from the understanding's fixation upon the form of religion, its use of images and figures to express what transcends these limited representations. The antithesis results as well from the understanding's inability to comprehend religion's spiritual content.

Religious representation is a partially spiritual expression of a fully spiritual reality. The representation, then, is internally at odds with its content. Within each religious tradition the believer realizes in some degree that the expressions used for divine matters are not meant literally but point beyond themselves. All religious representation is finite and to some degree external to the divine. This fact is characteristic of all religious awareness as instanced in humanity's unhappiness in being set over against God and in the religious recognition of humanity's need to be related to God. Religion is the awareness of being related to God while yet being in a condition of separation from God.

Religions and their myths, symbols, signs, and analogies are not equal but are categorized as they more or less perfectly reveal God and his activities as spirit. Because it is the nature of spirit to disclose itself wholly to spirit, Hegel argues that revelatory (*offenbare*) religion is the perfection of religion as religion. In other words, revelatory religion is the realization of the concept of religion (LPR I, 146; V3, 59). Religions and their forms of expression are evaluated according to the degree of their realization of the concept of religion. While at first sight Hegel's evaluation of actual religion appears as an external criterion imposed from the rational standpoint, he claims only to bring to light the course by which the concept "has forced [*gedrängt*] itself into the world in order to bring itself to consciousness of itself.... A purely philosophical treatment" must be, Hegel claims, only "a treatment of what is" (LPR I, 146; V3, 59).

The reconciliation of religion and philosophy is based, then, on the speculative thought of what religion is, namely, God's coming to self-consciousness through human consciousness. Religion's self-understanding is grounded in speculative philosophy's recognition that God works the relationship of God and humanity by lifting up the human spirit to the divine in the divine's own process of realization. Because religion and philosophy are the means for absolute spirit to reveal and to realize itself, they are identical in content. The philosophical expression of religion's truth is the outcome of the internal process of the concept of religion.

Religion itself manifests this process toward rational expression because representational expression of absolute truth contains within itself its own self-transcendence. Hegel notes that, while many brilliant minds have found satisfaction in religious truth, the human spirit also seeks further satisfaction in rational insight so that the truth is no longer external or contingent to oneself (cf. LPR I, 250; V3, 158–59).

The seeming contradiction of religious and philosophical truth is resolved for Hegel, as always, in dialectical fashion. It is philosophy's role to transmute (*verwandeln*) the content of religious representation into thought. Religion is the self-consciousness of absolute spirit in representational form. Speculative philosophy is the same self-consciousness of absolute spirit but in conceptual form (LPR I, 333; V3, 235).

In changing the form, does philosophy change the content? This is the question to be answered. It is clear that Hegel was fully aware of the difficulty that comes forth when philosophy tries "to separate in a content what belongs to the content as such, which is thought, from what belongs to the content of the representation as such" (LPR I, 404).[3] To ordinary consciousness, the transformation (*Umformung*) may seem to be destruction, but that is clearly not Hegel's thinking on the matter (LPR I, 404; V3, 299).

The precise way in which Hegel's claim can hold true must be investigated. A number of critics are convinced that Hegel's speculative rendering of Christian doctrines radically alters these doctrines. Hegel may use the traditional terms for doctrines of the Christian religion, they claim, but the meaning is only Hegel's.[4] Charles Ping, for example, claims "this rational philosophy of religion, far from receiving the content of religion, determines the content for itself."[5] In Ping's appraisal, for example, Hegel's speculative transformation of Christian faith subsumes the uniqueness of the Christ event into the universality of the idea, making Christ a derivative notion of the Hegelian system. Ping adopts a Kierkegaardian critique of Hegel. These criticisms will be dealt with more at length later, but it is sufficient for now to note that there are many who argue that Hegel's transformation of Christian doctrines is a "transubstantiation" as well.

It has been noted before but merits repeating that the philosophy of spirit cannot be merely a philosophy of God in the abstract but must be a philosophy of God in the concrete. It must be a philosophy of religion in which the object is God as he has revealed himself, God as spirit (cf. LPR I, 115–20; V3, 33–37). Philosophy cannot explain itself apart from religion; nor can religion explain itself apart from philosophy.

The self-explication of the concept of religion follows the one method of all science. Parallel to what is done in the *Encyclopaedia of the Philosophical Sciences,* § 566 and following, Hegel applies the method of the self-explication of the concept in three moments to the philosophy of religion. The first moment is the concept in itself as universal, compared to a seed that internally contains its teleology. The second is the determination of the concept as it develops in finite forms that are externally connected. The third is the reestablished (*wiederhergestellte*) concept as the true infinite that contains in unity its moments of differentiation (cf. LPR I, 174–76; V3, 83–84). The three moments of the concept are the logical basis for Hegel's phenomenology of religion — the rational means by which to grasp the appearance of actual religions. Hegel's *Lectures on the Philosophy of Religion* are structured according to the logical basis of religion: first, the concept of religion, which treats the universal form of religion; second, determinate religion, which describes particular religions as these contain "the path to the concept, religion only in terms of the stages of this path, the limited forms" (LPR II, 95; V4, 2); and third, the consummate religion, in which actual religion is perfectly at one with its concept, in contrast to determinate religions in which each is only a partial realization of the concept.

The concept of religion in general unfolds in three moments that correspond to the three moments of the concept in general as outlined in the second part of the *Science of Logic*.

> In the first instance, it is the *pure concept* or the determination of *universality*.... Because the concept is a totality, and therefore in its universality or pure identical self-relation is essentially a determining and a distinguishing [*Unterscheiden*], it therefore contains within itself the standard by which this form of its self-identity, in pervading and embracing, no less immediately determines itself to be only the *universal* over against the distinguishedness of the moments.
>
> *Secondly*, the concept is thereby posited as this *particular* or *determinate* concept, distinct from others.
>
> *Thirdly, singularity* is the concept reflecting itself out of the difference into absolute negativity. This is, at the same time, the moment in which it has passed out of its identity into its *otherness*, and becomes the *judgement*. (SL, 600–601; W6, 273–74)

In the concept of religion in general, then, these three moments are (1) God *a se* as undifferentiated universality, (2) the self-differentiation of the content of religion into the human subject and the divine object, and (3) the reestablishment of the unity between God and the human in worship. Because the concept of religion is the self-mediation of absolute spirit, the absolute realizes itself in the movement from self-unity to self-differentiation to self-reestablished unity.[6]

The first moment cannot properly be a moment of religion because religion arises only in the relation of God to finite consciousnesses. But the universal is essentially a distinguishing and explicitly contains this distinguishing, so that from the religious standpoint we can think back to God as abstract and universal — a thought that is present in some form in every religion. The second moment concerns the awareness of God in the division of the human subject and the divine object. Religious awareness arises through the mode of representation by which we know God and yet are separated from God. The third moment is the practical stage of the cultus by which the human subject in his or her heart is reconciled with God.

While the entire course of spirit's self-mediation is contained in the concept of religion in general, the concept has to realize itself gradually and partially in determinate religions as these are the necessary means for the full actualization of spirit. "Determinate Religion" then is the second major division of the *Lectures on the Philosophy of Religion*. The complete reconciliation of concept and reality takes place in revealed religion, where the content of religion is fully one with the concept of religion, i.e., the unity-in-difference of God and humanity as expressed in the Incarnation. Thus "The Consummate Religion" is the third major division of the *Lectures*. We are able to reason to the concept of religion *per se* and to discern the necessary, inner connection of religious phenomena because the concept has been made manifest in the Christian religion. What at first appeared to us as a succession of externally related events now from the standpoint of its concrete result reveals its logical beginning, which eternally contains the circular course of its entire development.[7]

This logical form of religion (which is the truth-content of religion) frees itself from the confining form of representational expression through philosophy's explication of religion. For Hegel it is not that philosophy transforms religion into pure thought but that religion transforms itself by the internal dialectic of the concept of religion. Because the content of revealed religion is spirit, it follows that the essential structure of rational thought[8] and the forms through which thought develops itself are implicit in the content of the Christian religion.

Religion in its characteristic mode of finite representation cannot bring about by representational means its transformation into thought and its reconciliation with philosophy. The overcoming of the antithesis of religion and philosophy "is to show forth the rationality of religion [*die Vernunft der Religion zu zeigen*] ... to reconcile reason with religion in its manifold forms [*Gestaltungen*]" (LPR III, 247; V5, 175). While this reconciliation must occur in the pure categories of rational thought, it is the outcome of the one spirit at work within religion and philosophy. This unity of spirit is the basis of Hegel's synthesis of religion and reason. In this synthesis, philosophy has the advantage over religion in knowing its true content rather than merely representing it and believing it (ILHP, 141; H, 192).

> Philosophy indeed can cognize its own forms in the categories of the religious representational mode [*Vorstellungsweise*], and even its own content in the content of religion and give it its due; but not conversely, the religious representational mode does not apply the criticism of thought to itself and does not comprehend (*begreift*) itself, and in its immediacy is therefore exclusive. (Enc § 573, R, p. 381)

Here we touch upon the much-discussed issue of precisely how in Hegelian thought philosophy is superior to religion. The full working out of this issue must wait upon the presentation and development of a number of elements in Hegel's philosophy. Further, a satisfactory resolution of this issue for contemporary philosophy and theology must draw out the lines of what is implied and underdeveloped in Hegel's thinking on this matter, though clearly Hegel's thinking is of enormous value in helping to think through this matter. By way of setting forth the problem now and anticipating our answer, we should note the following.

The "superiority" of philosophy to religion is in the comprehension of religious truths. Philosophy has the form of thought; religion does not. While philosophy can understand itself and religion, "religion does not understand philosophy" (ILHP, 142; H, 192). Because philosophy conceives the divine on its own resources — that is, it bases itself upon reason alone without dependence upon representations — philosophy reconciles religion with itself in the unity of truth and thus is religion's "inherent justification" (ILHP, 147–48; H, 199). Philosophy justifies religion because the absolute truth of religion cannot be founded upon contingent pictorial and historical forms.

To the religious mindframe, this setting of religion's justification seemingly outside itself appears as an arrogation on philosophy's part when, in fact, the religious critics of Hegel argue, the truths revealed in Christianity, such as the Incarnation and Trinity, were not reached by purely rational means, and it is questionable whether human reason without benefit of revelation could have arrived at them. This objection is true but not incisive. The preeminence of philosophy over religion is not chronological or genetic in foundation but logical and ontological and concerns only the form of religion's mode of expressing the truth. Furthermore, philosophy does not impose itself upon religion from outside since (1) religion is implicitly rational in its quest for absolute truth, (2) "the philosophy of modern times ... has arisen within the Christian world" (ILHP, 142; H, 192), and (3) doctrinal and theological developments demonstrate religion's own need to harmonize its faith with reason, as for example, "the Scholastics ... comprehended [*haben ... begriffen*] the Church's dogma in thought" (ILHP, 141; H, 192).

The agreement of religion and reason, a oneness in truth, cannot be established or demonstrated except from the standpoint of reason, which is properly the standpoint of philosophy. It is not a matter of harmonizing a philosophy with the given of faith, as was the case for the early church fathers. The issue is rather the determination of the truth of Christianity, and that is, and has always been, a work of reason. For Hegel, reason in relation to religious revelation has the character of neither a *via negativa* nor a *praeparatio evangelica*; rather, it has a positive and internal role in receiving revelation since it is the nature of spirit to be wholly manifest, that is, perfectly intelligible. Reason is the ultimate justification of religion, for if it does not express the truth, religion has no claim to allegiance, and all the other reasons to believe — feeling, enthusiasm, cultural identity, desire, security — cannot hold. While religious people may think Hegel's philosophy displaces religion (an issue that will be discussed), in fact, for Hegel philosophy sustains religion by bringing forth its true content. "Sustained [*erhält*] by philosophy, religion receives its justification from thinking consciousness" (LPR III, 346; V5, 268), or, as Hegel strikingly expresses this point at the end of his *Lectures on the Philosophy of Religion*, the content of religion "takes flight into the concept." Whether in fact Hegel succeeds in preserving the authentic content of religion through the speculative change in form is the question we will investigate, but it is only philosophy, not religion, that can judge the question.[9]

## The Elements of the Argument

### Religious Content and Its Speculative Transformation

When people profess a religious belief or profess disbelief or doubt, there must be a content or objective reference of this belief, disbelief, or doubt. In the Christian religious tradition, this content has been set forth in creeds and articles of faith (though even without such a formal and systematic presentation the faith is recognized as having content). When people profess a faith, as for example, in the creed, We believe in one God, presumably they profess the same thing, even though those who are making a sincere profession are of differing levels of maturity, intellectual sophistication, and cultural background — children and adults, uneducated and well educated, second-century Greek, twelfth-century Italian, twentieth-century Papuan. Certainly there are differences not only in how they believe, but in precisely *what* they believe.

Nonetheless, *what* they believe is in some fashion the same. If the *what* is not the same, then people are merely using the same words and/or participating in the same actions without objective reference.

We see, then, that in speaking of the content of religion (for our specific purposes, the content of the Christian religion), we must distinguish objective and subjective elements. We distinguish two elements of religious faith: to wit, the apprehended and the apprehending. That is, we can speak objectively of what is apprehended in belief and subjectively of the mode in or by which it is apprehended.

Further, we need to distinguish faith and knowledge. We take it as evident, as Aquinas (*Summa Theologiae* 2a2ae, I, 4–5) and others have shown, that no one can both believe and know the same thing at the same time. Believing and knowing are mutually exclusive acts of human consciousness. Hegel gives his own more specific development of this fact. According to Hegel, faith means that there is the subjective certainty of faith's object. Faith rests upon an imperfectly mediated testimony of the spirit. Knowledge, by contrast, means insight into the necessity of the objective content of what is known (LPR I, 388; V3, 284). Faith possesses its content in a form not wholly mediated by thought. But Hegel notes that when speaking of the Christian faith one is not speaking of a merely subjectively immediate content but an objective content that to some degree has been mediated by thought. "The Christian faith entails an authority of the church," and moreover this faith is "an objective, in itself rich content, a system of doctrine and of cognition" (Enc § 63, R). What one believes on the testimony of the spirit is true but is not explicitly known in the form of truth. Faith and knowledge then are not opposed but are different levels in the progressive activity of the one spirit.

Because religious faith is a subjectively different mode of apprehending the divine than is knowledge, the confusion develops that religious belief arises from feelings rather than from an objective content. Hegel spent great energy countering this view in order to show that faith has its basis in thought. Feeling concerns the nature and degree of personal involvement of a subject in a content. Feelings as such are not good or bad, right or wrong, and so feeling cannot be the basis of religion because feeling as such can be as much religious as irreligious. Feelings must be about "something," and that something has an ontological priority when one is searching out the foundations of religion. Clearly the content of a feeling can be separated from its subjective locus, which indicates that feeling as a form is external to its content. "Any content can be in feeling, just as it can be in thought generally" (LPR I, 390; V3, 286).

In order to develop Hegel's argument that the essential content of religion is thought and to provide the ground for the identity of content through speculative transformation, it is necessary to consider more closely his attack against those who sought the foundation of religion in feeling.

Hegel offers a simple proof that religion is essentially rational and cannot be founded upon feeling. He reasons that because human beings are distinguished from the animals by thought, and we are religious creatures by that which is distinctively characteristic of us, then thought is of the essence of religion. Conversely, because animals have sensation (*Empfindung*) and feeling (*Gefühl*), they should not be incapable of religion if religion were a matter of sensation or feeling (LPR I, 209–10; V3, 118). No doubt, in the 1821 lectures, Hegel has Jacobi in mind, among others, and in the later lectures, Schleiermacher, as the object of his criticism.[10]

Hegel makes the same point in the 1824 lectures but within the context of a more extensive polemic against subjectivistic theologies. God is for thought, not feeling, because "only human beings, not animals have religion, and humanity distinguishes itself from the animals by thought" (LPR I, 273; V3, 178–79).

In these 1824 lectures, Hegel amplifies his demonstration of the inadequacy of feeling as a basis for religion and makes more precise the place of feeling within religion. Feeling is a form that may receive various contents, and the content it receives is contingent or accidental to the form of feeling, so that God as a content of feeling has no superiority to any other content of feeling (LPR I, 272; V3, 177–78).

Hegel readily acknowledges that religion should be in one's "heart," but he makes clear that "heart" does not mean the coming and going of momentary and fickle feelings. On the contrary, when Hegel explains what it is to have a content in the heart, it reminds one of Pascal's use of "heart," wherein the individual in his or her deepest self is identified with the content "as a continuing, fixed mode of my existence" [*als fortdauernde, feste Weise meiner Existenz*] (LPR I, 174; V3, 178–79).

It is manifest from what Hegel says that the content of religious subjectivity is the supremely important matter for the foundation and definition of religion. When considered in isolation, feelings are simply empty forms that may be occupied equally well by good or bad, true or false contents. If truth is the holding fast on the part of the subject, as Kierkegaard would later claim, then the basest convictions are on a par with the noblest in the measure that they are equally held fast. Clearly, such a subjectivistic notion of truth and religion is antipathetic to Hegel's whole philosophy.

Faith, then, is not simply a subjective orientation but the unity of the subjective form of certainty and the objective creedal content. At first, "the genuine content" [*der wahrhafte Inhalt*] of faith is given externally in representation and memory and then becomes for the subjective consciousness "something interior, that has occupied and pervaded the heart [*das Gemüt*] and in that truth finds itself in self-consciousness and in its essential, permanent being [*Bestand*]" (F-M, 228; F-L, 246; W11, 43–44).

The 1822 essay quoted here, which Hegel wrote as a foreword to Herman Hinrichs's *Die Religion im inneren Verhältnisse zur Wissenschaft,* is a concise statement of Hegel's conception of the relation of faith and reason. It criticizes the attempt to found religion apart from a rational knowledge of God by showing the emptiness of religion and philosophy without the knowledge of God. Without such knowledge, the [human] spirit is left "partly with appearances and partly with feelings for only its sustenance [*Ergehen*]" (F-M, 228; F-L, 245; W11, 42).

Clearly, the "needs of the spirit" motivate Hegel to restore the knowledge of God to religion and philosophy which are "empty shells" without this knowledge. He is acutely, and even painfully, aware that because faith and reason touch the depths of human consciousness, disharmony between them is disharmony in the human subject that cannot be satisfactorily allayed save by being reconciled according to the demands of the spirit. As one studies Hegel, it becomes increasingly manifest that he is responding to a deep and pervasive existential problem that most of his contemporaries and predecessors seemed not to have discerned with the same shadowless clarity, viz., that the human spirit must, by its own deepest drives, be scientific and religious, and that any opposition between these drives engenders profound discord in the human spirit. If faith and reason avoid conflict by faith's renouncing any claims to substantial meaning and by reason's renouncing any claims to truth, then the absence of conflict is "a superficial barren peace," with the result that the opposition of faith and reason has been "overlooked, ... not overcome" (F-M, 227–28; F-L, 245; W11, 42).

Having shown that feeling is a form external to the divine content of religion, we have yet to seek to distill the content of religion that Hegel claims to be transferable into philosophy. This transference cannot be simple because of the inextricable connection of form and content. The *content* of religion is the content *of religion*, i.e., it has its determination as religious. Hegel has pointed out the mistake made by the understanding in thinking that the content of anything is essential and independent while its form is unessential and dependent. In distinction from matter that cannot exist without form yet can be thought in abstraction from form, content "is what it is only because the matured [*ausgebildete*] form is included in it" (Enc § 133, *Zusatz*).[11] There is an essential correlation of form and content that can, as Hegel indicates, be seen in everyday experience, e.g., when we recognize that a genuine work of art is one whose form and content are thoroughly identical or when we recognize that *Romeo and Juliet* as the story of two tragic lovers has its greatness in the form Shakespeare gives to this story (Enc § 133, *Zusatz*).

On Hegel's own grounds, how then can we change religion's proper form without thus changing its content? The question arises as E. Fackenheim has presented it when he says that if the representational form is essential to religion then philosophy cannot transform religion into philosophy without loss of religion's content: if philosophy does so transform the representational character of religion, then it would seem the representational form is unessential to religion.[12] As we will see, the identity in content cannot be conceived straightforwardly but only as a mediated, dialectical identity or identity-in-difference.

> It would be a simplistic misunderstanding of the Hegelian concept of the identity of content between religion and philosophy if that identity were conceived as a tranquil, constantly available tautology. This identity is to be understood as a "dialectical," living identity, one not excluding difference, but itself fully realized only as the result of a process of mediation.[13]

This identity in content is analogous to the personal identity of one's lifetime, which is the same through the change in moments from childhood to old age. This image is one Hegel himself uses to describe the absolute idea as its method or course of development. In looking back, the absolute is contained in each of its moments but only emerges as fully developed in its outcome as the old man who

> pronounces the same religious statements as the child but for whom the meaning has his whole lifetime ... and what we have now is the knowledge that the content is the living development of the idea. This simple retrospect is contained in the form. Each of the stages hitherto considered is an image of the absolute, but at first in a limited mode, and thus it drives itself onward to the whole, the unfolding of which is what we termed method. (Enc § 237, *Zusatz*)

The logic, the method of the absolute, is the structure of reality and the foundation for Hegel's claim that the true content of religion is identical to the content of philosophy, an identity enriched and fulfilled through the necessary course of its concrete manifestations.

*The Logical Elements*

IDENTITY

In the *Science of Logic* (411 f; W6, 38 f), Hegel shows that any assertion of identity implies distinction. Sheer identity, abstractly understood, is, in its content, nothing. Hegel treats identity under the category of essence, the second moment of the great triad of the logic (being, essence, and concept). In contrast with being, or the sphere of immediacy, essence is the sphere of mediation[14] and contains the movement of negation within itself. The sphere of essence has a dual character: its inner, essential being and its outer, nonessential being, which "shines" or seems to be. The dialectic advances to the thought that the essential and the nonessential are correlative, that is, are related by the activity of negation. This negative self-relation is "the *shining* [or *seeming*] *of the essence in itself*" [*das Scheinen des Wesens in sich selbst*] which Hegel calls *Reflexion* (SL, 409; W6, 35). The first moment of reflection is identity, which is essence as "sublated immediacy" or "*essential* identity." "It is equality-with-self that has brought itself to unity" as a "pure origination [*Herstellen*] from and within itself" (SL, 411; W6, 38–39). Hegel makes clear that the true conception of identity is in contrast with the "*abstract* identity" as thought by the understanding. Abstractly considered identity is on first thought completely empty, unmediated, and indeterminate. Such thinking about identity as sheer self-sameness is not precisely false, but it is trivial or silly, for Hegel's point is that one cannot think identity except as the movement of self-negation containing the moment of distinction within itself. The thought of identity in contrast with (in distinction from) distinction is not a thinking of identity as outside distinction, as the understanding would have it, but is an inner movement of identity, "identity as distinction that is identical with itself" (SL, 413; W6, 40). The conceiving of identity returns into itself as "*determination* of simple equality with itself" (SL, 413; W6, 41). Rather than placing identity and distinction alongside each other, external to one another, the categories of identity and distinction mediate one another. "A consideration of everything that is, shows that *in its own self* everything is in its self-sameness distinct from itself ... and is in its own self this movement of transition of one of these determinations into the other" (SL, 412; W6, 40). In general, the movement of dialectical thought is a process of self-mediation by the inner force of negation. Nothing is simply itself but is in relation with what is not itself and emerges from this opposition to sublated unity. We must keep this movement of self-negation in mind in order to understand Hegel's exposition of identity. John

Burbidge expresses well this self-contradictory character of the concept of identity by saying:

> *Identity* can only be thought by an intellectual activity that differentiates what it is not from what it is, and identifies that *not* to be inextricably entwined with what it is. This *not* or moment of *pure difference* is an *essential determination* of its meaning.[15]

Any judgement of identity, then, is essentially relational and contains within itself distinction. Hegel's examination of the law of identity and the law of contradiction demonstrates that nothing is simply itself. The judgement "A=A," if it asserts anything, implies that the predicate is distinct from the subject, otherwise the proposition could not be formulated. Identity cannot be true in itself; rather, identity is "the passage beyond itself into the dissolution of itself" [*das Hinausgehen über sich in die Auflösung ihrer selbst*] (SL, 415; V6, 44). To say "A is not-A" is to show more clearly that everything contains its distinction within itself. That which is negated of A is related to A in the very act of negation (cf. SL, 416; W6, 45). In contrast to the superficial way they are commonly understood, the laws of identity and contradiction are really synthetic statements that have their ground or basis in the whole system of thought and reality. The laws of identity and contradiction, which seem lifeless on first encounter, reveal within themselves a movement beyond themselves into their dissolution.

The truth of identity is dialectical. The categories of the logic of the understanding "concern only the correctness [*Richtigkeit*] of cognition, not the truth," and as such "they are unserviceable for the higher, for example, religious truth" (SL, 38; W5, 29). The true conception of identity, by contrast, is determinate, i.e., self-mediated, containing distinction within itself. The conception of identity as simple immediacy moves out of itself; it mediates itself, toward determination. This concept of identity as determinate must be kept in mind as we examine what it means for Hegel to claim that the content of absolute religion is identical with the content of absolute philosophy. For Hegel, the content of the Christian religion is the determination of the concept of religion, and it is this determination that is the dialectical conception of identity. In another way of saying the same, religion and philosophy have the same object and content: God, who is absolute identity, the entire movement of self-differentiation in unity with itself.

> Identity in its truth, as ideality of what immediately is, is a high determination for our religious consciousness as well as for all other thought and

consciousness as such. One can say that the true knowledge of God begins when we know him as identity — as absolute identity. (Enc § 115, *Zusatz*)

Hence we see that the identity in content of religion and philosophy cannot be conceived as a tautology because even "A=A," if it is not a silly expression, must be a dialectical truth.

FORM AND CONTENT

We have now to look at the relation of form and content as explained by Hegel in his *Encyclopaedia of the Philosophical Sciences*, part 1 (1830) and in the *Science of Logic* and to apply this explanation to the specific form-content of religion.

Hegel treats content and form in § 133–34 of the *Encyclopaedia* as the explication of appearance (*Erscheinung*). Phenomena form an interdependent world that appears to our consciousness. Unlike Kant, for whom the phenomena are forever separate from the real, for Hegel what is real must appear. Appearances then are not illusions but the moments of the reality which appears,[16] though it is only the total progression of the appearance (the manifestation of spirit to spirit) of the absolute that is fully real. What appears is the content, and the way it appears is the form, but since what appears is the way it appears, form and content are equal. Phenomena together form a pattern or world which is "the law of the phenomenon." The law is not itself a phenomenon but appears as the pattern or interrelation of the phenomena. Individual phenomena are unstable, but the pattern of their appearing is stable. This law or pattern is the form in which the content appears. But content cannot be formless, so there is an inner, immanent, stable, essential form of appearance and an outer, constantly changing, inessential form of appearance. Thus there is a doubling (*Verdopplung*) of the form. "At one time it is reflected into itself; and then it is identical with the content. At another time it is not reflected into itself and then is the external, indifferent existence in the content" (Enc. § 133, R). The absolute relationship (*Verhältnis*) of content and form is their *Umschlagen* ("turning over," "reversion" — Wallace translates "reciprocal revulsion") of one into the other. Errol Harris explains this mutual change or oscillation of form and content by a concrete example: "Form, as the law governing appearance (e.g., the law of falling bodies, that they accelerate 16 feet per sec$^2$) is simply the content of the phenomenon (what the falling body does) and the phenomenal content is just the form in which the law is actualized."[17] The relation of form and content is a moment in the dialectical movement toward the whole. André Léonard, for one, has noted the key role that the *Umschlagen* plays in the Hegelian dialectic.

> The *Umschlagen* is one of the most important determinations of the logic because it reunites, in the very center of the unfolding of the end, the immediate and the mediate, being and essence, which are the two fundamental coordinates of the logos.[18]

In the relation of form and content, Hegel is, of course, explaining a fact of experience: that there is order in the midst of change, that the world that appears to us acts according to laws. The content of this world is moving and dynamic. It is the developed (*entwickelte*) form (Enc § 134) that requires the double movement of the form (inwardly and outwardly) for its mediation so that it can come to be in and for itself. Form and content then cannot be grasped as fixed coordinates, as the understanding attempts to do, but they can only be truly grasped as moving or dialectical. Form and content are what they are as a relation (*Beziehung*) of identity that is distinction (Enc § 134).

Form and content receive a somewhat different, though complementary, treatment in the *Science of Logic*. Both the *Encyclopaedia Logic,* or "Lesser" *Logic,* and the *Science of Logic,* or "Greater" *Logic,* treat form and content as subcategories of "essence." The "Doctrine of Essence" makes explicit and mediate what had been implicit and immediate in the "Doctrine of Being." Each category of essence is a contradictory pairing of moments, the point being, as Mure points out,

> that not one of these coupled moments can be thought without *eo ipso* thinking more than that moment; and this "more" is not an external addition, but the truth of the "first" moment, which was only "first" because it was to be followed. This is precisely the nature of dialectical movement.[19]

Hegel follows the dialectical movement of thought from within as it becomes increasingly concrete. In this process of concretion, essence determines itself as ground, and ground "further determines itself as *form* and *matter* and gives itself a *content*" (SL, 445; W6, 82). By ground is meant "the unity of identity and distinction" (Enc § 121) as it is the source of explanation of the unity of reality as thought in its moving, contradictory moments.

When moving through the stages of the development of the concept of ground — form and essence, form and matter, form and content, ground and grounded — one has always to envisage the goal of the entire logic, i.e., the absolute idea. The end of the dialectic is the unity of inner content and outer form in which the process of reasoning is its own content. All the stages prior to the absolute idea are provisional and proleptic stages of the concretion of the absolute idea.[20] In the absolute idea, form and content coincide perfectly — namely, in explicit fashion — for the form of absolute thought is the circular method that is its own content. This content is the "completed [*vollendete*] totality" that contains all the determinations of thought as sublated and concrete (SL, 825; W6, 550). As Hegel has said in the introduction to the *Science of Logic*, the content of logic is "*the exposition [Darstellung] of God as he is in his eternal essence before the creation of nature and a finite spirit*" (SL, 50; W5, 44). Here, "before" is to be taken as logical priority because we can think this "eternal essence" only with the recognition that nature and finite spirits actually exist.

As has been noted, ground is the principle of explanation of the systematic whole that contains within itself the movement into an explicit, patterned diversity. Ground, then, is the restless duality of ground (*Grund*) and grounded (*Begründete*), *explicans* and *explicandum*. Ground implies distinction within its identity, for there must be something of which it is the ground, viz., the grounded.[21] At first thought, ground and grounded are the essential and its external result, but on further thought the ground is the source of explanation only in relation to that which it explains, so that ground is equally grounded and grounded is equally ground (cf. SL, 457; W6, 97). At a further, higher stage of dialectical determination, we distinguish the determination of ground as matter and form within the movement of ground in its initial abstract moment as "the unity of identity and distinction" (Enc § 121), or as "*essence that in its negativity is identical with itself*" (SL, 447; W6, 84). Matter and form are correlative determinations of the inner movement of the ground. Each explains the other. By matter is here meant the prime matter of Aristotle,[22] the pure potency to be informed, and form is the determining or defining element of the matter. Matter is conceived, then, as utterly indeterminate, purely plastic or formable, a mere abstraction. By characterizing matter as "formable," we are indicating that matter only has its meaning — or better, its definition — through form. Equally, form only has its meaning or definition by that which it "forms" or defines, namely, matter. Thus form is not external to matter. "Matter contains form locked up within it and is absolute susceptibility [or "receptivity," *Empfänglichkeit*] to form only because it has form absolutely within itself" (SL, 451; W6, 90). In the transition to form and content, form becomes the indeterminate element. Content is formed matter, the substrate of form and matter. Mure explains the dialectical movement from form and matter to form and content as "the passing of matter which was only implicitly form, into content which *is* form."[23]

As with every transition in the logic, the later stage must be a higher, more determinate, more concrete stage of what precedes, hence content and form are further determinations of matter and form. Stace explains this movement of the relation of matter and form to content and form by saying:

> In matter and form the two sides are indifferent to each other. The matter is regarded as *formless*, and the form as *matterless*. Each disregards the other.... But in content and form the two sides are so far from being indifferent to each other that they completely interpenetrate and determine each other. It is now seen that there is no such thing as formless matter. Even the bare matter has form in itself and when so regarded it is not matter, but content.[24]

Ground, the principle of explanation, has become determinate in the content. As determinate ground, "form and content are themselves one and the same identity" (SL, 457; W6, 97). At the level of determinate ground, the content is still other than its form and the form remains external to its content, but in their dialectical course, form and content cannot remain external to one another, for in their ground the content is "the identity of the *ground* with itself in the *grounded*, and of the *grounded* in the *ground*" (SL, 461; W6, 102).

In the world of appearance (*Erscheinung*), the content shows forth its form, and content is what it is because of its form. The form and content are respectively the how and the what of the appearance (we can recall Harris's example of the law of a falling body and its activity).

At a higher level of appearance, we distinguish the inner (*das Innere*) and the outer (*das Äussere*). The understanding tends to fix these forms as separate and empty, but in dialectical thought they are seen as aspects of one identical content.[25] In the *Encyclopaedia of the Philosophical Sciences*, § 140, *Zusatz*, Hegel demonstrates the understanding's mistake of separating the inner and outer dimensions of phenomena and of making what is inward the essential and what is outward the nonessential. Even in ordinary experience, Hegel notes the importance that we give to the outward appearance as an indication of the inner reality. We see it is false to speak of a person's inner disposition in separation from outward actions when in truth "a man is what he does" and "by their fruits shall you know them."

A further explication of content occurs in the category of actuality, because content is what is actual (*wirklich*) or concrete (Enc § 143, R).

When anything is thought to have many possibilities besides its concrete actuality, these possibilities are mere abstract forms that are imposed upon a content from outside. It is the actual systematic whole that decides what is possible and what is not. A true conception of a content, then, has its possibilities depend upon itself, "upon the totality of the moments of its actuality" (Enc § 143, *Zusatz*, p. 284).

Actuality is the unity of what is inner nature and outer manifold appearance as a content utters or externalizes itself (cf. Enc § 142). The absolute content displays itself in such a way that its manifold appearances (the outer) are "*one* substantial [*gediegene*] identity" (SL, 531; W6, 188), the inner, and this content is "*one identical substrate* [*Grundlage*]" and "*one identity of form*" (SL, 529; W6, 186).

In the section immediately preceding the category of actuality in the *Science of Logic*, inner and outer were opposed forms that lacked their mediated identity. That which was outward, the multiplicity of appearance, was thought unessential and had to find its ground in the inner, and that which was inner had only an inner, immediate unity that did not include its manifold manifestations, and so the inner was external to that of which it was to be the essential, viz., the manifold of appearance (cf. SL, 527–28; W6, 184–85). "The transition [*Übergehen*] of each into the other ... is their mediated identity; for it is precisely through its other that each is what it is in itself" (SL, 528; W6, 185). In the process of concretion, inner and outer, then, reveal themselves as inseparable sides of one content.

We have always to keep in mind that the totality is present in each category and is the foundation of all identity and distinction. The totality as teleological unites the content in its inner and outer forms. What shows itself outwardly is in actuality what it is inwardly. The goal of complete manifestation, transparent thought, is implicitly operative at each stage.

Every finite, contingent phenomenon as finite falls into the *Abgrund*, it vanishes in relation to the absolute, but this *Abgrund* is the *Grund* for the subsistence (*Bestehen*) of finite things. Finite things are real only in as far as the absolute shows in their showing: "er *ist* Schein, insofern *das Absolute in ihm scheint*" (SL, 532; W6, 190).

We think here perhaps of Spinoza's modes as they exist in utter dependence upon God, though for Spinoza only God exists, and therefore it is contradictory to think of modes as existing. Hegel's thinking is that everything, every moment, has the content of the whole, but its finite form negates its infinite content. By its finite form it disappears into the *Abgrund* of the absolute from which it has its *Grund* as a moment containing the absolute. For Hegel, the absolute is "its *own* exposition" [*eigene Auslegung*] (SL, 530; W6, 187). "Form and content dissolve in the absolute," so that "the content of the absolute is simply *to manifest itself*" (SL, 536; W6, 194).

## The Specific Argument for the Identity in Content of Religion and Philosophy

It is now our task to apply Hegel's reasoning about the discrepancy of the inner and outer forms of one content to the relation between religious representation and absolute knowledge. Falk Wagner in an article on "the *Aufhebung* of religious representation in the philosophical concept" says that the possibility for the changeover of the religious content into the philosophical content is based upon the fact that "the content's own form consists in the form-unity of content and form, but the form as form remains exterior to the content."[26] Our task is to clarify what it can mean for Hegel to claim that religion and philosophy are identical in content. Complicating the explanation is the fact that "form" is used in differing but related meanings. We cannot be simpler than the *Sache* to be explained, in this case the absolute content of religion and philosophy. We distinguish form and content and explain a transformation of content. The content of the absolute religion has a form (namely, religious form) that is external to the content but as joined to the content gives that content a religious form. The unity of the content and form must have its unity from the form (it is a *religious* content), hence there is a "form-unity," as Wagner says. For example, if the Trinity is explained as the unity of three persons — father, son, and holy spirit — an explanation that many people find neither entirely intelligible nor entirely nonsensical, there is a content with a certain mode of presentation, namely, what Hegel calls a representational form. The form and the content are one, and we might say this form-content unity is a "representational content." But when we begin to perform speculative surgery on this form-content, we find a dissonance between the form and the content, and the content emerges with a speculative form, indicating from the philosophical standpoint that the representational form that configured the content in its specific way was a religious form-content unity, or a representational form-unity, and the form was all along external to the inner content, which finds suitable form only in pure thought. We are using "form" and "content" analogously. By "analogously," here we mean that the terms have differing but related meanings, proportionate to each phase of the explanation. In our explanation, form and content change in the respective positions they hold in the course of explaining the change.

In another way of explaining the same, we can say the representational form-content of religion is sublated into the thought-content in the thought-form of philosophy. We will speak later at length of the meaning of sublation, but to understand what we are saying, consider Hegel's explanation of the "absolute" in book 2, "The Doctrine of Essence" of the *Science of Logic*, where the absolute is not the fully subjective, concrete absolute of the "absolute idea" but the indeterminate, substantial identity of Spinoza's absolute. This absolute determines itself from within as a movement from indeterminacy to determinacy, which appears as an outwardization of the absolute's inner self-determination. Consider *how* Hegel explains this movement of thought determination. The absolute as the one, simple substance

> is the identity of inner and outer. But the movement of reflection [the outward show of the inner ground] thus stands *over against* the absolute identity of the absolute. In this identity it is sublated and thus is only the inner of it; but as inner it is *external* to it. (SL, 531; W6, 189)

We see that dialectical thought requires analogous thinking — thinking that moves with the thought-determinations. When sublated, the movement of reflection is *within* the absolute but *external* to it as the simple identity that is not yet the dialectical identity of the absolute idea. What is important to see here for our purposes is that we must think movingly in the movement of the thing, otherwise we become confused when the import and application of the terms change, e.g., the way we see Hegel using "inner" and "outer." So in regard to our specific problem, the *content of absolute religion* (which is a unit) has an outer form. This form-content unit is sublated in philosophy, and the new form-content unit must be thought at a new level of thinking that recognizes an identity in content between the religious and philosophical forms. But the identity is a sublated identity so that the identical *content* has an analogous meaning, namely, content #1 *as* religious content and content #2 *as* philosophical content.

Further, with the aid of Rohs's explication mentioned above, we can say that the content has a content-determination within itself and a form-determination outside itself. The former belongs to the self-identity of the content, and the latter to the distinction within the content. The form-determination, the outer of the content, is the source for the differentiation of the religious content into purely speculative form where it is one with its content. What had been outer form-determination vanishes in the inner content-determination, and the absolute content is wholly and utterly absolute form, which is the absolute idea — the goal of speculative philosophy.

## The Argument for the Identity in Content 59

The content of religion is infinite and absolute, but it has a form-determination as religious that is finite and contingent. Because the form-determination is finite, Wagner says, "the religious content can be detached from the representational form and sublated into philosophical knowledge."[27]

We must remember, of course, that the content that is fully sublated in speculative philosophy is the content of the Christian religion in which the absolute content has come to its fullest form as religious. Other religions have not the fully expressed content of the absolute; consequently, their translation into rational form does not yield the absolute idea.

The sublation of the religious content into knowledge occurs because the restrictive form-determination of the infinite content-determination is negated. It is necessary to emphasize that the logic of Hegel is testimony to the power of negation. To speak facilely of dialectical thought as thesis-antithesis-synthesis is readily to fall into a fixed way of thinking, when thought rather has to move in thinking. The *Aufhebung* of the religious content into speculative content is an immanent tendency of the religious content itself, not only of its external form. The content is contradicting itself and must move. The *Aufhebung* is a destroying, a preserving, and a moving forward (with the emphasis upon these terms as verb forms). Hegel is not claiming to invent the dialectic but only to observe it and describe it from within. Do we not make better sense of the phenomena by recognizing the fact of this immanent tendency? That is Hegel's question as we look upon the multiplicity before us and seek to give it unity.

To many religious people this speculative transformation of Christianity appears as a change in the substantive content. Certainly there is change. *Aufheben* means destruction — not *only* destruction, of course, but clearly destruction. There is negation of the form-determination of the content. How this negation occurs can only be seen from the side of philosophy. That the content can be recognized as identical is a philosophical and not properly a religious recognition. It is reason that clearly discerns and explicates the movement.

Even upon rational investigation, however, the question for many remains whether the content can be called identical. In part the problem is that many do not grasp identity dialectically but statically, and we must keep in mind the Hegelian notion of identity. In part, however, Hegel did not carry out completely the implications of his own thinking in regard to how the Christian content is transformed yet identical in philosophy.

We can agree with Wagner when he says that Hegel draws one-sidedly on the sameness of content in religion and philosophy without emphasizing that the religious content in its detachment from the form of representation and transference to the concept is changed. By so doing Hegel leaves underdeveloped the basic insight of his philosophy, namely, that the movement from one level of consciousness to another can only take place by negation.[28]

The content of the Christian religion has been negated not *in toto* but in its form-determination. The finitizing form of figurative expression that originally brought the absolute down to the human level is dissolved with the concomitant movement of human thought to the level of the infinite. Throughout this movement the content of religion cannot be grasped and observed by itself apart from some formal determination since there is no formless content. Hence the inner and outer elements of the religious content are sublated in the new content at a more inclusive level of consciousness, and at no moment is there a static, isolated content to investigate.

A further point to note is that the absolute idea whose determinateness "has not the shape of a *content* but exists wholly [*schlechthin*] as *form*" (SL, 825; W6, 550) is a goal, we would argue, completely achieved only with regard to logic and to the structure of subjectivity, but not with regard to and from the perspective of existing reality because the concept is not yet fully actual, but the final cause is active in the continuing development of reality in time.

Can speculative philosophy claim to be God's thought *tout court*? Can philosophy slough off the restrictions of representational expression and emerge in the pure form of divine thought? The following chapter on religious representation will help fill out the meaning of the speculative transformation of religion's content and indicate some of the problems inherent in human language.

## The Summary of the Argument

To summarize the conclusions of this chapter, we can say that religious representations that reveal the divine — i.e., have the true content — are outwardly at odds with the ground from which they emerge, viz., God. They are partial, inadequate revelations of God that remain distanced from the innermost reality to which they point. In relation to one another, the various representations remain only externally united. Through the reasoning process they are brought into relation to one another, their surface contradictions are removed, and the truth that they reveal is brought more fully to light. This reasoning process in its goal is precisely what Hegel means by absolute knowledge as goal. What is outward is fully identical with what is inward. The inner and outer forms of one content are identical. The ground for the possibility of this process of approaching the truth is that the totality is immanent in each moment, drawing it onward.

# 3
# Representation

## General Considerations

The previous chapter has set forth the relation of form and content and the dialectical nature of the identity in content of absolute religion and speculative philosophy. It is now fitting to explicate more fully the proper form of religion, namely, *Vorstellung,* or representation. Hegel's treatment of representation is not limited to the religious sphere. We shall of course focus upon the religious form of representation, thus recognizing that what is said of representation as genus applies to religious representation as species. We shall proceed by sketching the relation of representation and thought and the problem of this relation in the philosophy of religion. We shall then consider in greater detail Hegel's treatment of representation and related notions, first in the *Science of Logic* (with reference to the "Lesser" *Logic* of the *Encyclopaedia*) so as to establish that for Hegel from the standpoint of his system there is a moment of pure thought prior to the realphilosophical and representational spheres, and then in the *Phenomenology of Spirit*, the *Philosophy of Spirit* (or part 3 of the *Encyclopaedia of the Philosophical Sciences)*, and finally the *Lectures on the Philosophy of Religion*. While the treatment of representation in these works is largely the same, there is a complementarity among them as well as a notable shift in approach and attitude between the *Phenomenology of Spirit* and the *Lectures on the Philosophy of Religion*. This close look at Hegel's treatment of representation will aid in clarifying the problem of the identity and change in the content of religion as sublated in philosophy by showing the nuances and implications within Hegel's treatment of religion and philosophy. It is neither possible nor desirable to consider every instance of Hegel's use of *Vorstellung*. It is enough to present his main considerations and explanations, especially as they concern religious representation. Lastly, we shall indicate the continuity between religious representation and conceptual thought and the difficulty of achieving pure thought without residue of representation.

Representation employs images in a universal way that has not yet the form of thought.

> Representation has already brought the sensible into the inner dimension; the content is of a sensible kind, but thought has already ventured into it, although it has not yet fully penetrated or dominated the content. (LPR I, 334; V3, 235)

The "not yet" is important because in the Hegelian dialectic representation is on the way to conceptualization. When the understanding works upon representations, it congeals them, connecting them *nebeneinander*, as Hegel says, by "a bare '*also*'" [*das blosse Auch*] (Enc § 20, R, p. 73). Reason, on the other hand, allows the spiritual dynamism of the representation's interiority to rise from "not yet" thought to actual thought, i.e., it allows the thought-content to become the thought-form. In general, Hegel says, "philosophy does nothing else than transmute [*verwandeln*] representations into thoughts" (Enc § 20, R, pp. 73–74).

Representations are not only thoughts in sensible form but the abstract notions of God, right, and duty (Enc § 20, R, p. 73) and the conceptions of science and mathematics, such as Newton's idea of force and the mathematical infinite. In general, representations are the products of the intelligence that are externally connected and not integrated internally and wholly into the system of thought. As given in representation, the object is set before (*vorgestellt*) the subject, as over against the subject. The object is received passively, without the conscious appropriation of the subject as active in receiving the content. In rational thought, by contrast, the mind is active and cognizant of its making intelligible the content of its thought. The otherness of the object is encompassed within the mind's self-knowledge of the union of itself and its object.

Representations are not false when taken as the necessary stages or moments of spiritual development, but they are falsified when the understanding fixes upon them as given. Reason, by contrast, seeks the conceptual grasp or comprehension of the simply and immediately given elements. Reason cannot be satisfied with apparent contradictions and seeks to resolve the contradictions according to rational necessity, that is, according to the internal relation of the elements. In short, rational thought mediates the multiple, immediate, representational data.

Representation mediates the subjective forms of consciousness and thought in such a way that the concrete and singular content of subjective experience is transcended. The singular intuition is subsumed into a representation with a universal content (cf. Enc § 454). Representation, then, points beyond the particular image and by the fact of being a representation implies that its truth is in what is thought and not in what is presented. "It sublates the unity of intuition, rejects the unity of the image and its meaning, and brings this meaning into prominence for itself" (LPR I, 240; V3, 149). For the religious consciousness, representation is the sublation of its finite modes that yet retains these finite expressions and at the same moment recognizes through them their eternal and infinite content. Thus religious representation holds within itself the dialectical tension of an infinite content in a finite mode. Representation has as its destiny the destruction of its own image because the images cannot adequately carry what is laid upon them, namely, a transcendent meaning.

This inadequacy of the representation by its own means to express its thought-content is the basis of Hegel's argument for its inherent need of rational transformation. Religious expression itself demonstrates this inadequacy. Religion has as its object the absolute and is the means for relating the divine and the human spirit, yet religious representations such as God, Creation, the Incarnation, the Fall, and the immortality of the soul present an inadequate and, often enough, conflicting notion of the divine reality. Religion attempts by figures, symbols, stories, and analogies drawn from ordinary experience to express a wholly spiritual reality. Religious representations succeed in the measure that they point beyond themselves; but when taken as the ultimate expression of the divine, they fail because they cannot found or justify the truth they contain nor reconcile the conflicting claims among them. According to Hegel, only philosophy, speculative reason, can demonstrate the essential interconnectedness of the elements and bring to light the logical necessity of the truth given in representation.

In Christianity, the recognition of the conflicting claims of religious expressions and of the need of rational harmonization is, of course, not new. Abelard (1079–1142), for example, in *Sic et Non* collected conflicting statements and inconsistencies in the Scriptures and church fathers so as to invite the reader to investigate their true meaning. Abelard accepted that the truth was contained in the authoritative statements of the tradition but that the truth could not emerge unless the apparent dissonance was resolved through the application of logic to theology. The means by which to discern true from false arguments was what he termed "dialectic." For Abelard, dialectic could not found the truth of church doctrines, but it could make clear the statements of the authorities and show the reasonableness of what is believed on authority.

In its time, Abelard's method was controversial because it seemed to subject divine authority to human reason. The conflict between Abelard and his contemporaries parallels the conflict between Hegel and his contemporaries. What is new, however, is the identification in Hegelian philosophy of human and divine reason. Hegel's philosophy is absolute idealism; reality is the process of thought thinking itself, so that the absolute is thinking itself in our thinking the absolute. For Hegel, therefore, religion in its mode of representation imperfectly apprehends the divine and has its perfection in pure thought.

The medievals agreed that at least some divine truths were beyond the power of human reasoning. The most intellectualist of the medieval theologians, such as Abelard and Aquinas, argued that certain truths were suprarational, but not irrational, and that belief in these revealed truths could be shown not to be in conflict with reason. It was generally agreed that God exceeds the powers of the human intellect. The mystics, especially, in their writings asserted the inadequacy of our thought to contain the divine, which exceeds the grasp of our categories and language. By contrast, for Hegel mysticism in its properly speculative sense means that which exceeds the understanding, so that the mystical, for Hegel, is the rational (cf. Enc § 82, *Zusatz*). "The mystical is not concealment of a secret, or ignorance, but consists in the self knowing itself to be one with the divine being [*Wesen*] and that this, therefore, is revealed" (PS, 437; W3, 526).

From the standpoint of the Christian theological tradition, Hegel has radically developed the notion of revelation and divine truth. Religion as the union of the divine and human must have as its condition of possibility the human knowledge of God. The only God we can affirm is God in some way known. A God completely beyond the world is an unintelligible abstraction. When one asks about God *a se,* one implicitly supposes in the question the God who is being-for-consciousness. When we speak of God-in-himself, we necessarily speak of God-in-himself-for-consciousness. However, we need not conclude that this being-for-consciousness "exhausts" God's being-in-himself since God transcends every particular state of human consciousness.[1]

Can philosophy apprehend God in conceptual form more adequately than the parabolic and analogical form of religion? Moreover, can there be a purely rational knowledge of God? Copleston says, "Hegel attempted to do what cannot be done, namely to make plain to view what can only be simply apprehended through the use of analogies and symbols."[2] Similarly, David Tracy in his work *Blessed Rage for Order* argues that metaphor and symbol disclose what cannot be adequately conceptualized in the expression of the limit-situations of our everyday activities that can properly be named religious.[3] According to Tracy, a conceptual analysis is necessary in order to judge the cognitive claims of religious experience and language. However, this conceptual language "does not claim to capture the full existential meaningfulness of the originating language" (148). Hegel's thought in this regard, he says, is "correctly considered unavailable for contemporary retrieval" (164, n. 12). A conceptual understanding of God must rather be evaluated on how well it harmonizes with the Scriptural meaning of God, so that the gulf is bridged between the God of the philosophers and the God of the Scriptures (184). Furthermore, Tracy understands Hegel to claim that the sublation of representations into concepts renders the representations no longer necessary so that the ground of religion falls away in the light of philosophical knowing (161). This last point will be discussed later, but the question is posed whether Hegel can sustain his claim to translate the content of religious representations into conceptual form (even as a goal). In order to answer this question we must look at Hegel's treatment of representation.

## Hegel's Treatment of Representation

*Representation within Hegel's Logic*

IN THE *SCIENCE OF LOGIC*

As said above, in chapter 1, logic is the form of thought, therefore the delineation of the form of thought must eschew intuitions and representations if it is to express thought in its purity. A number of examples from the *Science of Logic* will demonstrate Hegel's aim.

In the *Science of Logic,* chapter 1, "Being," remark 1, Hegel concerns himself with being in its purest form. As such, being cannot be limited by anything outside itself, since pure being is all inclusive; nor by anything within itself, since an internal limitation of being would make being a determinate this or that. The thought of pure being is without determinate content, and as such it is nothing. On first encounter, this identification by Hegel of being and nothing seems nonsensical, but for Hegel to think in such a way is to persist at the level of understanding, to make a category mistake, and to confuse determinacy with indeterminacy. To think together being and nothing is to think becoming — that is, to think dialectically — since being and nothing are opposite and identical, and becoming is their perpetual negation and preservation. The ancient formula *ex nihilo nihil fit* does not truly express becoming, which is, in one of its formulations, the passing of nothing into being. Hegel says Christian metaphysics implied the thought of becoming in its doctrine of *creatio ex nihilo* but "understood this proposition synthetically or merely representationally [*bloss vorstellend*]" (SL, 84; W5, 85).

Here Hegel points to an expression of truth that is yet impure and inadequate because the content is not purely in thought but in representations. Ordinary consciousness has difficulty with pure thinking and so becomes perplexed because it brings "representations of something concrete" into logical statements, "forgetting that what is in question is not such concrete something but only the pure abstractions of being and nothing" (SL, 85; W5, 87). Hegel is showing the confusion that results from introducing concepts of determinate things into pure, abstract ways of thinking.[4]

Hegel wishes to counter the tendency of raising *das Vorstellen* to the level of *reinen Gedanken* in the manner that Parmenides mistakenly did (SL, 88; W5, 90). At the conclusion of chapter 1, remark I, Hegel states clearly his purpose in the *Logic*, viz., to prevent cognition (*das Erkennen*) "from applying to God the determinations and relationships of the finite" (SL, 90; W5, 92).

Hegel's denunciations of the uncritical use of representations do not apply only to religion but to metaphysics, physics, and mathematics as well. A quantitative understanding of infinity in physics speaks of the infinitely great and the infinitely small, but these quantitative notions of infinity are, in fact, "representational images" [*Bilder der Vorstellung*] which Hegel calls, in metaphorical language of his own, "nullifying cloud and shadow" (SL, 238; W5, 276). In contrast with this faulty understanding of infinity, only speculative reason can demonstrate the true meaning of these representations of infinity.

Symbols too are "shadowy" ways of expressing a thought-content. In a criticism of symbolism in a remark on the concept, Hegel notes that numerical and spacial relationships distort the inner whole of logic. "The concept as such can only be essentially comprehended [*aufgefasst*] with spirit" (SL, 618; W6, 295). Hegel goes on to say that symbols are useful for suggesting and intimating the truth of the concept, but they are unsuitable "for expressing and cognizing" [*auszudrücken und zu erkennen*] the concept because they remain exterior to that which they express. What Hegel says of symbolism applies *a fortiori* to any theology that would place symbols above conceptual thought (we can think here of David Tracy).

> What in symbols is an echo of a higher determination, is only truly known through the concept and can be approximated to the concept only by

separating off [*Absonderung*] the sensuous, unessential part [*Beiwesens*] that was meant to express it. (SL, 618; W6, 296)

Hegel says it is foolish to think that more may be expressed through symbols than in thought. On the contrary, whatever truth is contained in symbolic expression is veiled until made explicit in the form appropriate to its truth (SL, 215; W5, 248). "In symbols the truth is dimmed and veiled by the sensuous element; only in the form of thought is it fully revealed to consciousness: the meaning is only the thought itself" (SL, 215; W5, 248).

It is Hegel's constant claim that only spirit can know spirit, and any mode of expression that retains spacial and temporal forms remains outside the spiritual content it expresses and as such is not equal to what it attempts to express. The object as given in intuition or representation remains foreign and external to thought. An object of consciousness is only truly itself, *an und für sich*, in thought. "In intuition or representation, the object is an appearance" (SL, 585; W6, 255). As an appearance it remains set over against consciousness, but when truly grasped the object is pervaded by thought and has its determinations entirely in thought.

In studying Hegel it is noteworthy how he associates expressing and cognizing, *ausdrücken* and *erkennen*. Language and thought are not accidental to one another, so that reason and language develop dialectically, one with another: "Da der Mensch die Sprache hat als der Vernunft eigentümliche Bezeichungsmittel" (W6, 295; cf. SL, 618). *Eigentümliche* here indicates that language is a means that is the property of reason, that is to say, that language belongs to reason as reason's own, and any other means of expression is a stepping away from full conceptual truth. Philosophy's proper task then is to translate the representations of ordinary discourse into concepts.

> Philosophy has the right to select from the language of common life which is made for the world of representations, such expressions as *seem to approximate* the determinations of the concept ... for common life has no concepts, but only representations, and to cognize the concept in what is otherwise mere representation is philosophy itself. (SL, 708; W6, 406)

Representations have their place (and thus their truth) within the whole of thought because spirit and the concept have the power and the freedom to externalize themselves in the diversity of nature and yet remain one and complete. The mistake is not to recognize the representations as only "traces and inklings" [*Spuren und Ahnungen*] of the concept and to take them rather as a faithful copy (*treuem Abbild*) of the concept. "Spirit ... engages in *Vorstellen* and runs riot [*herumtreibt*] in its endless variety," which is to say spirit freely externalizes itself in representations and makes them "footprints" of itself (SL, 608; W6, 282).

IN THE "LESSER" *LOGIC*

Hegel begins the *Encyclopaedia of the Philosophical Sciences* by noting that philosophy must suppose a certain concern with the immediate objects that consciousness represents to itself because in the order of time consciousness

> makes representations of objects, before it makes concepts of them, and that it is only through these representations and by recourse to them, that the thinking spirit rises to know and comprehend thinkingly. (Enc § 1)

But this acquaintance with the objects of representation soon proves inadequate to a thinking comprehension of these objects (Enc § 1).

Hegel treats representation as a kind of knowledge (*Erkennen*) between *das Sinnliche* and *der Gedanke*. Sense concerns the apprehension of unrelated individuals. *Das Vorstellen* may have its content from sense, yet as something universal or simple. But representation may also derive its content from self-conscious thinking, as in law, morality, and religion. This latter mode of representation may be harder to distinguish from thought, yet it shares with the first, more sensible mode of representation the character of being individualized. Implicitly (*an sich*), the representations express mental determinations (*geistige Bestimmungen*), yet they stand isolated in their universality and remain outside one another (*aussereinander*). As with the understanding, the representational elements lack internal relationships. Although the understanding supplies the necessary connections between the elements, it does so as a form of external connection that places the elements in relation to one another (Enc § 20, R).

*Representation in the* Phenomenology of Spirit

In contrast with the view that truth can be known only in intuition, feeling, or religious experience, Hegel asserts that truth is scientific in form, that is, it exists only in the form of the concept (cf. PS, 4; W3, 14–15) or, in other words, its content is the concept. The purpose of the *Phenomenology of Spirit* is to investigate the forms of consciousness as they lead to absolute knowledge and from this perspective to comprehend all the forms of consciousness as the self-movement of spirit as the totality. In order to accomplish this goal one must take on the strenuous effort to think in conceptual terms (*die Anstrengung des Begriffs*). Representational thinking and formal thinking, which Hegel calls *Räsonieren*, resist the more tiresome form of thinking in concepts: the first because it is immersed in matter and finds it difficult to rise to the purely conceptual level, the second because it prefers the form of argumentation in freedom from being determined by the content of thought (PS, 35–36; W3, 56). These contrasting forms of thought are the moments of faith and pure insight. Faith has a spiritual content but without insight or intellectual penetration. Faith is thought — a fact, Hegel notes, that is often overlooked. However, faith reduces its content to representation as something beyond the world of sense that is "essentially an 'other' in relation to self-consciousness." Pure insight, by contrast, will not accept any content that is not the product of its own self-consciousness. Hence it has the form of truth but is spiritually vacuous (PS, 324; W3, 394). The opposition of faith and insight cannot be resolved at the level of their opposition but only in the concept that can recognize their opposition as an essential moment of itself (cf. PS, 36; W3, 56). Thought, then, has to rise out of thinking based in images as well as from the hollow reasoning of Enlightenment thought if it is to achieve true, scientific knowledge in which spirit is conscious of itself in purely conceptual form.

Religion is the consciousness of the absolute but not yet in the form of self-consciousness (PS, 410; W3, 495). In Christianity, the revelatory religion, "spirit has attained its true shape [*Gestalt*], yet the shape itself and the representation are still the unvanquished aspect from which spirit must pass over into the concept" (PS, 416; W3, 502–3). This true shape is God as the activity of self-mediating subjectivity.

The section of the *Phenomenology of Spirit* on "revelatory religion" is a translation of Christian representations into a conceptual synthesis. When dialectically conceived, the representations become moments of the whole movement of reality as available to consciousness. By contrast, the understanding fixes upon representations which, when thought together, are in conflict, and thus it fails to recognize the inner dialectical movement of opposing representations. Hegel is arguing that "neither the one nor the other has truth; the truth is just their movement" (PS, 427; W3, 568). Hegel is claiming that the finite, externally connected representations demonstrate in the thinking-through of their oppositions the internal necessity to be reconciled because reality is a dialectical movement of thought.

The representations of the Christian community have absolute spirit as their content; but, when not mediated by rational thought, they remain obstacles to the self-consciousness of absolute spirit.

> The content is the true content, but all its moments, when placed in the medium of representation [*in dem Elemente des Vorstellens*], have the character of being uncomprehended, of appearing as completely independent sides which are externally connected with each other. (PS, 463; W3, 556)

The claims of the Christian religion must be reinterpreted in purely conceptual form if their truth is to emerge. The content of the truth is there, implicitly, but in untrue form, and the history of consciousness that Hegel traces in his *Phenomenology of Spirit* is for human consciousness to come to the speculative awareness of the divine-human relation that has been revealed in the Christ event. The Incarnation as a historical event has taken place, but according to Hegel its speculative truth is now beginning to emerge.

> All that now remains to do is the *Aufheben* of this mere form, or rather, since this belongs to consciousness as such, its truth must already have yielded itself ["have arisen," *sich erheben haben*] in the shapes of consciousness. (PS, 479; W3, 575)

The religious community has awareness of the meaning of the Incarnation, but it has not delved to the full truth of this mystery until it knows conceptually the dynamic reality of God becoming human. The full implications of this mystery, while given in religion, cannot be brought to light in purely rational terms because in the mode of representation the full truth of the God-human relation is external to the believer.

> The representational thinking [*das Vorstellen*] of the [religious] community is not this conceptual thinking; it has the content, but without its necessity, and instead of the form of the concept it brings into the realm of pure consciousness the natural relationships of father and son.... The object is revealed to it by something alien, and it does not recognize itself in the thought of spirit. (PS, 466; W3, 560)

Because of the difficulty of thinking in pure form, the self-consciousness of the religious community resists thinking its content in conceptual form and clings to the external elements of the faith content with the result that "the inner element of faith has vanished" (PS, 466; W3, 560).

While in the *Phenomenology of Spirit* Hegel acknowledges the truth content of Christian representations, he emphasizes that these representations are obstacles to the autonomy that is proper to spirit. That autonomy is achieved only in absolute knowledge. The Christian religion reveals the absolute in representations that are externally related to one another and to the human consciousness, and the barrier between human consciousness and its object has not been overcome at the religious level.

When the barrier is overcome, human consciousness is divine consciousness. "Knowledge of the absolute" in its Hegelian meaning is an objective and a subjective genitive. Feuerbach drew the conclusion from Hegel's philosophy that human self-consciousness at the level of absolute knowledge is simply the absolute, and thus he transmuted theology into anthropology. However, Lauer says we can interpret Hegel to say only that "consciousness of self short of consciousness of the 'absolute' is not consciousness of the whole self."[5] We cannot *simpliciter* equate the human and the divine. At the level of absolute knowing, human consciousness recognizes itself as a moment of the inclusive infinite. The infinite spirit is active, immanent, and conscious within the community of human spirits, but the absolute exceeds all its particular manifestations, though it of course occurs in and through them. That Hegel's conception of the divine-human relation is different from the common, religious way of conceiving God's relation to humanity is clear. The question, though, is how we are to conceive adequately the relation of God and humanity when we realize that we are spirits and God is spirit and that to be human is essentially to be *capax dei*. Hegel's purpose in the *Phenomenology of Spirit* is to investigate the development of human spirit. In doing so, he must of necessity find the representations of the divine-human relation deficient and self-contradictory as commonly understood and must reinterpret them in wholly rational terms.

*Representation in* The Philosophy of Spirit

Part 3 of the *Encyclopaedia of the Philosophical Sciences* contains, perhaps, the most complete, general treatment of representation. It is titled the *Philosophy of Spirit* and is divided into "Subjective Spirit," "Objective Spirit," and "Absolute Spirit." The first two divisions concern spirit in its finite, determinate shapes, while the third concerns infinite spirit as the goal or truth of its prior, finite manifestations. In "Subjective Spirit," under the subheading "Psychology," Hegel treats the "universal modes of the activity of *spirit as such*" (Enc § 440, R). "Psychology" is further divided into "theoretical spirit," which treats the subjective integration of the objects of consciousness, and "practical spirit." Representation is treated under the former.

In § 446–64 of "theoretical spirit," Hegel explicates the stages of intelligence (*Intelligenz*) as it increasingly liberates itself from sensation in its movement toward pure thought. The ascending stages of this division are intuition (*Anschauung*), representation (*Vorstellung*), and thought (*Denken*). The first stage, intuition (*Anschauung*), is already above feeling (*das Gefühl*) in that intuition has some subjective awareness. Intuition means a kind of intellectual perception in which the mind knows its object as singular and immediate. In § 448 Hegel distinguishes two moments that consciousness finds in the unmediated given of intuition. The first is attention (*Aufmerksamkeit*), by which the mind focuses upon the intuition as one's own. The second moment outwardizes the stuff or material of the intuition as an object (*Gegenstand*) existing *over against* consciousness. This object, however, as Hegel says, is a "relative other" [*relatives Anderes*], for consciousness objectifies what is subjectively present. These two moments of attention and externalization together constitute intuition. Because what Hegel says at this point is integral to its German expression, it seems best to quote Hegel's own words and then to paraphrase them.

Die Intelligenz als diese konkrete Einheit der Beiden Momente, und zwar unmittelbar in diesem äusserlich-seienden Stoffe in sich erinnert und in ihrer Erinnerung-in-sich in das Aussersichsein versenkt zu sein, ist *Anschauung*. (Enc § 449)

In intuition, the external material of perception is brought inward. The externally given material is internalized as one's own. What one senses is sensed as "out there," but it is "out there" as an activity of the mind and so is inward. This bringing inward is the recollecting of what has been perceived. As explained in the *Zusatz* of § 449, for intuition, in distinction from representation, the "objectivity of the content" is preponderant. While for representation the subjectivity of the intuited content becomes preponderant at this level of a more general understanding of representation.

The second moment of theoretical spirit is representation, which in turn is divided into three stages — recollection, imagination, and memory. Representation first appears as *erinnerte Anschauung* (Enc § 451), recollected/inwardized intuition. Representation has subjectivized the given material of intuition, though not so completely that the intuited material is still not present as a particular image, albeit inwardized, in the mode of representation. As with everything in Hegel's philosophy, representation can ultimately only be understood in relation to its lower and higher moments. Specifically with regard to representation, it is only from the perspective of thought that representation can be cognized as a movement away from the unmediated, particular, objective content of perception toward what is recognized as inherently mediated and subjective. In this first stage of breaking from intuition, the subject becomes conscious of transforming an image of a particular thing in direct perception of that thing into the mind's own time and space by means of an image that frees the referent of the image from the spacial-temporal determination that it originally had in intuition (cf. Enc § 452). This act does not occur deliberately.

The next phase of representation is imagination (*Einbildungskraft*), which, as the term indicates, is the power of forming images. In contrast with recollection, the intelligence is active in bringing forth the images from within itself (cf. Enc § 455). Here again three ascending stages are distinguished. First, the mind merely reproduces images. Second, the mind relates or associates the images according to its subjective aims. Third, the mind employs symbols and signs by which it posits an identity between general representations and particular images (cf. Enc § 455, and R).

It is under the third stage of imagination that Hegel treats symbols, signs, and language. A symbol expresses a content similar in essence and concept to the content of the intuition it employs, as, for example, an eagle symbolizes strength because the eagle is perceived as strong. A sign's content is other than the content of its perception, as, for example, a flag. In contrast with much present-day thought about symbol, Hegel argues that signs are a higher stage of spiritual development than are symbols because the intelligence shows greater freedom in the use of signs than in the use of symbols, as the mind arbitrarily connects the general meaning of signs with their sensuous material (cf. Enc § 457, *Zusatz,* and § 458, R). A sign relinquishes its own self in its meaning as, for example, a flag has no intrinsic meaning apart from what it signifies. Hegel treats language as a "product of intelligence for manifesting its representations in external elements" (Enc § 459, R, p. 271). In verbal expression, Hegel finds the highest expression of thought at the level of imagination because the word disappears in what it signifies. The formation of written language manifests further development in comparison with spoken language. In particular, an alphabetic, written language is above a hieroglyphic one since that which belongs to the mind cannot be given a pictorial sign. Alphabetical writing "takes the mind from the sensuous concrete to attend to the formal, sounded word and its abstract elements and gives foundation to the subject's interiority and makes pure what it is essentially" (Enc 459, R, p. 276).

In memory (*Gedächtnis*), the stage of representation closest to thought, the intelligence inwardizes the signs. An idea is joined to the intuition of a verbal sign (Enc § 461–62). Hegel's example of memory in the *Encyclopaedia of the Philosophical Sciences,* § 462, "remark," is illustrative. "Given the name lion, we need neither the intuition of the animal, nor its image even: the name alone, if we *understand* it, is the unimaged simple representation. We *think* in names." In the *Zusatz* of § 462 Hegel offers further reflection on the relation of thought and language. We think by means of language, yet language is external to thought in the sense that it is the instrument of thinking. Thus, paradoxically a word is an *innerliches Äusserliches.* Words are not limitations on thought but the means by which thought comes to be. Hence the ineffable (*das Unaussprechliche*) is not something excellent but a kind of cloudy thinking seeking clarity. Here we are reminded of Hegel's statement about language made in the *Science of Logic* in the context of his criticism of symbolism which we quoted earlier, that "in language man has a means of designation peculiar to reason" (SL, 618; W6, 295). For Hegel, nothing in principle can impede "the courage of knowing," the power of spirit, in its quest of truth (ILHP, 3; H, 6). As Malcolm Clark points out in his study of representation, the opposition of reality to its being comprehended in thought is the dialectical struggle of reason itself, therefore one cannot be satisfied with speaking of the absolute as "ineffable." He says Hegel's

> rejection of an "ineffable" simply beyond language is not incompatible with a deep sense of that externality of language which is at the heart of meaning: indeed, his dialectic may be seen to spring from the embarrassment of a thought that is present to itself only in the alienation of its expression.[6]

In reflecting upon Hegel's theory of language, we are reminded of Wittgenstein's famous statement that "philosophy is a battle against the bewitchment of our intelligence by means of language" (*Philosophical Investigations* § 109). For Hegel, the recognition of the struggle of language to express pure thought without residue of finite particularity is already a dialectical advance in that the knowing subject can begin to sift out the finitude and particularity of its expression as it moves toward the expression of the infinite and universal.

The paradox of language is that it is both identified with thought and opposed to it. The reason for this duality is the relational character of identity. To realize that thought is other than its expression is to recognize that (1) it is other, and (2) that it is *of thought*, immanently in relation to that which is other than itself. Thought comes into its own only through what is not itself, viz., language that has its origin in nature. Thus, philosophy constantly struggles to say what it means through the spiritual purification of its language, yet thought cannot transcend its language, and so thought and its expression develop dialectically. Of course, it must be recognized that language is not completely external to thought, but that language implicitly contains the thought that issues from it. In the *Realphilosophie,* language and thought develop in tandem, and through the springlike force of opposition they unwind from within through the sublation of their own finitude. Hence, a word, as Hegel says, is an *innerliches Äusserliches.*

"Ineffable" cannot be the final limit of human thought but only the limit that in being recognized as limit is already being surpassed. Thought and language are a dialectical coupling in the spiraling movement toward absolute knowledge.[7] Thought is not something behind its language, but thought is its own linguistic expression. Yet there is a continual alternation within this identification of thought and its expression. In one moment the expression is more than the particular thought-content — the expression of the thought is the essential element. In another moment, thought is more than its particular linguistic expression — now it is the thought that is the essential element. This correlative tension of thought and expression in the sphere of the *Realphilosophie* is the dialectical force that moves toward ever more fully adequate thought in more fully adequate expression.[8]

We see, then, that for Hegel representation is the intermediate stage between intuition and thought. Like sensation, it contains spacial and temporal expression and a plurality of elements. Like thought, it is recognized to express inner and universal truths. The thought element of representation is expressed in determinate spacial-temporal terms, and as such this thinking remains bound to the partiality of a subjective standpoint. Furthermore, not all representations are on the same level but order themselves in the measure that they are pervaded by spirit.[9]

Dominique Dubarle makes an insightful application of the divisions of representation in the *Philosophy of Spirit* to differing forms of religious expression in relation to thought.

> From the point of view of the reconsideration of religious knowledge, one can say that in a certain fashion the epistemology of the narratives of religious events, those that concern the life of Jesus which the evangelists present for example, depends on the gnoseology of *Erinnerung*, and in the same way the epistemology of believing theology, as that of the *Summa* and the traditional treatises, depends according to Hegel on the gnoseology of *Gedächtnis*, while the epistemology proper to philosophy, that of Hegel, depends on the gnoseology of *Denken*.[10]

The differing levels of representation in relation to thought in the revealed religion, historically realized as the Christian religion, will be implied in Hegel's treatment of representation in the *Lectures on the Philosophy of Religion*, to which we shall turn shortly.

The last section of part 3 of the *Encyclopaedia of the Philosophical Sciences*, "Absolute Spirit," describes the ascending stages of the consciousness of the absolute idea in art, religion, and philosophy. These stages of the absolute idea parallel the stages of theoretical spirit — intuition, representation, and thought.

Art is the presentation of the idea in sensuous form. It is spiritual content in material, external form. The highest form of art as art is that which achieves the greatest harmony of spirit and matter. This art Hegel terms beautiful and associates with the art of classical Greece. Beautiful art makes what is sensuous and natural wholly the expression of itself. "It is the inner form which utters [*äussert*] only itself" (Enc § 562, R). But the highest form of art is still limited because it is bound to sensuousness. Thus, Hegel says, "Beautiful art has its future in the true [*wahrhaften*] religion" and so passes into revealed religion (Enc § 563).

It is in the nature of spirit to be self-revealing. Hence, the religion which has the absolute spirit as its content must be the religion of which God himself supplies the content, or better, is the content, through self-revelation (Enc § 564). In the "remark" of § 564, Hegel sharply criticizes theologians, whose task it is to elucidate rationally the given of faith, for facilely accepting that we cannot know God. It is contrary to the notion of revealed religion and to the notion of God as spirit, to asseverate that God is unknowable. The human spirit cannot be content merely with the representations of faith but must move from them to reflective understanding and then to conceptual thought.

As given in representation, the knowledge of God is thought in finite, subjective, reflective categories (*Reflexionsbestimmungen*) by which events are externally connected one to another as a succession of appearances (Enc § 565). The religious mode of thinking divides form from content and distinguishes the form of revealed religion into three spheres or elements. God reveals himself in the first sphere as a self-remaining, eternal content; in the second sphere as a differentiation from his eternal essence into the world of appearances; and in the third as the reconciliation of the alienated world with his eternal essence (Enc § 566).

These three spheres correspond to the moments of universality, particularity, and singularity and together constitute one syllogism of the absolute self-mediation of spirit's self-revelation, which representation expresses in a cycle of concrete shapes (*Gestalten*) (Enc § 571).

If this self-differentiation and this self-reconciliation are understood abstractly and formally, then the process is thought as a result of God's arbitrary will, which makes this process of God vain, willful, and accidental. It is here that philosophy rises above simple faith and gives this content the form of truth by knowing the process as "an indivisible coherence [*Zusammenhang*] of the universal, simple, and eternal spirit in itself," as "the spirit's closing into unity [*Zusammenschliessen*] with itself" (Enc § 571), a closing philosophically seen as necessary since it is the very nature and movement of spirit as such to reveal and reconcile, to differentiate and return.

Art expresses its content in the mode of intuition, and religion in the mode of representation. Philosophy is the cognition of their concept, the science of their spiritual content (cf. Enc § 572). Philosophy knows the necessity or inner coherence of the content that art and religion express in their respective forms. The concern here is the content of the absolute religion, and so Hegel says "philosophy determines itself as a cognition [*Erkennen*] of the necessity of the *content* of the absolute representation" (Enc § 573). By the absolute representation Hegel means that only God and nothing else is represented. The absolute representation is the content of absolute religion, whose content is philosophically cognized as absolute subjectivity inclusive of its activity of self-othering.

All religions and philosophies, Hegel says, proceed from the same need, viz., to grasp a representation of God and his relation to the world (Enc § 573, R, p. 389). This common need of religion and philosophy arises from the nature of the human spirit to be itself fully by knowing itself as spirit, as well as from the nature and character of absolute spirit to know itself in and through this movement of finite spirit knowing beyond itself. "Religion is the truth *for all*" (Enc § 573, R, p. 379), but the human spirit in its desire to know cannot be wholly satisfied with the relatively disjointed representations of God and his relation to the world. Religion acts rightly in disdaining a philosophy that rejects religion because of religion's surface contradictions but fails to see religion's infinite content. But Hegel makes clear that religion cannot reject the philosophy that comprehends the infinite in thought, because the content of speculative philosophy is religion's own content, namely, God and his relation to the world (Enc § 573, R, p. 389). Hegel has consistently argued that speculative philosophy is already (but of course not only) interior to revealed religion and that religion misunderstands itself when it takes its modes of representation as the highest form of truth and thus undercuts its own foundation and leaves itself vulnerable to "rationalist" philosophy. Religion can be the truth for all only if it has its fulfillment in *begreifende Vernunft*.

## Representation in the Lectures on the Philosophy of Religion

Despite a longstanding philosophical interest in religion and a frequent treatment of it in his works, it was not until 1821 in Berlin that Hegel gave a series of lectures on the philosophy of religion. He took up the series again in 1824, 1827, and 1831, each time revising and developing the structure and content of his thought. These series demonstrate the seriousness with which Hegel as a philosopher studied religion and attempted to give religion systematic expression.

Hegel defines religion as "the self-consciousness of absolute spirit" (LPR I, 318; V3, 222). Religion, then, is not simply a human concern but is God's own activity as mediated by human spirits. This self-consciousness of spirit takes place in the mode of representation (LPR I, 141; V3, 55) by which God gives himself, or appears, to human beings. As speculatively defined in this way, religion is the relating of opposing sides — finite consciousness and infinite consciousness — in one subject that holds together this opposition (LPR I, 211–12; V3, 119–20). As such, the content of this consciousness is not of "something true, a this or a that" [*nicht eines Wahren, dieses oder jenes*], but the concrete universal (LPR I, 205; V3, 114), God as essentially related to finite spirit. Because the content of religion is God in relation to finite spirit, the religious sensibility (*Empfindung*) of the human subject is in an inner conflict (*Kampf*) that must issue into a representation that distinguishes the finite spirit from the infinite spirit (LPR I, 216; V3, 124). In other words, the infinite content of religious sensibility cannot rest in finite consciousness but must set itself over against the finite subject as an infinite object in the form of representation. Religious sensibility is not lost in representation but is sublated; sensibility "nourishes itself ... through the representation" (LPR I, 218; V3, 127).

In complementarity with the speculative definition of religion there is the phenomenological determination of religion in the process of the ascent of finite consciousness to the absolute. In terms of the history of consciousness, it is the religious standpoint that recognized the infinite wealth of all that is over against the finitude of every particular thing (LPR I, 222; V3, 130–31). "God" is the name that means the "absolute, all-encompassing fulfillment" (LPR I, 230; V3, 139). The result of the phenomenological investigation of religion turns back upon itself, and this result of the appearance of religion is recognized in the "speculative turn" as the foundation or truth of the appearance. Philosophy cognizes the logical necessity of given religious representations as moments within God's internal self-development and of the development of the universe insofar as the latter is *an sich* divine (LPR I, 231; V3, 140–41).

From the standpoint of our investigation of representation, we have to realize that Hegel is not simply dealing with religious representations as observable data that manifest a historical progression in humanity's self-understanding of its relation to the divine, but that Hegel is attempting to demonstrate the foundation and logical necessity of these representations as manifestations of the movement of absolute spirit.

Representation is based upon images; but in contrast with images, it is universal because it raises the image from the level of sense experience to the level of the universal and so is thought-full (*gedankenvoll*) (LPR I, 238; V3, 148). In a figurative way of speaking, Hegel says thought has "ventured into" [*hineingewagt*] the content of representation, but thought does not "permeate" [*durchdringen*] the content (LPR I, 334; V3, 235).

Because of their elevation above the particularity of sense images, religious representations can express true doctrine. But Hegel is clear that religion expresses a true content only in the measure that religious expression rejects its sensible and figurative form and rejects any sensible and figurative content. Religious representations work the truth by rejecting their figurative form as well as any figurative content "insofar as religious opinion [meaning, *Meinung*] was bound up with the figurative [*Bildliche*]" (LPR I, 239; V3, 149). This "insofar" is the important qualification that Hegel adds to his claim about the truth of religious representations. Whatever part of the representation's content that is sensuous or figurative must be removed. The divine content of religion must be unhusked from its finite form in order for religion to be what it essentially is: the self-consciousness of the divine through human consciousness. Hence there is a struggle within religion because its representations have a figurative form and content that as figurative obfuscate the true content. Religious truth is essentially veiled and requires a labor of the spirit to bring it into clear view.

Because representation is between intuition and thought, it is in "constant unrest" [*beständiger Unruhe*]. It negates its figurative character but remains tied to it. Representation "is still essentially entangled [*verwickelt*] with it [the sensible] and needs it and this struggle [*Kampfes*] against the sensible in order to be itself" (LPR I, 241; V3, 150).

In order for a representation to express religious truth, like a man handcuffed to his enemy who must cooperate with his enemy in order to move toward his goal yet remains at enmity, the true content must negate its figurative content while yet being bound to that figurative content.

As explained in chapter 2, there is an inner content-determination of the content of religious representation that is identical with the content of philosophy — that content is the self-consciousness of absolute spirit. Religion and philosophy do not differ in this content because there cannot be two kinds of self-conscious spirit (LPR I, 333; V3, 235). In other words, it is the oneness of God's being and activity of self-manifestation or spirit as a process of self-return through the mediation of finite spirits that allows Hegel to say that religion and philosophy are one in content. The truth of religion is its concept whereby the content of religion "accords with the concept of spirit," i.e., God's means of appearing is equal to his concept (LPR I, 332; V3, 234).

Yet there is the content of religion that is not identical with the content of philosophy, that is, the content of representation as a form-content unity that includes (albeit in an unsteady way) its sensuous manner of representing. This content has an outer form-determination that has not yet been dominated by its wholly spiritual, inner content-determination. The conflict and "constant unrest" of representation belong within the representation's content as a complex form-content unity. The sensuous form does not touch the inner content but is external and accidental to the content of religion, because finite and infinite spirit relate to one another by spiritual means, not by sensuous means.

Hegel grants the difficulty of precisely separating out what belongs to the essential content of a representation and what belongs to the representation alone as representation, but he never compromises the principle of their distinction. The accusation that philosophy's *Umformung* and *Übersetzung* of religion constitutes a *totale Veränderung, Zerstörung* is the mistake of "ordinary thinking" that is incapable of dealing with the divine content (LPR I, 397; V3, 292). The problem only appears at the level of the understanding, whereas reason is able to separate out the essential content from the content's particular, contingent religious formulation.

That the transformation of the content of religious representation is not a destruction of the content is manifest in the fact that within religion there are different degrees to which thought has "penetrated or dominated" the content of representation.

In the *Philosophy of Spirit* we saw that religion belongs to the sphere of absolute spirit between art and philosophy (Enc § 553 ff.), and we saw that representation has stages in the ascent of spirit to thought (Enc § 451–64). It will be helpful to keep these divisions in mind as we study religious representations in their various degrees of permeation by thought.

Religion, along with art and philosophy, belongs to the universal standpoint. Within this common relationship to the universal, art, religion, and philosophy are distinguished as they are respectively determinations of *Anschauung, Vorstellung,* and *Denken* (LPR I, 234; V3, 143). While distinguishable, each of these three forms of absolute consciousness essentially moves through one another (*läuft durcheinander*) (LPR I, 234; V3, 143).

Art stems from the desire to present the spiritual idea for consciousness by means of intuition (LPR I, 235; V3, 143-44). In order for the spiritual idea to present itself to consciousness, the spectator — more widely, the community — completes the work of art by annulling the exteriority of the work and raising it into identity with itself (LPR I, 236; V3, 145)

The anecdote of the Turk who, when shown a painting of a fish, accused the artist of not painting the soul is an example for Hegel of how the spirit and truth of art (and of religion) reside in the spiritual community — "the spectator, the community, is the soul" (LPR I, 237; V3, 146). Art, like religion, comes to completion when the human spirit recognizes spirit in the object.

Artistic truth, then, is not merely correctness (*Richtigkeit*) — the agreement of the artwork with its known object (as one could think of the example of the fish, wherein the painting of a fish correctly depicts a fish). In the truer sense, artistic truth is the "correspondence [*Zusammenstimmung*] of the object with its concept," (as when the power of universal spirit is recognized in the painting of a fish) (LPR I, 235; V3, 144). The true content of art and of religion, in their respective forms, is absolute, universal spirit. Not to grasp their spiritual content is to remain at the finite level of the understanding.

Hegel's comparison of art and religion is significant for the clarification of his thought about representation because, as the artistic image, merely as an image, is lifeless, so too the representation, merely as a representation, is lifeless. The truth of either art or religion is the correspondence of the artwork or the religious representation with its concept. Their truth depends essentially upon the community that through spiritual "seeing" recognizes the spiritual content in the artwork or in the religious representation. Art is religious for Hegel, and religion, in its turn, is philosophical because art, religion, and philosophy are united in the forming power of spirit.[11] Through artistic activity the human spirit (the artist) forms natural materials into an artwork, and the human community brings the artwork to completion by recognizing the presence of spirit in the material form. Religion is higher than art, though, in that religious representations explicitly point to the divine and, in comparison with art, the representations are "not bound ... to the form of immediate intuition" (LPR I, 238; V3, 147).

As spirit "comes more into its own," we can distinguish ascending levels of representation. As said before, the essential feature of representation is that the spiritual content is put forth in an accidentally connected manner rather than as rationally necessary. Hence Hegel distinguishes the ascending levels of representation as, first, of the sensible, and, second, of the non-sensible. To the first belongs the conveyance of an inner meaning by the use of images. Religious history also belongs to the sensible realm, as its outward form is empirical. The Jesus story (*die Geschichte Jesu*) is an example of the sensible representation. What appears to the senses is the story of a man, by which Hegel means the recording of the perceptible events of Christ's life. The other aspect of the Jesus story is inward and is the object of reason (LPR I, 399; V3, 294). This inward dimension of the story emerges only in the spiritual community. While the imagistic and historical modes of representation belong to sensible expression, there is as well a non-sensible *Gestaltung* of representation to which belong the notions of creation and even of "spirit" itself (in its religious meaning) (LPR I, 400–401; V3, 295–96). A notion like creation is not bound to any sensible image, yet as long as it is merely presented as true without showing its rational necessity, simply as an act of the divine will, it belongs to the realm of representation. The distinguishing characteristic of representation, then, is a spiritual content in a particular, contingent form, "taken as isolated in its determinacy" (LPR I, 404; V3, 299). In distinguishing as he does various contents of representation, primarily the sensible and the non-sensible, Hegel indicates a hierarchy of representations as they become more independent of intuition and approach more closely thought.

We note a further ascent in the levels of religious representation in that Hegel also indicates that there is a greater domination by thought of Christian doctrines than of Christian symbols and stories. Because for Hegel the Christian religion is essentially a teaching, its representations of God and God's activities are universal in meaning and hence are immediately thoughts (LPR I, 106; V3, 24), that is, the doctrinal representations of Christianity are thoughts that have not yet been fully mediated in the form of thought. It is on the basis of its doctrinal character, then, that Hegel can say that "the Christian religion has essentially within itself *Erkenntnis*" and that this *Erkenntnis* brings about the development of a form of thought that opposes the religious forms of representation and feeling (LPR I, 106–7; V3, 25).

Two points are significant to note in this context. One is the emphasis on Christianity as doctrinal. Since the doctrinal representations are more "thoughtful" than other types of representations, Christianity in this developed form as doctrine is essentially knowledge and hence not far from speculative expression. The second is the transitional character of this doctrinal knowledge that stands over against feeling and representation and must have rational expression because it is knowledge.

Because the Christian religion is essentially *Erkenntnis*, philosophy of religion has a twofold purpose: to demand (1) that science (*Wissenschaft*, systematic knowing) take serious consideration of religion, and (2) that religion have the courage of knowing (*Mut des Erkennens*) (LPR I, 109; V3, 26–27). Nothing less than the reconciliation of knowledge and religion in the unity of truth can be satisfactory to the thinking person. When science remains separated from religion, and religion from science, each is one-sided and thus untrue. The opposition is false in origin and arises from wrongly conceiving knowledge on one side (as in the understanding) and religion (as irrational) on the other side.

As stated before, art, religion, and philosophy are spheres of absolute spirit. All arise in their respective forms by the self-same activity of absolute spirit. Hegel can claim that religion and philosophy agree in content because they agree in the activity of the infinite, which is thinking reason that contains and maintains the finite as a moment of itself. Religion and philosophy are both the activity of thinking reason, though religion is naive or unself-conscious (*unbefangene*) about this truth (LPR I, 302; V3, 206). Hotho's notes (which likely are a commentary on Hegel's words at this point) state that "philosophy is reason in the mediated form of thought, whereas art portrays reason immediately in time and space, in stone and sound, while religion internalizes [*erinnert*] this externality" (LPR I, 302; V3, 206–7). Religious truth is expressed in representations, many of which retain a spacial-temporal surface but whose content is recollected and interiorized from its immediately given, material form.

Although the most extensive treatment of representation in the *Lectures on the Philosophy of Religion* occurs in volume 1, "The Concept of Religion," brief consideration should be given as well to the placement of representation in "The Consummate Religion."

In the course of the series of *Lectures on the Philosophy of Religion*, Hegel came to integrate a dyadic formulation of the objective (God) and subjective (finite spirit) elements of religion with a triadic formulation of absolute unity, difference or diremption, and unity-in-difference as found in the *Encyclopaedia of the Philosophical Sciences*, § 566.

In volume 3 of the *Lectures*, "The Consummate Religion," Hegel in 1821 distinguishes an outer triad of "abstract concept," "concrete representation," and "cultus," and an inner triad of God in himself, God in creation, and God in history constituting "concrete representations." Interestingly in this 1821 division, the second person of the Trinity belongs to the third division of the inner triad. In the later lectures Hegel changed this division so that the third person of the Trinity corresponds to the third division of what in 1821 is the outer triad. In commenting on this "trinitarian" division of Hegel's treatment of consummate religion, Dale Schlitt says, with particular reference to the 1821 *Lectures*,

> it is as if Hegel, who had so clearly and exhaustively discussed the three moments of the concept in the *Logic* as universality, particularity, and individuality, cannot refrain from speaking of the determinations of the concept without at least affirming a structural parallel between the three moments of the concept in the *Logic* and the three elements of "concrete representation" as moments of the consummate religion. (V5, 15)[12]

From 1824 onward, representation in volume 3 of the *Lectures on the Philosophy of Religion* is treated as the second element of the development of the idea of God, which corresponds to the second moment of the Trinity *ad extra*. The first element in this division is the idea of God in and for itself; the third is the community. The condition of possibility for distinguishing these three spheres of the economic Trinity is the immanent Trinity, i.e., the divine unity, diremption, and return of the Trinity *ad intra*. From 1824 on, the overall structure of volume 3 of the *Lectures* is divided according to a speculative interpretation of the Christian religion that translates the representation of the Trinity as Father, Son, and Spirit into the concept of the Trinity as the three moments of the idea: self-identity, self-differentiation, and self-return. The second element of the Trinity *ad extra* encapsulates the movement of the divine life from inner unity to differentiation to reconciliation.

Ultimately, then, Hegel's entire philosophy can be viewed as a "thinking backward" from the Christian religious representation of the Trinity to the pure form of the absolute idea whose content is *"the exposition of God as he is in his eternal essence before the creation of nature and a finite spirit"* (SL, 50; W5, 44).

The sphere of representation is, then, "the divine history ... , God as having his determinate being in the world" where he appears to finite spirit (LPR III, 187; V5, 121). Representation is the element of self-externalization that has its "return" in the cultus or spiritual community in which human spirits are raised to the level of infinite spirit as the all-inclusive unity-in-difference.

## The Problem of Religious Representation

With reference to the "Greater" and "Lesser" *Logics*, the *Phenomenology of Spirit*, the third part of the *Encyclopaedia of the*

*Philosophical Sciences*, and the *Lectures on the Philosophy of Religion*, we have presented Hegel's conception of representation and its place within his system of thought. We have now to clarify the Hegelian meaning of religious representation and to offer an interpretative evaluation in answer to certain questions that present themselves. Can the expression of speculative thought more adequately apprehend the divine than representation, and if so does representation drop away, and therefore religion itself, for those who can think at the conceptual level? Hegel's answer to the first part of the question is clear, though contested. Representation is an inherently limited form that partially veils its divine content, which content can become transparent in pure thought. Hegel's own answer to the second part of the question is unclear and seems to shift somewhat from the *Phenomenology of Spirit* to the Berlin lectures on philosophy of religion, but a fitting interpretation can be offered.

## *The Doubleness of Representation*

Religious representations mediate the divine and the human, the infinite and the finite. Finite spirit is both finite and spirit. As finite, it is immersed in the realm of unmediated nature and intellectual darkness, alienated from God. As spirit, it has its "citizenship in heaven" and is like unto God, who is pure spirit. At this point Hegel's philosophy can be read to agree with the whole Christian religious tradition that the finite, human spirit is *capax dei,* and that through time and labor by the initiative of divine grace it may overcome (at least in some degree) its separation from God.

Religious representation points beyond itself. It presents (from *praeesse*, "to be in front of") a universal, infinite content in particular, finite form. Hence within representation there is an inherent tension between the inner content and outer form. To the atheist, this tension is a contradiction. If religious representations say anything, their content is human. They are radically and completely anthropomorphic. We need think here only of Feuerbach. This atheistic reduction of representation negates the absolute content of representation and fails to conceive the true nature of the infinite. Nonetheless, the finite character of representation does obstruct its infinite content and partially explains the atheistic tendency to reduce all representations to a purely human content. In order for representation to express the absolute, the tension of inner content and outer form must be reconciled.

William Desmond points out the double way in which representation functions.

On the one hand, we need to pass through and beyond its mere sensuousness, in order to apprehend its non-sensuous content. On the other hand, since we have to pass through the sensuous form to attain contact with the content, invariably the sensuous form seems to separate us from the content. As a mediator, the sensuous form of representation both unites us with the content and separates us from it.[13]

Hegel himself points out this double character of representation wherein "the idea is veiled at the same time it is unveiled"; the essence (*Wesen*) shows (*Scheint*) in the appearance (*Erscheinung*), at the same time the essence is only appearance (ILHP, 39; H, 57). The recognition of this difference between a representation, and its meaning indicates the need to unclothe the meaning for thought. In general we see that representation has a mediating and a transitional role in revealing the absolute.[14] The double character of religious representation is present throughout Hegel's philosophy. Earlier, in the *Phenomenology of Spirit*, Hegel emphasizes the character of representation as hindrance to absolute knowledge. Later, in the *Lectures on the Philosophy of Religion* from 1824 on Hegel emphasizes the character of representation as facilitation.

From the standpoint of the goal of thought, representation holds a central and necessary position in mediating the opposition of infinite and finite according to the dialectical character of reality as thought. In the ascent of human consciousness, the mind must first form representations before forming concepts (cf. Enc § 1). As long as the human mind does not fix upon the finite form but allows the content to purify itself in the rational comprehension of spirit, representation will not permanently separate the human and the divine. Hegel's intention is to negate the untrue form of representation and to make explicit the self-consciousness of the tension and instability already implicit in representation. The *Aufhebung* of religious representation into conceptual form is not, from the philosophical standpoint, an extraneous reworking of representation but is internal to representation because "religious representation initiates a questioning of itself."[15] Hegel has noted that representation as "constant unrest" mediates intuition and thought, so that spirit from within representation wars against its figurative form (LPR I, 241; V3, 150).

## The Continuity of Representation and Thought

Paul Ricoeur points out that it is crucial to the Hegelian meaning of the sublation of religion in philosophy to recognize the inner dynamism of religious representations. The images and figurative modes of religious expression, he says, are not extrinsic additions to the spirit of a culture that produces its religious representations; rather, these representations encapsulate the whole progress of spirit to that moment. This internal movement of religious, figurative expression means that reason's speculative explication of religious expression is not an addition alongside the religious but a dialectical working out from within of the representations themselves. "Religious representations are not inert contents, but processes traversed by an inner dynamism toward the speculative mode."[16]

Religion itself then, if it is true to its inner drives, is thrust on its own initiative toward conceptual thought. Religion battles against its own idolatrous tendencies. However, according to Hegel religion by its representational mode alone cannot unite the human and divine without recognizing its destiny in *begreifende Vernunft*. The representations of religion must be *aufgehoben*. It may at first seem contradictory to say, on the one hand, that representation is raised to the level of pure thought by philosophy as a purely speculative activity and, on the other hand, that religion of itself purifies representation according to its inner truth. These assertions are contradictory, however, only when religion and philosophy are defined exclusively of one another. The very fact that religion tends toward the rational clarification of its own representations is an indication of the continuity of religious representation and thought. As will become clear in the argument of subsequent chapters, the content of religion has its destiny in thought, and philosophy as the activity of pure thought has its embodied life in rational religion, so that ultimately absolute religion and absolute philosophy have a sublated unity.

For Hegel, absolute religion and absolute philosophy are different languages to express the same truth. Hegel's efforts are principally (and necessarily) concerned to translate the content of religion into the form and language of conceptual thought so as firmly to found this content in the form of the truth. However, most interestingly, and most strikingly, in his 1829 review of Karl Göschel's *Aphorismen über Nichtwissen und absolutes Wissen im Verhältnisse zur christlichen Glaubenserkenntnis*, Hegel looks favorably upon the idea of a reverse direction, namely, from conceptual thinking to representation. For Hegel, speculative truth once established through the rigor of conceptual thinking is then in the position "to look after" and "to care for" [*pflegen*] representation and faith (cf. W11, 377).

> If with respect to the aforementioned boundness [*Gebundenheit*] to the form of thought this [form of thought] will be paramount in a logical elaboration, so must it be all the more welcome to find in a writing such as this one [viz.,

Göschel's] the speculative concepts elaborated to the [point of the] recognition of their agreement with religious representations and the words and signs of the one translated into the language of the other. (W11, 379-80)

Clearly, philosophy is superior to religion in respect to demonstrating the truth,[17] but (at least by his later years) religious representation has an established and enduring place in Hegel's philosophy.

## Thomistic Analogy and Hegelian Representation

The sophisticated religious consciousness has always recognized the insufficiency and translucency of its figurative form of expression but has not been inclined to think that any thought of the divine could be transparent. At this point a comparison of Aquinas's notion of analogy with Hegel's notion of representation and their positions in their respective philosophical systems may help clarify precisely how we are to interpret the relation of religion and philosophy in Hegel's thought.

Raymond Williamson in his study of Hegel's philosophy of religion says in an endnote that thoughtful religious people have always recognized that myths and other figurative discourse about the divine are never to be taken literally but as pointing beyond themselves to their ultimate basis. Williamson notes that this recognition about religious language is not new with Hegel. Aquinas's theory of analogy is the classic example of this recognition, though the Protestant tradition with which Hegel was acquainted had little regard for Aquinas's thought. Here Williamson makes a statement that invites further consideration. "Hegel's comments about religious language may be seen as providing the same realization as the doctrine of analogy — for his own tradition, which he found to be so ensnared in the narrow confines of literalism."[18]

We should first note that Hegel's use of the word "analogy" has no special philosophical significance for him and is loosely grouped with other "indeterminate forms" (cf. LPR I, 334; V3, 235). In Aquinas's thought, on the other hand, "analogy" is the word that denominates the link between human thought and divine reality as founded upon the link between created being and divine being and is of central importance in Aquinas's epistemology.

In order to understand Aquinas's notion of analogy we must distinguish it from univocal predication in which the concept has an identical meaning in every instance, as, for example, "Socrates is wise" and "Plato is wise." In analogous predication there is a sameness and a difference in the predicate itself, as, for example, "Socrates is wise" and "God is wise." That which is the same in both predicates is the *res significata;* that which is different is the *modus significandi*. The sameness of the thing signified is not a univocal but an analogous sameness, that is, the *res* which the concept signifies applies differently to each subject. Questions arise, then, as to the nature of the unity of the analogous concept and the extent to which the thing signified can be differentiated from the mode of its signification.[19]

From the ontological standpoint for Aquinas, that which applies to God and world has its primary and proper meaning in God and applies in a derivative and secondary sense to creatures, because ontologically creatures are the effects of their creator. In the order of knowledge, however, our concepts are applied properly and primarily to the things of our experience and then by analogy (i.e., improperly and secondarily) are applied to God. In Aquinas's philosophy of analogy, then, the order of knowledge is inverted in relation to the order of being, so that the thing signified by the concept which first had its proper application to creation and only an improper application to God now, from the ontological standpoint, is recognized to have its proper application to God and only improper application to creation. This transmutation of a humanly derived meaning into a divine meaning takes place by changing the mode of signification of that which the concept signifies from its limited, imperfect form in the world to a higher, more perfect mode of signification in God. The thing signified, which in the created order had a definite and comprehended content, has in God an indefinite and not fully comprehended content.[20] The content of the concept in God is open and wide relative to its defined meaning in the created order. The mode of signification is changed from a finite to an infinite form, and the thing signified is transferred from creation to God. The struggle of analogous predication in theology is to move from the natural world in which our knowledge originates to the divine in which the meaning of our concepts finds its perfection and its ontological origin. The ontological basis of analogy is in the likeness of effects to their cause. We are able to rise to a knowledge of God because his effects are to some extent like his essence. In order to know God we must move away from the finite and sensible toward the infinite and non-sensible.[21]

It is evident that there is a likeness, albeit complex, between Aquinas's analogy and Hegel's representation. That which is analogously expressed of God really says something of God but is limited by the form of its expression, viz., human experience as embodied in language. The content of the expression struggles to break out of its limited form, and succeeds in doing so in the measure it makes expression refer to its illimited and perfect content. Human thought is able to achieve some knowledge of God because the ideas of our knowledge ultimately have their foundation in God and when transferred to God return, as it were, to their ontological source, as when we know what wisdom, goodness, and being mean in the worldly sphere and then know by way of analogy that God is wisdom itself, goodness itself, being itself. Knowledge of God is knowledge of the cause from the effects. The human mind is able to rise to God because the world is the effect of God.

For Hegel, the religious representations point beyond themselves but do not fully achieve what they point toward because of the finitude and particularity of their forms; nonetheless, that to which they point is the infinite and universal. For Hegel nothing is apart from God, and the rising from the natural world to God through human thought is itself the immanent activity of infinite spirit returning to itself as the inclusive unity of God and world.

Both Aquinas and Hegel indicate the limitations of figurative language about God, and both attempt by means of rational thought to show how such language can properly express something of God. Whatever its form, what is truly thought of God must have its ontological basis in God. For Aquinas, analogy changes not only the mode of signification of its concepts but transfers the thing signified from its epistemological origin in human experience to its ontological origin in God. For Hegel, the transition from religious representation to speculative thought is not only a change in form of expression but a dialectical *Aufhebung* of its content. The content is moved from a finite to an infinite plane. Furthermore, Hegel's sublation of religious truth in philosophical truth parallels Aquinas's rational explication of the workings of analogous predication.

Are then Aquinas's notion of analogy and Hegel's notion of representation the same? Without trying to appear facetious, the precise answer is that they are analogous. The two philosophical systems cannot simply be conflated. The relation is complicated because it seems that Thomistic analogy is not only to be compared to Hegelian representation but to Hegelian dialectic, moreover in a way relative to each philosophical system. For Aquinas, the relation between God and world is intrinsically analogical by way of efficient and final causality. For Hegel, the relation is immanently dialectical as to ground and end. As regards our knowledge of God, for Aquinas our highest knowledge of God is analogical — imperfect, indirect, and partial. Only in this regard is Thomistic analogy, in Hegelian terms, representational. As regards our ontological relation to God, for Aquinas all things causally participate in God as their source and goal as a relation of finite being to infinite being.

> Because we come to a knowledge of God from other things, the reality [*res*] in the names said of God and other things belongs by priority in God

according to his mode of being, but the meaning of the name belongs to God by posteriority. And so he is said to be named from his effects. (*Summa Contra Gentiles* I, 34, 6)

For Hegel, the infinite is the inclusive, immanent, dialectical process that is source and goal of its own movement of self-determination in and by finite things. To think this dialectical process is to be one with absolute, infinite spirit. The philosophies of Aquinas and Hegel cannot, then, be compared straightforwardly. In certain respects, to think analogously is to think, in Hegel's terms, representationally; in other respects, it is to think dialectically. The problem for both philosophers is the same, namely, the relation of infinite and finite, in thought and in reality. For Aquinas, the two sides are ontologically related causally by participation, and this relation is thought and expressed analogously. For Hegel, the relation is dialectical, partially and externally thought and expressed in representation, and only adequately thought and expressed in dialectical thinking. Both philosophers are concerned to explain how it is that we can know God. While for Aquinas the human soul can never achieve full knowledge of God, for Hegel it must be remembered that the human spirit as human — i.e., as finite — cannot know the absolute. However, by contrast for Hegel, the human spirit knows the absolute as the human spirit is raised to the level of the absolute in the absolute's knowledge of itself as mediated through human spirits. For Aquinas and Hegel, God is truth, the completely transparent knowledge of the whole of reality. In our opinion, however, Hegel brings out more clearly than Aquinas the essentially relational character of what it means to say God knows himself perfectly. All knowledge must include opposition that is thought together as a dynamic unity-in-difference.

This Hegelian reading of Thomistic epistemology and metaphysics may not commend itself to many Thomists and Hegelians, but it would be untrue to the spirit of either philosopher to disdain bridge building between philosophies and in any way to stymie our intellects in the attempt to know and think all things together.

This comparison of Aquinas and Hegel has the purpose here of clarifying Hegel's thinking about representation and its religious import. One point to note is that Aquinas's doctrine of analogy is recognized as integral to the religious tradition (even as dominated by that tradition), and it arose in an epoch when philosophy and theology were distinguished but not separated. This integration of philosophy within the religious tradition is exemplary for the interpretation of Hegel's thought because it shows rational thought at work within religion. William Desmond claims that Hegel does not draw out the implications of the fact that the sophisticated religious mind concerns itself with the difficulties inherent in its religious expression; to show that Hegel does not fully recognize the implications of this fact, he quotes Hegel's statement that "the religious consciousness [*Vorstellungsweise*] does not apply the criticism of thought to itself, does not comprehend itself, and is therefore, in its immediacy, exclusive" (Enc § 573, R, p. 381).[22] In fairness to Hegel it must be said that when the religious consciousness gives rational explanation of its representations, it is thinking philosophically and not properly religiously, because the specifically religious mode of thinking is *Vorstellungsweise*. Desmond's criticism at this point may not be incisive; but it is true, as Hegel recognizes, that there is a religious self-consciousness of the problem of anthropomorphism and an effort within religion to correct rationally any relations to a false idea of God as is evident, for example, in the philosophy/theology of Aquinas. We must remember that Hegel's polemic against religion's *Vorstellungsweise* occurs in the context of the thought of Kant, Jacobi, Schleiermacher, *et alii*, and more widely in the context of thought deriving from the divorce of faith and reason in the late Middle Ages. We can agree with Desmond's attempt to show "the continuity of religion and reason in a manner consonant with Hegel's view, and ... the internal resources of religion itself which preserve it against the onslaughts of an exclusively negative, 'critical' rationality."[23] Hegel himself appears to have grown in his recognition of the continuity of religion and reason within religious self-consciousness, as is evident in the *Lectures on the Philosophy of Religion*.

## Reason within Religion

We have established that there is a gradation in the levels of representation that form a continuum between intuition and thought according to their greater permeation by spirit and their lesser entwinement with contingent and external elements. Hegel's recognition of an ascending ladder of representations within religion is important for the philosophical evaluation of religious representation. By emphasizing the inadequacy of every religious representation in relation to its philosophically transformed content, one tends to take a negative outlook toward representation in Hegel's philosophy of religion. On the other hand, by emphasizing the process of rational purification of representational expression within religion itself, one tends to take a more positive outlook toward representation. According to Paul Ricoeur, Hegel's own thinking about the value of religious representation manifests such a change in attitude and emphasis. Ricoeur notes that Hegel's theory of representation in the *Phenomenology of Spirit* emphasizes the *Aufhebung* as destruction because of Hegel's "impatience" with the resistance of representations to conceptual thought. This "impatience" with any figurative expression, Ricoeur points out, is the result of Hegel's recognition that the "determinateness" of figurative expressions constrains the development of spirit. There is a tendency to stay at the figurative level, which is spirit in an unmediated form rather than to recognize the self-destructive tendency of these representations in their path toward absolute spirit. As should be clear, the problem for Hegel in the *Phenomenology of Spirit* is not with religious expression *per se* but with all uncritically accepted formulations of reality. Thus the representations must be, in figurative expression of our own, "cracked open" if the truth of what they contain is to emerge in transparent form.[24]

Since figurative expression is not the adequate form of the self-consciousness of spirit, philosophy must sift out the figurative elements so as to achieve the purely conceptual truth within the figurative expressions. But Ricoeur asks how the process of philosophical interpretation can be carried out if the historical dimension is removed. "To what extent is this reduction of the historicity, say, of the life of Jesus, compatible with the claim that the Absolute has been revealed in 'this' man?" (83). The question is central to the assessment of Hegel's philosophy of religion. In what degree and manner does conceptual thought do away with religious representations, or precisely how do the representations remain essential to their rational elucidation?

Ricoeur says that, in contrast to the *Phenomenology of Spirit*, the *Lectures on the Philosophy of Religion* present the *Aufhebung* of the representations more in the sense of a preservation, but that is because in the *Lectures* Hegel focuses upon the rationally developed representations of the Christian doctrinal tradition rather than upon the stories and symbols of religious expression. This change in focus means that Hegel's philosophy need not be as destructive of religious discourse in its progress toward absolute spirit because it is clear that "philosophy has to deal with a religious discourse that theology has already brought to its dialectical expression" (85).

Because absolute knowledge does not create its object but rather recapitulates the process that has preceded it, and because the dialectic is the accumulation of its interior dynamism rather than an external addition of phases, Ricoeur is led to assert that absolute knowledge is not a final stage displacing the other stages but is the thoughtfulness of all the stages. "Absolute knowledge ... is not a supplement of knowledge but the thoughtfulness of all the modes that generate it" (86). Religious stories and symbols are not abolished in thought but are continually interpreted in conceptual thinking according to the inner movement of the representations themselves. Philosophy of religion aims at conceptual thought by retaining its basis in the mediating shapes of representational thought (88). At this point we are in agreement with Ricoeur, but we should be clear that Ricoeur has adapted somewhat Hegel's own position as to the final stage of the dialectic. In the *Phenomenology of Spirit*, for Hegel, absolute knowledge is the thoughtfulness of what went before, as Ricoeur notes, but, in contrast with Ricoeur, it is also a going beyond what went before. It is the final shape of self-consciousness and, at this stage in Hegel's thought, is the initial moment of logical thought. As the final moment, it includes the moments of its development and in that sense transcends them. As the culmination of a process by which the absolute appears to human consciousness, absolute knowledge is the final stage of knowledge that for the Hegel of the *Phenomenology of Spirit* leaves representation behind. By the time of his *Lectures on the Philosophy of Religion*, Hegel tends to the view of the continuation and preservation of representation as rationally clarified. This change in view appears to us to arise from the inner working of Hegel's own thought as the actualization of the concept and the movement of sublation, so that Ricoeur's understanding of absolute knowledge as preserving in thought what has gone before makes better sense of how we are to think of dialectical progression and, as will be seen, how we are to conceive the relation of religion and philosophy. This continuity in the relation of religion and philosophy, the recognition of religion's self-conscious questioning of its symbols and stories, and its effort to purify itself of false images, especially as seen in the developments of the Christian doctrinal tradition, together indicate that the question of the relation of religion and philosophy in Hegel's thought (at least from the Berlin period) is better posed in conciliatory than conflictual terms.

In order to help make our interpretation of Hegel's philosophy concrete, we should consider that too often we overlook the fact that religious language and practice arise in a social context in a continual process of human activity and reflection. The authors of Genesis, for example, were seeking, by means of the Creation accounts, to make sense of certain aspects of the human situation. The faith community of the Jewish people, characterized as a *Volksgeist*, engendered and accepted these myths as an authentic expression of the human relation to God. The continuous faith interpretations of these stories through the ages testify to their richness. The meaning and interpretation of these stories arose according to a hermeneutic development in response to deep and pervasive human questions. The myths need never be interpreted in ways contrary to reason, and the sophisticated religious consciousness has been self-correcting in this regard. Imagination, feeling, wonder, and intellection form (at least ideally) an interrelated whole in human religious life. Moreover, while religious teaching is not purely philosophical, it is still cognitive in a wide sense, otherwise it should not be knowable or receptive of assent. Augustine noted this fact in his Sermon 43, quoted in chapter 1 above, when he said, "Understand that you may believe," since no one can believe what is said unless he or she understands (to some extent) what is said. Hegel's claim to translate the representations of the Christian religion into purely rational form is simply in his eyes the one activity of the same spirit that first engendered and fostered the representations and gave them meaning. As Jaeschke notes,

> the passage from [representation] to conceptual thought must be carried out from a position which does better justice to that truth which is also representation's own truth — better than representation itself does.[25]

In a way representation has a priority over conceptual thought not only in chronology, nor even only in its universal availability as "religion is the truth *for all*" (Enc § 573, R, p. 379), but in the fact that image, symbol, and story more deeply engage the whole human person — intellect, imagination, and feeling — than any pure thought can do because religious representations are palpable and grasp the human person in a psychic and emotional unity. Philosophy has priority over representation, however, as it brings forth the truth and corrects error. Philosophy, though, can only bring forth the truth already present. In this regard, representations are essential to set the truth content before human consciousness and raise human consciousness to the divine.[26] If God is not a determinate representation for human subjectivity, then religious feeling lacks foundation. There can be no *Erkenntnis* of God without a representation as the intended object of the religious consciousness (LPR I, 192–93; V3, 101–2). The antipathy of philosophy and religion arises when religion finally fails to give primacy to an objective moment as inclusive of the subjective moment and prefers feelings to objective truth.

In calling attention to the fact of reason within religion and religion's embodiment of rational thought in religious expression, life, and practice, we are emphasizing the continuity of religion and philosophy and arguing that religion is not subsumed or obviated in its philosophical comprehension. We need not interpret philosophy's sublation of religious representation primarily as cancellation of religious expression.

Clearly there is a process of struggle and violence involved in the use of representational language to arrive at conceptual thought. In a passage that Rosenkranz records from an introduction to some lectures on the system of philosophy in Jena, Hegel is recorded as noting the inevitable struggle that results from trying to express the infinite by means of representations as exemplified by Böhme's mystical expression.

> The modern mysticism [i.e., Böhme's] is of a darker cast and a more sorrowful kind [than oriental mysticism, which cancels its images as it uses them]. It steps into the depths of the essence with common, sensible representations and fights to make itself master of it and bring it before its consciousness. But the essence will not let itself be grasped in the form of a common sensible representation. Any representation of this kind that it is grasped in is inadequate. It is only made to fit the essence by violence, and must equally violently be torn [away from it]; it presents only the battle of an inward [essence] that is fermenting within itself, and cannot advance into the clear light of day, feels its incapacity with sorrow, and rolls about it in fits and convulsions that can come to no proper issue.
>
> The clear element is the universal, the concept, which [is] as deep as it is extensive in its revelation that leaves nothing veiled.[27]

By contrast with Hegel's thinking in his Jena period (at least as refracted by Rosenkranz), we see a somewhat different emphasis on the value and role of religious representation in Hegel's 1829 review of Karl Göschel's *Aphorismen über Nichtwissen und absolutes Wissen im Verhältnisse zur christlichen Glaubenserkenntnis.* In answer to the question posed by Göschel "whether in its progression philosophy might not gain in clarity and determinateness if it would *join itself* more resolutely *to the word of God,*" and even whether "the *representation, the shape*" [*die Gestalt*] might not be the highest form of the truth rather than thought (W11, 377), Hegel repeats the fact that conceptual thought is gained by violent struggle with representation. But he makes his assertion with a strikingly different emphasis on the rebound of the achievement of conceptual thought within faith and its expression.

> With regard to himself the reviewer [Hegel] cannot dismiss what the author [Göschel] claims in the passage cited. The author has herewith touched upon a most interesting question [*Gesichtspunkt*] — the coming-over [*Herübergehen*] in general *from representation to concept* and *from concept to representation,* a coming-over-from and a going-over-to [*ein Herüber- und Hinübergehen*] which is present in scientific meditation and which is here required also to be expressed everywhere in scientific presentation.... [This] reviewer should recall, at least with a view to offering an apology for the incompleteness of his work in this respect, that indeed the *starting point,* which also the author names, chiefly imposes to join oneself more firmly to

the concept wrung from the representation often in hard struggle and to the concept's course of development, as its expression in pure thought is called. [It also imposes] to follow more strictly in its track in order to become sure [of the development] of the concept and to restrain forcibly the distraction, which representation in its many-sidedness and the form of contingency in the connection of its determination brings with it. This many-sidedness brings the danger of complacency too close by relaxing the rigor of the method of thought. The [herewith] attained greater stability in the movement of the concept will allow one to be without concern for the seduction of representation and [will allow one] to give freer play to representation under the rule of the concept. Just like the certainty, which is already present in divine faith allows originally to be calm vis-à-vis the concept as well to be in the concept without fear concerning its consequences as also less troubled about its consistency which when faith is presupposed does not have to prove itself to be free. (W11, 378–79)[28]

In this later view of Hegel, religious representation gains stability, certainty, and freedom "under the rule of the concept" and is no longer an obstacle course to be gotten through on the way to conceptual thought.[29]

*The Achievement of Conceptual Thought*

If one grants that representational expression can by degrees approach the full truth, the question remains whether conceptual expression can ever achieve the full truth in the pure form of truth without admixture of a limiting form. In other words, can God be known as God knows himself or must philosophical expression remain always "at a distance" and remain inherently representational itself?

David Tracy, we recall, claims that conceptual expression is less adequate than metaphor and symbol in disclosing the divine. For Tracy, reason has only a regulative function for religion, and in this regard he appears to take a Kantian position. Aquinas's position appears closer to Hegel's in that he identifies being and intelligibility so that the mysteries of faith are reasonable and in principle knowable. Because of the finitude of our intellects, we remain always unable to comprehend the divine, though by analogical predication we can rise from the sensible basis of our mode of knowing to knowledge of the supersensible. Knowledge by analogy, however, is still "at a distance" and is not knowledge of God as God knows himself. For Hegel, of course, the conceptual knowledge of God is God's self-knowledge, though as a process immanent in human spirits. Dubarle indicates an important difference, though, between the two philosophers in regard to the relation of thought and reality. When Aquinas says that "things have the same disposition in truth as in being" [*sic enim est dipositio rerum in veritate, sicut et in esse*] (*Summa Contra Gentiles* I, 1, 2), he means that when the human intellect has a true knowledge of God, the knowledge of the being of God is proportionate to the human mind and not simply identical to the being of God. For Hegel, the true knowledge of God is no longer "simply an 'isomorphism' between the disposition of the thought and the disposition of the thing ... the speculative truth is the *identity* of the thought to the Truth."[30] What has provoked so much discussion is Hegel's claim that speculative philosophy can achieve this identity of thought and divine truth. Though in contrast with what Aquinas says, it may be that Hegel's ultimate identification of thought and reality accords better with the radical implication of Aquinas's acceptance of the perfect intelligibility of being.

Raymond Williamson questions Hegel's claim that philosophy can provide absolute knowledge. Williamson asserts that "no finite mind can fully grasp, and no finite language can adequately express the Absolute."[31] Religious language is allusive because all expression of the divine is allusive: "No linguistic expression or concept ... can embrace ultimate reality: all our expressions and concepts are nothing more than signs or symbols."[32] Williamson claims that even Hegel's concept of spirit is a symbol.

Williamson's assertions, however, do not precisely connect with Hegel's thinking because finite mind and language do not *qua* finite know the infinite; it is rather the encompassing nature of the infinite activity in finite spirits that raises them to the level of the infinite. For Hegel, the true infinite itself constitutes and is constituted by the relation of finite and infinite. God is the wholly affirmative principle that determines the finite and particular moments within the infinite. For Hegel, it is the true infinite that constitutes the religious standpoint by which the human subject surrenders its particularity and becomes "interwoven with the thing itself" [*in die Sache hineinverflochten*] (LPR I, 283–84; V3, 188). It is this foundation of religion that is the foundation of Hegel's philosophical claims as well. By contrast, it would be impossible to found religion upon the finite subjectivity of reflective consciousness which thinks in finite categories because, rather than God, the single subject is the affirmative (LPR I, 300; V3, 205) and no relation to the infinite can be established merely from the finite standpoint considered in isolation from the whole.

Anselm Min offers a Hegelian answer to those who would deny the possibility of a rational knowledge of God.[33] He points out that Hegel never denies the finitude of human reason. Human reason arises within history, in a struggle with contingency and irrational elements. Only the absolute, true infinite can completely realize the unity of all elements and seeming contradictions; the absolute idea has "within itself the highest degree of opposition" (SL, 824; W6, 549). Reason transcends the finite but is mediated through the finite. Human reason cannot prove, for example, the necessity of the Incarnation prior to its being given, represented, to human reason. But once given, reason can recognize the Incarnation as rational, i.e., as logically necessary.[34] In the Incarnation, the dialectical character of divine and human reason becomes manifest as the necessary condition of the Incarnation as God's self-revelation.

Hegel's philosophy would be merely abstract reflection without the concrete content of the Incarnation. Religious consciousness knows the Incarnation, though imperfectly in the form of representation. Perfect knowledge of the content of the Incarnation is achieved in speculative reason according to the systematic interrelations of the whole. The Christian mysteries, then, are necessary to the philosophy of absolute spirit, not as a set of historical, contingent facts, but in their universal significance. The philosophical comprehension of the Christian representations is the interpenetration of the religious and philosophical consciousness in such a way that, as Min says, we possess "faith informed by thought and thought given its content by faith."[35]

We see, then, that for Hegel rational comprehension is the fulfillment of the revelation of the divine that begins in representations. Spirit reveals itself to spirit, and the rational elucidation of representations is the continuation of the process of revelation. In a sense Hegel is bringing forth in a more radical way the scholastic insight of the identity of being and intelligibility. Because all that is is oriented to being known, the opposition of reason and religious revelation breaks down as they merge into one movement of divine activity. Finite spirit's knowledge of God is God's knowledge of self. If God is perfectly known to himself, then that self-knowledge is of and for spirit, and every finite spirit, as spirit, must as it grows in knowledge grow in the knowledge of God. The finite, frail character of human knowing is constantly being sublated as mind moves from the level of faith and of understanding to the level of reason.

*The Problem of the Linguistic Expression of Conceptual Thought*

Hegel's claim to achieve the level of pure thought in his philosophy by the supersession of all representational modes of thought is problematic and requires some explication. The problem can be stated as an antinomy. Language is the expression of thought, and yet language as a form of representation opposes thought. We recall from the *Encyclopaedia of the Philosophical Sciences* that "we think in names" (Enc § 462, R), and in the *Zusatz* of § 462 Hegel adds that "to want to think without words ... appears as an *Unvernunft*." The reason we must think in language is that

> we only know our thoughts, only have definite, actual thoughts when we give them the form of *objectivity*, of a *being distinct* from our *inwardness*, and therefore the shape of *externality*, and of an externality too, that at the same time bears the stamp of the highest *inwardness*.... The word is such an *innerliches Äusserliches*. (Enc § 462, Zusatz)

Similarly, we recall Hegel's statement in the *Science of Logic* that "in language man has a means of designation peculiar to reason" (SL, 618; W6, 295). Hegel says as well that *"language* is the work of thought" (Enc § 20, R, p. 74).

Because thought and language are interwoven in their dialectical development, how can thought, even at the level of absolute spirit, escape from the externality of language if language, as Hegel argues, remains always a form of representation and representation does not have the form of pure thought? Mure states well the dilemma (one might argue, the antinomy) of Hegel's philosophy.

> In all thinking language survives to subserve thought as its indispensable expression. Without discourse thought cannot fulfil itself as thought. But this dependence of thought for the fulfilment of its own nature upon a lower, still sensuous phase of spirit precludes the perfecting of this fulfilment. Even philosophical thought is an incomplete synthesis of language with thought. It can never quite pass from meaning to truth, from reference to an object to utter self-identification with its object.[36]

Mure's conclusion is that "the problem of expression is not in Hegel's philosophy completely solved, and that on Hegel's own theory of language pursued to its conclusion no complete solution is possible."[37] Is Hegel wrong in claiming to achieve the pure form of thought? "Language is the work of thought," and "we think in names." There can be no human thought without language because we can only have thoughts in objective form, that is, in words that make the thoughts external to us. A word, then, is an *innerliches Äusserliches* (Enc § 462, *Zusatz*),[38] and the absolute knowledge, which must be the thinking of the absolute, inevitably, it seems, remains representational, an "inward externality."

At this point we return as a point of reference to Aquinas's theory of analogous predication. In answer to the question of whether anyone in this life can see God's essence, Aquinas reasoned that we cannot comprehend the divine because as corporeal beings our power of intellection is founded upon sensation. By our natural powers we can only know the forms of material beings, and so we cannot naturally know God, the pure form of existence, as long as we remain corporeal beings. Only in the beatific vision will we know God's essence through the activity of divine illumination within our intellects (*Summa Theologiae* Ia, 12, 4, 11–12). We know God naturally only through his effects, and hence our expression of the divine must always remain analogous. Hegel appears not to have reasoned that we must transcend our bodily existence in order to achieve absolute knowledge nor that our highest present achievement of thought must always remain embedded in the natural order.

Does Hegel achieve, as he claims,[39] absolute knowledge such that in this knowledge all representation drops away in the sphere of pure thought, a state that may be compared in religious terms to the beatific vision,[40] or is Mure correct in arguing that thought can never wholly escape externality because the language by which we think remains always residually representational, or is there some other interpretation that may resolve this problem of the achievement of philosophical thought? In order to formulate our own solution, let us briefly consider some thoughts of Hans-Georg Gadamer on language and thought vis-à-vis Hegel so as to understand more clearly our difficulty.

Gadamer draws from Hegel the contextual, historical nature of human thought but separates himself from Hegel's argument that there is a moment of fulfillment in the process of thought, viz., absolute knowledge. For Gadamer our knowledge is never complete but is continually opening out to new horizons. In Hegel's terminology, for Gadamer knowledge has a "bad infinity" — endlessly progressing without a final moment of inclusion. "For Hegel," Gadamer says, "it is necessary, of course, that the movement of consciousness, experience, should lead to a self-knowledge that no longer has anything different or alien to itself."[41] *Contra* this position of Hegel, Gadamer's position is that "the dialectic of experience has its own fulfilment not in definitive knowledge, but in that openness to experience that is encouraged by experience itself."[42]

In regard to our particular problem of the relation of thought and language and the achievement of thought, Gadamer makes clear that we think and have truth and a world only by means of language.[43] In this respect Gadamer is in fundamental agreement with Hegel, as shown by Hegel's statements (cf. Enc § 20, R; § 462, R and *Zusatz*; and SL, 618; W6, 295). He differs, however, from Hegel as regards the outcome of the dialectic. In contrast with Hegel's view of logic as the immanent self-activity of the concept, hermeneutical experience "resembles a dialectic, an activity of the thing itself," but is not "an experience of thinking in the same sense as this dialectic of the concept, which seeks to free itself entirely from the power of language."[44] As finite and situated, whatever we say (and think) according to Gadamer always points beyond itself but never achieves its object *sub specie aeternitatis,* as Hegel claims for the moment of absolute knowing.

> There is no possible consciousness, however infinite, in which the "object" that is handed down would appear in the light of eternity. Every assimilation of tradition is historically different: which does not mean that every one represents only an imperfect understanding of it. Rather, every one is the experience of a "view" of the object itself. (430)

Rather than definitive expression, Gadamer speaks of a linguistic event — as a poem, for example — that does not express a thing but opens us to a world (427–28). Because we are finite and historical by nature, perfect knowledge is an implicit but unattainable goal — "we never achieve anything but an ever more extended aspect, a 'view' of the world" (405).

Gadamer, for our purposes, may be described as an "open ended" Hegelian. He is a Hegelian who argues that experience and thought are continually developing in a dialectical fashion. They aim at an ever-widening view through the "fusing of horizons" (273f, 337f) but, as radically finite, can never attain absolute knowledge.

> Our human nature is so much determined by finitude that the phenomenon of language and the thinking wherein we seek to get hold of it must always be viewed as governed by the law of human finitude. Seen in this way, language is not a transitional form of thinking reason which is perfected when thought becomes completely transparent to itself.[45]

The question we pose is whether Gadamer can argue that truth is a goal immanent in its process of becoming and yet impossible of attainment. Can one speak of a process of development without implying an end? A related question concerns the "bad infinite," where there is merely endless succession without an overreaching moment of inclusion. If there is no definitive moment of inclusion of the dialectical process, then the moments of the process remain over against one another, ununited.

We now return to our question of whether or in what sense Hegel can claim to achieve the definitive moment of absolute knowledge. In reply to Mure, who claims that thought remains always at a distance from its object because thought cannot free itself of the inherent sensuous externality of language, we answer that the externality of the fact of language is not of itself an insuperable obstacle to pure thought because the language by which we think is not itself the object of our thinking but yields itself up to the content expressed, as a ladder by which we attain a certain height is no longer needed once we have reached that height. The recognition of the linguistic limitation of thought is, in a dialectical fashion, the self-surpassing of that limitation.[46] We can recall Malcolm Clark's insight that Hegel's

> rejection of an "ineffable" simply beyond language is not incompatible with a deep sense of that externality of language which is at the heart of meaning: indeed, his dialectic may be seen to spring from the embarrassment of a thought that is present to itself only in the alienation of its expression.[47]

Externality and opposition, the characteristic elements of representation, are within absolute spirit as its condition of possibility. The inner *logos* is correlative with its outer manifestation. Language is the externality of thought that brings the inner logic into unity with the outer manifestation, and this unity is absolute spirit. Hegel's goal is that we enter into dialectical thinking and in doing so become one with the movement of thinking itself.

Gadamer's criticism of Hegel may be stronger than Mure's in that it shows the radical finitude and historical conditioning of our thought and resonates with the hermeneutical character of our experience, as shown in the interpretation of texts, the meaning of artworks, and the fact of translation. These are instances of ongoing discourse. Philosophy, too, manifests itself as ongoing discourse. Without, however, a final goal to the ongoing discourse — namely, absolute truth — Gadamer cannot escape the charge of relativism as he claims to do.[48] Merold Westphal offers an interpretation of Gadamer's philosophy that may provide us a means by which to resolve our difficulty, namely, the Biblical notion of eschatology, which views history not as unending movement but as having a moment of fulfillment (e.g., the kingdom of God).

> Gadamer might well grant the theoretical possibility of such a historical transcendence of the normal limits of historical understanding. (How else avoid the charge of blatant dogmatism?) But his response to Hegel's actual claim would not be changed. It would take an eschatological transition far more dramatic than anything that took place in Hegel's life or since to merit being called the Kingdom of God. The promise of "liberty and justice" for all would have to become a reality and not merely a promise and a dream.[49]

Hegel's claim to achieve a decisive, absolute moment in which thought is perfectly at one with the entire movement of the concept is on Hegel's own grounds not achieved because, as we will see, truth is the whole, and until the world is entirely rational — in other words, without discrepancy between the ideal and the real — then knowledge of the absolute (which is the absolute's self-knowledge) is not achieved. Knowledge remains an ongoing "fusing of horizons." However, *contra* Gadamer, knowledge has a kind of realized eschatology with one, absolute goal that, as the true infinite, is immanent and operative in the totality of the finite moments. We can know the *eschaton*, under the form of eternity, as the form of the whole, but we cannot know the *eschaton* as fulfilled because it is not yet fulfilled. It seems to us that one can know the *eschaton* as eternally "already" without being able to know what the *eschaton* is since the temporal standpoint from which we think and the process of actual things which is time (Enc § 258, *Zusatz*, p. 50) are not yet fully overtaken by the eternal, and so from our temporal standpoint the knowledge of the absolute, decisive moment is yet open to ongoing development. The problem arises from thinking the eternal inclusion of the process of actual things, which is time as an actual achievement instead of as a goal. Absolute knowledge, then, is an actual achievement insofar as we grasp the eternal, but it is a goal insofar as the concept has not yet fully actualized itself in the world. Eternity, Hegel says, is "the absolute present, the now, without before and after. The world is created, is now being created, and has eternally been created.... Creating is the activity of the absolute idea" (Enc § 247, *Zusatz*, p. 26). "The world is now being created," and as a temporal process of the realization that is the eternal, absolute idea, the process is incomplete.

When we speak here of eternity it must be explained that we mean not only without beginning or end but timelessness. To say the eternal is timeless, however, says only what it is not without indicating what positive content can be given to this conception. In explanation, we should first note that there is nothing illogical or incoherent in the notion of timelessness. Timelessness is not a "square circle." Though difficult to conceive, it is not logically impossible. Second, eternity is not imaginable. It cannot be pictured but only conceived. It cannot adequately be represented but only thought. Third, to give positive content to the notion of eternity we must focus upon the meaning of "the absolute present, the now." We may think of time as a succession of "nows," but the now itself has no succession; temporally it is nothing. We are arguing that the goal of Hegel's dialectical process is a now, an absolute present, a final moment in which the process of finite things is thought at once, *tota simul*, in Boethius's words. In the end, the multiplicity of the whole is known in a single thought, and that thought is eternal. As the summation of the process of its own engendering, this final moment is not one last moment in the succession of moments but transcends the succession of moments by perfectly including them. The final moment of inclusion then, the true infinity, is on another level, so to speak, than the succession of finite moments because by containing these moments it transcends them. The whole is something more than the sum of its parts. If we are to make any sense of the attempt to think together time and eternity and the problem of Hegel's claim to achieve absolute knowledge, then it seems to us that we must deal with absolute knowledge as both eschatologically imminent and realized. When we deal with truth in chapter 5, we will more fully develop our meaning, but for now, as concerns representation in relation to pure thought, we can say that absolute knowledge, wherein the form of thought is the content of thought, is our goal as long as we dwell in the process of actual things, which is time, and the concept is not fully actual. However, our thought that the goal is eternally realized is true but is still a goal for us.

Curiously, we may be able to take a cue from Aquinas in attempting to resolve our difficulty, though our position is not properly Thomistic. Aquinas, we recall, reasoned that direct and fulfilled knowledge of God necessitates a transformation of the present bodily state to one in which our intellects are illuminated. In this state, the rational creature becomes deiform (*Summa Theologiae* Ia, 12, 5), and the body, which is proper to the human state, is perfected so as not to impede the perfection of knowledge, which is proper to an intellectual being (*Summa Theologiae* Ia, 2ae, 4, 6). The question we present to Hegel's exposition of absolute knowledge is: what transition must occur in our present state to bring about our deification and deiformity that the absolute may know itself in our knowledge of the absolute (as expressed in Enc § 564, R)? Is there not yet in this life an impediment to absolute knowledge? Aquinas's rational explanation of beatitude cannot be equated with Hegel's absolute knowledge but it suggests that our knowing requires a change and perfection of our bodily state. It seems to us that Hegel's exposition of absolute knowledge is a "glimpse" but not an actual achievement.

*The Meaning of Finality in Hegel's System*

There is yet a further, closely related problem in the consideration of what absolute knowledge can mean in Hegel's system. Is there a final goal and consummation of the dialectical process beyond which there is no further development, or is the "end" an ever-ongoing realization of the concept? In other words, is the *Zweck* of the entire dialectic attainable or not; or even what does attainable mean? On the one hand, how can there be a teleological process without an end that is in principle attainable (though not, of course, separate from the process of its own becoming), while on the other hand, how can there be an end to dialectical development that does not mean the death of spirit?

In order to answer our questions, we must consider Hegel's explanation of teleology. Hegel's philosophy is thoroughly teleological in that the process of the whole is a movement toward and by a single *Zweck*,[50] which is the self-actualization of the concept by which subject and object, content and form, perfectly coincide. In its realization, the end "makes itself into the other of its subjectivity and objectifies itself; having sublated the distinction of both, it has *only* closed together [*zusammengeschlossen*] *with itself* and *retained itself*" (Enc § 204). In other words, the concept realizes itself by its own inner dynamism. The goal of the dialectical process is not external to the process but wholly the activity of the concept "*through itself with itself*" (SL, 748; W6, 454). In an image that is frequent in describing Hegel's philosophy, "the circle closes" in the process of its realization.

> It can therefore be said of the teleological activity that in it the end [*Ende*] is the beginning, the consequent the ground, the effect the cause, that it is a becoming of what has become, that in it only what already exists comes into existence. (SL, 748; W6, 454–55)

Because the whole of Hegel's philosophy is teleological, it is important to illustrate what Hegel means by this category. Teleology is the self-determination, the self-generation of the whole. As such, it should not be equated with, but subsumptive of, the finite, external teleology of organic activity and conscious human behavior. The final cause moves its moments toward its own concrete realization. This movement is the concept in its own activity of self-realization. The means to the realization of the end is at once the object that the subject makes its own and also the instrumental power or urge of the means. The end acts through its means, as subjective agent, and the means brings about the end, as objective activity.

In his section on "Realized End" in the *Science of Logic*, as well as in *Encyclopaedia of the Philosophical Sciences* § 209 and *Zusatz*, Hegel states that it is the cunning of reason (*die List der Vernunft*) that makes an end appear other than its objective means. Also when dealing with finite ends, an objective means may be more "honorable" than the end it accomplishes. Here, Hegel uses the example of a plough because it outlasts its particular finite accomplishments (cf. SL, 746–47; W6, 452–53).

It is only in regard to the whole, however, the true infinite, that means and end and the cunning of reason can be properly understood. By the cunning of reason is meant that the concept is the immanent principle of all reality, which as infinite is able to subsume random events because of their finitude. Apart from the whole system, these events are nothing, except as the understanding thinks them *in abstracto*. But in relation to the whole all finite events are recognized as integral to the perfection of the whole. Though it is not Hegel's example, we may think of the "random" activities of atomic particles that *in toto* form perfectly ordered and predictable patterns (consider the disintegration of radioactive material) and that ultimately have their place in the cosmos.[51] The end, the true infinity, is the express realization of what had been implicit in the process — i.e., the concept — which is "to possess externality [*Äusserlichkeit zu haben*], yet in this external totality to be the totality's self-determining identity" (SL, 754; W6, 461).

We return to our question: Is there a final achievement of the dialectical identity of the elements of the whole without remainder or is the dialectical process perpetual becoming without final achievement of its purpose? The Hegelian answer to any such question, of course, must attempt to say, "Both." But how are we to make sense of the dialectic and Hegel's system as a whole?

It seems to us that Hegel's answer attempts to play off time and eternity in a speculative translation of what in theological terms is recognized as imminent and realized eschatology. Hegel's own writings appear problematic in regard to our question and demand clarification and interpretation. In his explanation of Hegel's category of teleology, Errol Harris's way of speaking participates in the difficulty. Consider the following.

> This process reaches its fulfillment in man's final awareness of his own membership in and union with the ultimate totality.... In this we become apprised of the fact that the Absolute Whole which is the Truth and the Good is eternally realized, and that the contradiction between what is and what ought to be, felt in us as desire and will, is a sort of illusion.[52]

Harris says as well that the infinite purpose is fulfilled "only because and by virtue of the fact that it is ceaselessly and unremittingly in process of realizing itself through the endeavor of the finite, in which the whole is immanent."[53] The same point is made again when he says, "The whole realises itself only through the continuous development of its moments into the complete totality."[54] The problem is in speaking coherently of "final awareness" and "fulfillment" as well as of "continuous development" "ceaselessly and unremittingly in process."

In one way, the interpretation of teleology as ceaseless progression and never-complete realization lends itself well to Hegel's dialectical movement, which is then comprehended in a kind of Spinozistic beatitude.[55] But we would counter that such an explanation is superficial and does not resolve the contradiction that arises from conflating *simpliciter* ceaseless activity and purposive activity. We cannot simply say we comprehend the whole movement *sub specie aeternitatis* and think that we have answered the problem, when in fact the "way things are" is not the way they ought to be. Nor is never-ending-better-comprehension a solution, as Gadamer seems to think, because it possesses the difficulties of the bad infinite. Moreover, there cannot be talk of progress and betterment without (at least an implicit) reference to definitive achievement. To say, "Endless activity is itself the end," as the words indicate, is a performative contradiction. If the activity is endless, then it has no end; if it has an end, then it is not endless.

Our own answer is that the *telos* of the dialectic is the complete overreaching of time by eternity in which there is no longer a further "horizon" or some remainder, but in which ideal and real are completely identical. This identity, however, is identity-in-distinction. It is the final moment and cannot be continuing and ceaseless because it is not temporal.[56] Is not such a final moment "static" and "dead," one might ask. We need to be clear, however, that if we speak of this moment as "static" or "moving," "dead" or "living," we are prone to speak figuratively and to become infected by the finite, temporal modes of thinking that characterize the understanding. This final moment is neither "static" nor "moving," "dead" nor "living," except insofar as our conception sublates these ways of speaking and thinking based on the images of ordinary experience. At this point we are expressing the goal that is not yet but can be thought as the goal. We are pointing toward the goal, which when and as achieved can only now be pointed toward and expressed in the paradoxical expressions characteristic of mysticism. The goal *as* achieved cannot be expressed in our present situation. We see through, and point beyond, the limitations of our language, which when the goal is achieved our spirit will have transcended. Simply stated, a goal cannot be conceived as an actual achievement while it is yet a goal. The problem arises from trying to think an eternal goal in temporal terms. What then Hegel expresses as absolute knowledge and absolute idea is the final moment of the dialectical process, but it is the final moment as goal, not as complete achievement.

At this point we are interpreting the meaning of the eternity and absolute nature of the goal of spirit in a way different from Hegel's own view. We find what he is recorded as saying suggestive, but problematic.

> The carrying out [*Vollführung*] of the infinite purpose [*Zweck*] is therefore merely to sublate the illusion that it is yet not carried out. The good, the

> absolute good, eternally accomplishes [*vollbringt*] itself in the world, and the result is that it is already accomplished implicitly and actually [*an und für sich*] and it need not first wait upon us. This is the illusion under which we live, and at the same time it is alone the actuation [*Betätigende*] on which the interest in the world is founded. The idea in its process creates that illusion for itself, sets another over against itself, and its activity consists in sublating this illusion. Only out of this error does the truth emerge, and herein lies the reconciliation with error and with finitude. Other-being or error, as sublated is itself a necessary moment of the truth, which truth can only be where it makes itself its own result. (Enc § 212, *Zusatz*)

This way of speaking of the removal of the illusion that the infinite purpose is not yet accomplished reminds one of Spinoza's movement from inadequate to adequate knowledge without any real change in the world (since for Spinoza the world as infinite and eternal is already perfect and has no *telos*) but merely a change in thought. However, in the light of Hegel's system we know that the whole is the activity of the concept, and the immanent goal of this activity is the perfect inclusion of the finite in the infinite, the temporal in the eternal.[57]

Hegel's position becomes clearer when we consider his synthesis of the good and will (Enc § 233-35; SL, 818-23; W6, 541-48). The contradiction that represents itself as an "infinite progress of the actualization of the good" (Enc § 234) has the character of the bad infinity because the will carries out the successive approximations of what ought to be, but the good, the conformity of life and reason, is never established. The contradiction is resolved for Hegel when the one-sidedness of the subjective purpose of the good is sublated, as is the one-sidedness of what in the objective realm opposes itself to the world (cf. Enc § 234). The sublation, or synthesis, is achieved in "the *truth* of the good," wherein "the good is attained in and for itself — the objective world is in and for itself the idea, just as at the same time it eternally posits itself as *purpose* and through activity brings forth its actuality" (Enc § 235). What this "truth of the good" means is that "unsatisfied endeavor vanishes when we cognize that the final purpose of the world is brought to fulfillment [*vollbracht ist*] just as it brings itself to fulfillment.... The good, the final purpose of the world, only *is* in that it constantly brings itself forth" (Enc § 234, *Zusatz*).[58] But what does it mean, we ask, that the *Endzweck* of the world is the continual *Hervorbringen* of this *Endzweck*? It seems to us that the *Endzweck* of the world requires that the infinite *Geist* know itself perfectly by the inclusion, and in that sense, the transcendence, of the temporal process, and that that inclusive moment be no longer temporal but absolute, infinite, eternal. As long as the purpose is temporally bringing itself forth, it is, from that standpoint, incomplete, and "unsatisfied endeavor" remains. In other words, how can there be satisfaction of the endeavor if endeavor and struggle are unending? Satisfaction of the endeavor implies an end to the endeavor, it seems to us. We would argue that the comprehension of the whole as ceaseless activity that is yet purposive is a contradiction that seems best resolved by distinguishing a goal as thought and a goal as fully achieved (at which point it is no longer properly a goal) and by a clarification of the meaning and relation of time and eternity.

In summary, we agree with Hegel that the language with which we think need not remain representational because in recognizing the restrictive character of language we have transcended the restriction. Furthermore, as an interpretation of Hegel's philosophy, we argue that absolute knowledge, thinking thought, thought in the pure form of thought is the goal at work as an immanent teleology in the dialectical process of reason. This absolute knowledge is compared to realized eschatology as an anticipation in time of what eternally is. "What eternally is" is only meaningfully explained as the thought of a goal presently bringing itself about, which in order to bring itself about must have in principle a final moment in which goal and achievement meet.

# 4
# Philosophy's Sublation of Religion

### Introductory Remarks

Having presented in chapter 2 the relation of form and content in religion and philosophy, and in chapter 3 the representational mode by which religion expresses its content, we have now to consider more closely the meaning of Hegel's claim that religion is *aufgehoben* in philosophy. We recall that we have argued that the content of religious representation is a nexus of an outer form-determination and an inner content-determination. In the sublation of representation in conceptual knowledge, the outer form-determination is annulled and the inner content-determination is preserved by being joined to the form-determination of thought. In the pure form of thought, there is no longer an opposition of outer form and inner content, so that the content is entirely the form of thought. We have further argued, in agreement with Hegel, that the absolute identity of form and content is achieved with regard to the structure of thought by transcending the inherent externality of language, which is the necessary means by which we think. In the process toward absolute knowledge, religious representation and philosophical thought form an ascending continuum. However, with regard to existing reality, we have adapted Hegel's thought by arguing that absolute knowledge is a goal not yet achieved in the realphilosophical sphere. We have now to present more fully Hegel's explication of philosophy's sublation of religion and to consider the implications of this sublation, namely, the precise manner in which philosophy is "above" religion and the precise manner by which religious truth is retained in the Hegelian synthesis.

The problem of religion's sublation in philosophy belongs to the wider problem of sublation in general. Hegel's overall concern to overcome alienation in all its forms has led many to think that the individual is subsumed, or "lost," within reason as the activity of the inclusive absolute. Do not the natural world, the human individual, the work of art, and the religious symbol resist subsumption within a wider whole, they ask. As we will see, G. R. G. Mure and Søren Kierkegaard, in differing ways, find Hegel's notion of sublation untenable. In answer to these criticisms, we will argue that Hegel's absolute spirit is not a monism (as that of Spinoza) but is what Hegel claims it to be: unity-in-difference. This unity-in-difference is achieved through the infinite, dialectical movement of the whole wherein the finite moments are united and sublated within the infinite movement of thought. This process of thought is at once the process of the world. This unity-in-difference of the whole is founded upon the idealistic principle that identifies being and thinking so that everything has its determination as sublated within the concrete, processional whole that is infinite, dialectical thought. In this view, sublation is not subsumption but dialectical integration. Each element of the whole must be conceived as what it is: an element in relational unity with all other elements. We will argue that nothing is ever "lost" in its sublation, and that religion in particular retains its integrity as rational religion in its philosophical sublation.

## Sublation as the Dialectical Movement of Concretion

### Dialectical Movement

To describe the dialectic is to think dialectically. In treating Hegel's philosophy, we have constantly to resist the tendency that we are somehow outside that which we describe. We have to realize that in thinking anything, we are implicitly thinking its opposite, for nothing can be conceived simply by itself but only in relation to what is not itself. For example, if we reflect upon the act of perception, we recognize that there is a perceived object and a perceiving subject that are joined in the single act of perception. Similarly, if we judge that a cup is on the table, we are implicitly judging as well that the cup is not anyplace else, so that what is affirmed is also a statement of what is not affirmed. Thus, affirmation and negation are joined in the single act of judging. When reflected upon, these simple examples of our mental activity point for Hegel to a profound truth, viz., that thought is the movement of uniting opposites, and that this movement of which we become aware at a certain point in our intellectual maturity is a movement already at work within the world as a whole. For Hegel, dialectical thought is its "own self-sublation of finite determinations [of thought] and their passing over into their opposites" (Enc § 81).

No finite thing can be conceived in isolation. Every determinate thing is defined by its opposite, which by opposing the thing, completes it. The principle of the relation of opposites is at once the inner principle of their distinction. The unification of differences that characterizes the movement of thought implies inclusion within a whole. Negation for Hegel is not an external means of contrasting isolated things but is an activity internal to the relational unity of things. Negation is "the foundation of all determinateness," and Hegel quotes Spinoza that *omnis determinatio est negatio* (Enc § 91, *Zusatz*). Everything is just what it is by not being another. Existence (*Dasein*), by which Hegel means determinate being, is the result of sublating together the two contradictory moments of the category of becoming (Enc § 89). Becoming then is the characteristic of the system of thought as a whole, for when we think being as an indeterminate whole (as when we think God *a se* apart from creation, that is, abstractly), we immediately think its opposite — nothing — and in thinking the one moment we necessarily think the other, and this thinking of their mutual opposition is becoming. By themselves, being and nothing are mere abstractions that vanish into one another in the concept of becoming. However, as Hegel notes (Enc § 88, *Zusatz*), we must make clear that being is not the thought of anything concrete but is a purely abstract category. "Becoming is the first concrete thought" or concept (Enc § 88, *Zusatz*) and is thus the principle and paradigm of the entire dialectical process of thought. "This unity of being and nothing ... forms once and for all the basis and element of all that follows" (SL, 85; W5, 86).

Every determination of thought then is a moment of becoming that includes negation within itself. Everything tends by its own inner movement to pass into its opposite. This inner force of negation is not simply cancellation of the first moment but preservation of the moment within a more inclusive synthesis because each moment is defined by what it excludes. Because negation yields a positive result, it is just as true of the dialectic to say *omnis negatio est determinatio*.[1]

At each phase of the dialectic, the whole process of becoming is at work. The unity of the whole is the dynamic tension of all elements as interrelated. Each determinate (finite, defined) element has its meaning only in relation to the whole, and if we attempt to grasp anything in isolation from its wider relations, then it loses its proper definition.

It is evident that in speaking logically (dialectic is a description of thought), we have been speaking metaphysically as well because for

Hegel logic is metaphysics, or in other words, reality is thought (or more precisely perhaps, we can only speak of reality as already available to thought). The categories of thought then are the structures of reality, so that the whole of reality is an infinite — i.e., all-inclusive — synthesis of the finite elements of the world in the process of its own becoming.

SUBLATION

Each phase of dialectical synthesis is an *Aufhebung* of its constitutive moments. In chapter 1, we had noted that the *Aufhebung* of Hegelian philosophy is at once a destroying, a preserving, and a moving forward, which is the dialectical movement of thought through the motor force of negation. It is now our task to present more fully Hegel's explication of sublation and to bring forth its implications for the philosophy of religion.

In the dialectical movement, opposites are united, or, more precisely, reconciled or mediated. In relation to their synthesis, the moments are recognized as partial and contradictory. As such, they yield themselves up by their own internal dynamism to the new phase of their reconciliation.

The term "reconciliation" is especially apt because there is "a making friends again" of the estranged elements. The unity that is achieved at each phase of the dialectic is the reestablishment of the unity that had been implicit from the beginning. In order for unity to come about, the inherent source of the prior opposition must give way to the synthesizing activity. In a way of speaking, there is an absorption or cancellation of the distinction within the higher, inclusive phase. However, we grievously distort the notion of dialectical unity if we conceive it as a monadic unity. Dialectical thought unites its opposites in a dyadic unity or, as it is so often described, as a unity-in-difference.

We describe dialectical movement by saying that the unifying or synthetic phase sublates its opposing moments, or, conversely, that the opposing moments are sublated in the new, more inclusive phase.[2] The seeming happenstance of the plurality of meanings of the ordinary German word *aufheben* that conveniently provides Hegel a means to express dialectical unity is in actuality for Hegel an indication that language is the objectification of thought.

> This double usage of language, which gives to the same word a positive and negative meaning should not be viewed as accidental.... [W]e should rather recognize in it the speculative spirit of our language rising above the mere "either-or" of understanding. (Enc § 96, *Zusatz*)

*Aufheben*, as the conjunction of *auf* and *heben*, literally means "to lift up" or "to pick up." This sense of "picking up" leads to its meaning of "to keep, save, or preserve" and leads as well to its meaning of "to set aside, cancel, abolish, deny." We note that all the meanings share the sense of transition because sublation is a movement. More than once Hegel takes note of this plural meaning. "*Aufheben* exhibits its true twofold meaning which we have seen in the negative: it is at once a *Negieren* and an *Aufbewahren*" (PS, 68; W3, 94). Similarly he notes in the *Science of Logic* that *aufheben* means *aufbewahren, erhalten* as well as *aufhören lassen, ein Ende machen* (SL, 107; W5, 114).

In the *Science of Logic*, under the category of becoming, Hegel speaks of the sublation of becoming and devotes a remark to the expression "to sublate." He describes the sublation of being and nothing as a "stable result" [*ruhiges Resultat*] or a "stable simplicity" [*ruhige Einfachheit*] (SL, 106; W5, 113). Mure notes that in this case, by *ruhig* Hegel means "not 'static' but 'poised,' or 'steady.'"[3] The dialectical unrest of being and nothing yields an equilibrium as a result of the self-destruction of its opposing moments (SL, 106; W5, 113). Becoming (which is the paradigmatic category of the entire dialectic) is a holding in balance. This poise of opposites, Hegel indicates, is not nothing but being (SL, 106; W5, 113) — that is, the third moment is the first, but as its result. The stability of becoming is only relative to the opposition of being and nothing, and so the indeterminacy of becoming passes over into determination as *Dasein*, which is the internal concretion or mediation by thought of *Sein* as an inner movement of self-determination.[4] It is necessary for us to describe the dialectic triadically as a means for us to enter into the movement of dialectical thought. However, if we fix upon the threefold form by which we describe the dialectic, as is the tendency of the understanding when we describe the dialectic as "thesis," "antithesis," and "synthesis," then we remain external to the movement. The dialectic is a movement of thought and hence can only be thought dialectically, i.e., in its own inner movement. For this reason, Hegel notes, we can variously describe the dialectic as a (1) unity, (2) duality, (3) triplicity, and (4) quadraplicity. The dialectic is (1) a single movement, (2) a movement from immediate unity to mediated distinction, (3) a movement from what is immediate to its negation to the negation of the negation, and (4) a movement wherein the negation of the negation as the moment of reconciliation is a fourth (SL, 836; W6, 564).[5] Obviously we cannot think the dialectic as elements added externally to one another. We see the need then to think the unfolding of the content from within as "a stable result," or as spirit, which as Mure well describes it, is "what-is-and-is-not-and-therein-becomes."[6]

Sublation is the result of mediation, which has "*in itself the determinateness from which it originates*" (SL, 107; W5, 113–14), which is to say that the originating unity and its negation only have their meaning and truth as opposing moments from the standpoint of their resultant reconciliation. As Mure says, "thesis and antithesis are already synthesis."[7] A common difficulty that we have in grasping the Hegelian dialectic is the seeming absurdity that the result is already in the beginning. The difficulty is overcome, however, when we recognize the capacity of thought to include the negative within itself. Like Hercules in his struggle with Proteus, the moment of sublation embraces its self-dissolution. "What is sublated is at the same time preserved; it has only lost its immediacy but is not on that account annihilated" (SL, 107; W5, 114). We must emphasize, however, that the result is the new and positive stage of the negation of the originating moment. Sublation is the process of becoming determinate. "Being and nothing are the same; *but just because they are the same they are no longer being and nothing*, but now have a different significance [*Bestimmung*]" (SL, 108; W5, 115). To think being and nothing is to think the pure movement by which one moment vanishes into the other (SL, 83; W5, 83).[8]

Every sublation is the truth of what precedes it and is the proleptic determination of the goal of absolute spirit. Each sublation is a progressive development of the whole as it brings into unity an ever-greater diversity, and the perfection of the dialectic is the holding of all moments together in thought. As mentioned before, the dialectical form of thought is as well the form of the world, and the union of logical form and the development of the world (nature, experience, history, and so on) is spirit. When we study the dialectic we are also studying the movement of the world as a whole. The content of philosophy, Hegel says, is actuality (*Wirklichkeit*), the region of spirit that is brought forth as world (Enc § 6). On first sight it would seem laughable that Hegel could claim the course of world events to be an entirely rational process, but he makes clear that no particular event or part of the world as particular is rational; only the result is rational. By referring back to his often misunderstood statement in the preface to the *Philosophy of Right* that identifies the rational and the actual, Hegel makes clear that the actual is not the chance occurrences, errors, evils, and transitory events that come into existence but is what is meant in religious terms by divine providence (Enc § 6, R). The identification of the rational and the actual is the immanence of the idea in the progressive unfolding of the world. What is taken up is rational, and what is left behind are the contingent, erroneous, evil, and transitory elements of the world. This taking up and leaving behind is sublation.

## THE SUBLATION OF RELIGION IN PHILOSOPHY

As stated in the previous chapters, the Christian religion and speculative philosophy have the same content, dialectically identified — viz., God as absolute spirit — but the religious representational form is inadequate to its purely spiritual content. God as spirit must reveal himself to spirit in complete transparency, i.e., purely in the form of thought, which is the form appropriate to spirit. "God is only God insofar as he knows himself; his self-knowledge is further his self-consciousness in human persons and human knowledge *of* God which proceeds to human self-knowledge *in* God" (Enc § 564, R). In absolute knowledge, the opposition of finite spirit and infinite spirit is overcome in the moment of the identity of absolute knowing, as human consciousness becomes divine consciousness in the one activity of spirit. In representation, by contrast, the finite spirit is kept yet "at a distance" from absolute spirit.[9]

However, already in revealed religion the separation inherent in representation is overcome when the divine spirit witnesses to itself in the believer. "Such a form of the finite representational mode is sublated in the belief in the one spirit and in the devotion of the cultus" (Enc § 565). In this view, philosophy frees the content of revealed religion from any restraints imposed by an external form and makes explicit the union of the divine and human spirit that is already implicit in the spiritual community. "Philosophy thus determines itself as a cognition of the necessity of the *content* of the absolute representation" (Enc § 573). We recall Hegel's words in the *Phenomenology of Spirit* in the chapter on absolute knowing.

> The *content* of representation is absolute spirit; and all that now remains to be done is to sublate this mere form, or rather, since this belongs to *consciousness as such*, its truth must already have yielded [*ergeben haben*] itself in the shapes of consciousness. (PS, 479; W3, 575)

The sublation of the content of revealed religion in philosophy is at once the emancipation of the content from its restrictive religious formulation and its cognitional determination according to the necessity of the content. This juxtaposition of freedom and necessity with regard to the same *Sache* is not without paradox. Hence, a word should be said in explanation of the Hegelian meaning of necessity because of the many questions that the term invites in the reader's mind, especially for our purposes, as concerns the ascription of necessity to God. Correctly understood necessity is determination according to the inner principle of the thing — in a word, according to its concept. "Necessity as such is implicitly [*an sich*] the self-relating concept" (Enc § 232). Necessity is the result of its own inner development and ultimately is the same as freedom. From the perspective of the end, all the elements together form an interrelated, systematic whole, but because the unity is prescribed from within — that is, not prescribed by anything outside itself — it is free.

> But, as we have already seen, the process of necessity is so directed that it overcomes the rigid externality which it first had and reveals its inward nature. It then appears that the members, linked to one another, are not really foreign to one another but are only moments of one whole, each of them in relation with the other, being at home [*bei sich*] and combining with itself. This is the transfiguration of necessity into freedom, and this freedom is not merely the freedom of abstract negation, but rather concrete and positive freedom. (Enc § 158, *Zusatz*)

Hegel's way of speaking of freedom and necessity reminds one of Spinoza — "that thing is called free, which exists solely by the necessity of its own nature, and of which the action is determined by itself alone" (*Ethics Demonstrated according to Geometrical Order*, part 1, definition 7) — but what is different from Spinoza's thought is that the whole is not conceived as abstract substance but as concrete subjectivity, developing according to its end. Necessity is the concept that turns back upon the multiplicity of its elements and includes them.

> The richest is therefore the most concrete and most *subjective*, and that which withdraws itself into the simplest depth is the mightiest and most all-embracing [*Übergreifendste*]. The highest, most concentrated point is the *pure personality* which solely through the absolute dialectic which is its nature, no less *embraces* [*befasst*] and holds *everything within itself*, because it makes itself the most free. (SL, 841; W6, 570)

Hegel explains the necessity of the concept in three moments: (1) the conditions (*Bedingung*), (2) the fact (*Sache*), and (3) the activity (*Tätigkeit*) (Enc § 148). These three moments are understood from the standpoint of the teleological activity that converts the conditions into the fact. Activity

> is the movement which translates the conditions into the fact, and the latter into the former as the side of existence [*Existenz*], or rather the movement which educes the fact from the conditions in which it is *implicitly* [*an sich*] present, and which gives existence to the fact through the sublation of the existence which the conditions have. (Enc § 148)

When these moments are looked at independently of one another — i.e., abstractly — the process appears as "*external* necessity" (Enc § 148), but from the standpoint of the total system, the outcome is the concretion of the inner principle of the whole, which is the concept.

When applied to God, this category of necessity explicates the inner principle of the determination of the whole, which is the "*pure personality*" that holds everything together in itself and "makes itself the most free" (SL, 841; W6, 570). God is the perfectly free agent of creation as well as the provident and wise agent of its destiny. The contradiction of ascribing freedom and necessity to God is only apparent.

> One has in no way to treat as mutually exclusive of one another the view of the world as determined through necessity and the belief in a divine providence. What underlies the thought of divine providence will hereafter be shown to be the *concept*. The concept is the truth of necessity and contains necessity as sublated within itself, just as, conversely, necessity is *implicitly* [*an sich*] the concept. Necessity is only blind so long as it is not conceived, and there is nothing therefore more mistaken than the reproach of blind fatalism, which is made against the philosophy of history when it considers its task as the cognition of the necessity of what has occurred. The philosophy of history contains therefore the meaning of a theodicy, and those, who mean to honor the divine providence by excluding necessity from it, in fact degrade it through this abstraction to a blind, irrational caprice. The unsophisticated religious consciousness speaks of God's eternal and immutable decrees, and therein lies the express recognition that necessity belongs to the essence of God. Man, in his difference from God, with his particular opinion and will, follows mood and caprice, and thus finds that by his action something quite other comes about than he had meant and willed, but God knows what he wills, is determined in his eternal will, neither by accident from within nor from without, and what he wills he also accomplishes irresistibly. (Enc § 147, *Zusatz*, pp. 289–90)

We must then at every stage bear in mind that necessity properly belongs to the systematic whole and that it is wholly an inner principle of the teleological development of spirit. When Hegel describes philosophy as the "cognition of the necessity of the *content* of the absolute representation" (Enc § 573), it is meant that philosophy thinks this content in its innermost unity. When sublated in philosophy, religion's content possesses the freedom of the truth.

It is evident that the meaning of the Hegelian sublation of the Christian religion in philosophy and the conclusions we infer from this sublation depend upon what we mean by the core of the Christian religion. If the core is (mistakenly thought to be) the assemblage of empirical-historical representations, which is the vehicle by which human beings initially encounter the Christian message and come to faith, then the content-form unity of this vehicle for Hegel must be dissolved so as to be purified of any contingent and external elements. If the core is the witness of the spirit that the divine has become human and dwells in the spiritual community, then Hegel's philosophy is explicated Christianity that brings forth this faith grounded in spirit from its immediacy to full awareness of its truth. Hegel himself is clear as to what must be the core of the Christian religion. The meaning and truth of the Christian religion cannot be based upon anything sensible — historical accounts, miracles, Biblical textual evidence — but upon the spirit, Christianity's conceptual truth. He is fond of quoting St. Paul that "the letter kills, but the spirit gives life" (2 Cor. 3:6; LPR III, 260; V5, 187; also LPR I, 167; V3, 77) and sardonically criticizes theologians whose emphasis upon exegetical investigations as a means to understand the Christian religion leads them to overlook the eternal truth that does not depend upon anything empirical or external (cf. LPR I, 339–42; V3, 240–42). The sensible is "the point of departure" for spirit to reveal itself but is not the ground of the truth of this revelation. The sensible subserves spirit so that "its relationship to the sensible is at the same time a negative attitude" (LPR III, 228; V5, 159). By emphasizing, as we have in the previous chapter, the doctrinal elucidation of the Christian representations within the Christian religion, we can interpret philosophy's sublation of religion as religion's self-understanding that makes explicit its implicit rationality.

That the Incarnation has brought about the reconciliation of God and humanity, that God dwells in the human heart, that the "hour is coming and has already come," that the divine presence is established in germ and must grow to completion "when God will be all in all things" are truths for Hegel whose meaning is made explicit in speculative philosophy. The truth of religion and philosophy is a content and a goal that belongs to the one divine activity in the development of thought and the development of the world. In the "Draft of the Inaugural Address of the Philosophical Teaching Post at the University of Berlin" delivered 22 October 1818, Hegel says,

> Philosophy has *the same purpose and content* as religion, only not as *representation* but as thinking. The shape of religion is therefore unsatisfactory for the higher *mature [gebildete] consciousness* — it must want to cognize, to sublate the form *of religion* but only so as to justify its content. This then is the true justification, not the historical, learned, external [justification]. The eternal does not have its foundation in the temporal, in facts, etc. The eternal is the *witness* of the spirit. (W10, 411)

The religious content as represented without its rational justification is a source of discontent to us as intellectual beings, but when the rational justification is given, it is the justification of the content of religion as religion's higher moment. Ultimately, religion cannot be founded upon anything foreign to the human spirit but only upon "the witness of spirit" that is the inner unity of the divine and human spirit. "The genuine content of a religion has for its verification [*Beglaubigung*] the witness of one's own spirit that this content conforms [*gemäss sei*] to the nature of my spirit and satisfies the needs of my spirit" (LPR I, 389; V3, 285).

For Hegel, the Christian representation has reached the zenith of the representational form of spirit, i.e., it comes as near to speculative thought as is possible for any representation because it expresses the absolute as self-conscious.

> In this religion [i.e., revelatory religion] the divine being [*göttliche Wesen*] is *revealed*. Its being revealed obviously consists in this, that what it is, is known. But it is known precisely in its being known as spirit, as being [*Wesen*] that is essentially [*wesentlich*] self-conscious being [or "self-consciousness," *Selbstbewusstsein*].... Spirit is known as self-consciousness and to this self-consciousness it is immediately revealed, for spirit is this self-consciousness itself. The divine nature is the same as the human, and it is this unity that is beheld [*angeschaut*]. (PS, 459–60; W3, 552–53)

Ricoeur says that this immediacy of the absolute in the person of Christ is the beginning point of its rational interpretation, i.e., the mediation of the content of this event into the explication of its universal, conceptual meaning. The presence of God to sensible religious intuition is the condition for us to achieve knowledge of the absolute and the absolute to become self-conscious. "Absolute knowledge is possible because there [in the Christ event] the Absolute has made itself known."[10] The sublation of all its moments in absolute knowledge is the mediatory process by which the universal becomes concrete. Without this mediation, the absolute could not be self-conscious — the revelation of spirit to spirit.

From the standpoint of absolute knowledge, what becomes of the moments by which the mediation of spirit is effected — in particular, what becomes of revelatory religion, by which the absolute becomes self-conscious? Our conclusions at this point must be tentative and anticipatory. If we can agree with Ricoeur, absolute knowledge does not displace absolute religion but is its "thoughtfulness."[11] Lauer draws a similar conclusion. He argues that philosophy's sublation of religious faith is the realization of faith in its fullness as it becomes "thinking faith."[12] "What begins in faith ends in thought, not because thought is different from and higher than faith, but because faith is fulfilled, as faith, in thought."[13] This interpretation of Hegel's philosophy will be more fully developed as we continue. Obviously our attempt to present Hegel's view of the relation of philosophy and religion leads us to interpretative developments that are not Hegel's own. The precise meaning of the sublation of religion in philosophy is ambiguous in Hegel, and it is our task to make precise philosophy's sublation of religion in the light of the Hegelian system.

## Mure's Criticism of Sublation

We must first point out that sublation cannot simply mean absorption since there cannot be dialectic without the inclusion of difference as difference. Errol Harris expresses this point well.

> Neither dialectic nor its product is flawed by difference. Without that its unity is not flawless but eviscerated; it is in fact destroyed. A flawless dialectic properly understood is one in which difference is completely *aufgehoben* without loss, and so completely retained, while transfigured in this retention to unity and wholeness.[14]

Hegel claims that rational thought can retain a tension of opposing elements; the immediacy of the elements is lost, but they are not annihilated (SL, 107; W5, 114). Nonetheless, to some it appears that sublation is a superseding of its constitutive elements that in order to emerge as a new phase must destroy its prior phases; or else to others it appears that the sublation fails because the particular, empirical, and contingent remain impermeable to the kind of inclusion Hegel describes. Kierkegaard may be counted among the former, and Mure among the latter. Let us first consider Mure's criticisms.

Mure questions whether philosophy as Hegel presents it can bridge all contraries in a consummate, absolute unity of thought. Specifically, he argues against Hegel's claims to unite the oppositions of universal and particular, *a priori* and empirical, necessary and contingent, intelligible and sensuous.[15] Because for Hegel thought must contain its other within the activity of thought itself, the question arises whether in the Hegelian sublation the other — i.e., the particular, empirical, contingent, and sensuous — can be taken up without residue. Let us consider what Mure says of the empirical over against the *a priori*, realizing that his criticisms, *mutatis mutandis*, apply to the other oppositions as well. Mure's thesis is that "philosophical thought can never sublate without residue the endless empirical flow, and is therefore empirically tainted"

(331). In other words, he claims that Hegel's philosophy remains fundamentally dualistic. Mure argues that

> the universal takes shape as the intelligible system which somehow is to be the whole truth of what was given as mere fact, but its necessary connexion is throughout hypothetical, wholly in the air, unless brute fact somehow persists and contributes to the categorical basis without which hypothetical thinking can neither begin nor conclude. (317)

Mure further argues that "the *Begriffsbestimmungen* of Nature, though they are thought-forms of the contingent, must have contingency in themselves" (330). In other words, he argues that empirically contingent content cannot be wholly sublated as empirically contingent. If Mure is correct, his criticisms would counter Hegel's (or any philosophical attempt) to think the whole, to bring all reality within the compass of dialectical reason.

In reply, we must ask whether there is anything that is a "mere fact" or a "brute fact." Are we to think a "brute fact" as a Kantian thing-in-itself? If so, then all the problems of Kant's distinction of noumenon and phenomenon confront us. We need to be clear that to know anything as a brute fact is to know it as a brute-fact-for-consciousness. Mure is concerned to ensure the novelty of continuing historical and scientific development, but we would argue that whatever new data emerge for philosophical comprehension, these data must be rational, intrinsically intelligible, if they are to be known at all.

It also seems that Mure confuses a moment of human consciousness with absolute spirit, which is the result and final goal of the ever-active process. Any sublation is the development of opposition that arises from finitude (e.g., the particular, empirical, contingent, and sensuous) and is a moment in the thrust onward toward the whole apart from which the finite can have no meaning. The "finality" of Hegel's system is the recognition that all limits are self-surpassing within the inclusive infinite and concrete universal. It is the totality of the process that is absolute and not any moment of the process, except as the whole is implicit in each moment.[16]

In reply to Mure's contention that Hegel's dialectic is flawed because the contingent and empirical cannot be overcome in human experience, Errol Harris argues that it is divine reason as immanent in human reason that validates the dialectic.[17]

> Unity in the final outcome is the Absolute, but it is not absolute in the course of the process nor in our finite consciousness. Nevertheless it is the immanence of the Absolute in both that makes us capable of the awareness of the necessity of the consummation and its implications in our experience. (294)

*Kierkegaardian Criticism of Sublation*

The resistance of otherness and difference to dialectical inclusion appears to many to make Hegel's claims untenable. Mure, on the one hand, as we have seen, questions whether thought can include the empirical and contingent and be the pure form of thought without remainder of empirical and contingent elements. Kierkegaard and his followers, on the other hand, question whether dialectical synthesis can preserve its constitutive oppositions, specifically the "either-or" that they claim radically characterizes human existence. Although we agree with Errol Harris that "Kierkegaard is astonishingly obtuse about the Hegelian dialectic" (113), we must respond to the Kierkegaardian critique of Hegel, especially as it concerns the sublation of religion in philosophy, because by so responding we bring into relief the precise meaning of the sublation and correct its misinterpretations.

Over against the unity of thought and being — i.e., being as available to thought or consciousness, which is the principle and result of Hegel's system — Kierkegaard asserts that the individual person is not simply a thinker who should (or even can) become one with the system of thought but that the individual ex-ists, or stands out from the whole. "The systematic Idea is the identity of subject and object, the unity of thought and being. Existence, on the other hand, is their separation."[18] According to Kierkegaard, the individual subject vanishes in the system of pure thought.

> He [the individual subject] becomes the pure abstract conscious participation in and knowledge of this pure relationship between thought and being, this pure identity.... The existing subject, on the other hand, is engaged in existing, which is indeed the case with every human being. (Ibid.)

Whereas Hegel takes the double usage of *aufheben* as an indication of "the speculative spirit of our language rising above the mere 'either-or' of understanding" (Enc § 96, *Zusatz*), Kierkegaard takes the "both-and" of speculative reason as the subsumption of the individual in "abstract" thought.

> Hegel is utterly and absolutely right in asserting that viewed eternally, *sub specie aeterni*, in the language of abstraction, in pure thought and pure being, there is no either-or.... Hegel is ... wrong when, forgetting the abstraction of his thought, he plunges down into the realm of existence to annul the double *aut* with might and main. It is impossible to do this in existence, for in so doing the thinker abrogates existence as well. When I take existence away, i.e., when I abstract, there is no *aut-aut*; when I take this *aut-aut* away from

existence I also take existence away, and hence I do not abrogate the *aut-aut* of existence. (270–71)

Clearly Kierkegaard finds it impossible that thought should be able to unify the diversity and oppositions of reality and to comprehend within a system of thought the human person as free. The difference in the two thinkers is manifest in Kierkegaard's calling Hegel's thought "abstract." Kierkegaard calls "abstract" precisely what is concrete for Hegel, viz., the unity-in-difference of dialectical thought — reality as mediated by thought. Kierkegaard's characterization of Hegel's philosophy as "abstract" is not simply a terminological difference but indicates a rejection of absolute idealism. Hegelians and Kierkegaardians can agree that if existence is not in principle ideal then it cannot be comprehended within the process of thought; they disagree as regards the ideality of existence. Kierkegaard's rejection of idealism, as will become more evident as we proceed, is problematic for religious thought, his own included.

For the present, we see most clearly the nature and implications of Kierkegaard's thought in his attack on Hegel's claim that the content of the Christian religion is identical with speculative philosophy and that the form of the Christian religion is sublated in philosophy.

Kierkegaard asserts that Christianity is not a doctrine but a way of being (339) that cannot be mediated and "become a phase of speculative thought" (340). Kierkegaard vociferates against any speculative transformation of Christianity before defining what Christianity is prior to its speculative comprehension. For Kierkegaard, the Christian is not one who knows Christianity but one who lives it. This antithesis of faith and knowing is further indicated when Kierkegaard eschews defining the Christian religion in terms of an objective, doctrinal content and rather defines the Christian religion in terms of subjective faith.

> Christianity is the precise opposite of speculation.... [I]t is the miraculous, the absurd, a challenge to the individual to exist in it, and not to waste his time by trying to understand it speculatively. If we are to have speculation within this presupposition, it will be the function of this speculation more and more profoundly to grasp the impossibility of understanding Christianity. (338)

Christianity for Kierkegaard is not an intelligible content that admits of rational justification, but an "existential communication" (339) to be held fast in faith, which if it were not absurd would not demand absolute trust.

It is clear that Kierkegaard's thought can only be characterized as fideism. If we call Kierkegaard a philosopher, it is only in the sense that he thoughtfully investigates as universal the meaning of personal choice and radical self-commitment. The opposition of faith and reason that characterizes Kierkegaard's thought has Hegel's philosophy as its focus, but its implications are problematic for the faith it seeks to defend.[19] We can admire an investigation of the subjective dimension of truth and the meaning of freedom as the characteristic of human existence, but his thinking, we hold, needlessly sets freedom and faith in opposition with the desire to know and does violence to the human spirit that of its nature must be rational. If there is not a rational basis for belief, as Kierkegaard asserts, then any belief, regardless of its content, is true in the measure that it is sincerely held fast. Our response to Kierkegaard's position can be developed further by means of Charles Ping's theological work, mentioned in chapter 2 that expresses a largely Kierkegaardian critique of Hegel's religious thought.

According to Ping, Hegel dispenses with the uniqueness of the person of Christ and of the individual believer's personal relationship to God in Christ.[20] The argument is that the Christ event in Hegel's philosophy is not accepted as an independent datum but is comprehended as the outcome of the activity of reason (294). Moreover, the timeless determination of the logical idea eliminates the uniqueness of any historical moment (312). Ping also indicates that for Hegel the difference between the divine and human is not absolute. The Christian paradox that the absolute existed in human form, an impossibility to human thought according to Ping, is rationally explained by Hegel and therefore made relative to human thought (297). Moreover, the relation of God and the human person in the Hegelian system supposes a continuity of reality that fails to recognize the discontinuous and dependent relation of humanity to God expressed in the Christian religion (307). Hegel's philosophy also eliminates God's freedom because divine activity is determined in servitude to the system. "God is conscious of himself in man, therefore, man in his rational comprehension is the determination of God.... God is the result of philosophy" (319).

Such criticisms as these are not untypical of those who assess Hegel's philosophy from the standpoint of a supposed self-understanding of the Christian religion, but they are in fact problematic in their own right and not forceful when subjected to philosophical analysis. In general Ping supposes the matter that demands to be investigated, i.e., an understanding of the content of Christianity. What does it mean to say God is infinite, absolute, free, and became man in the person of Jesus? Ping does not incisively reply to the Hegelian analyses that anticipate Ping's criticisms. Furthermore, he uncritically accepts the Kierkegaardian appraisal of Hegel's philosophy of religion without acknowledging its problems.

When Kierkegaard states that there is an absolute difference between God and the human person,[21] the question arises of how they can be related. One wonders what can be the conditions of possibility for religion if the difference between God and humanity is absolute and discontinuous. To speak of a "leap" explains nothing. Of course, Kierkegaard states that the relation cannot be explained: "In connection with the absolute paradox the only understanding possible is that it cannot be understood."[22] By "paradox" here Kierkegaard seems to mean "absurdity." If the Christ event is absurd, how can it be believed? If feeling, and not reason, is its foundation, then Hegel's criticism of a theology of feeling comes to bear. For Kierkegaard, the truth of Christianity is not a matter of reasons, proof, or argumentation but of faith or personal conviction.[23] Kierkegaard's approach to faith is clearly voluntarist rather than rationalist.[24] Our question is, what is the foundation of the individual will to believe? If it is God's initiative and that initiative can never be rationally appraised, then how can the believing individual be sure that the basis of his or her belief is God rather than a god of one's subjective creation? To Kierkegaard it does not matter that one pray to the true God but only that one pray in truth.[25] Because for Kierkegaard truth is subjective, any criticism that Hegel has changed the content of the Christian religion cannot be sustained on Kierkegaard's (or Ping's) own grounds. Truth for Kierkegaard is not an objective content but the firmness of subjective appropriation,[26] hence the issue of Christianity's true content (which Kierkegaard claims Hegel has distorted by inclusion within the speculative system) is irrelevant from a Kierkegaardian standpoint. It is important to realize that Hegel responds to subjectivistic views by pointing out that conviction for its own sake has no standard by which to measure its truth. "According to the modern view conviction as such, the mere form of being convinced, is already valid — the content may be whatever it will, there being no standard present for its truth" (Enc § 22, *Zusatz*).

Even though we find Kierkegaard's thinking about truth philosophically untenable, it is valuable to ask why in the first place Kierkegaard so strongly resists the philosophical comprehension of Christianity. It seems that the vehemence of Kierkegaard's reaction to Hegel is in part based upon an interpretation (we would argue, a misinterpretation) of sublation as absorption. In attacking Hegel, Kierkegaard perceives himself to be attacking a way of thinking that would make the human relation to God through Christ a moment among moments or a matter of intellectual thought that does not deeply engage the religious person in a way of life that is radically different from the life of the nonreligious person. It is the existential fact of singularity and difference that Kierkegaard wishes to protect from any subsumptive or leveling process. At a more general level, the problem confronting us as exemplified in the Kierkegaardian reaction to Hegel belongs to the perennial philosophical problem of the one and the many. Hegel's answer to this problem is the dialectic — the activity of spirit that is universal and concrete. Hegel expounds the dialectic in order to show that unity need not be conceived as sheer absence of determination. In this regard Hegel should be distinguished from other monistic thinkers. Parmenides, for example, begins from the insight that being must be one and concludes that change is an illusion, despite the fact that he can offer no coherent reason why one should have the illusion. The one-sidedness of Parmenides's thought should not lead one to disdain the fundamental insight that being is one. The case is similar with Spinoza. Spinoza is correct in the recognition that being is one, but he develops his thought in such a way that the world in its manifest diversity is lost (cf. LPR I, 377; V3, 274; also Enc § 50, R). Kierkegaard and others appear to interpret Hegel's system as a monism like that of Parmenides and Spinoza that does not permit difference to stand forth and that, by containing difference, erases it. It appears clear to us that Hegel explicitly responds to these critics who interpret speculative philosophy as an "identity-philosophy." "To speak of identity-philosophy is to stick with abstract identity, or unity in general, and to neglect the inherent determination of this unity, whether it is defined as substance or as spirit" (LPR I, 379; V3, 276). Kierkegaard misinterprets Hegel on this point. Moreover, Kierkegaard's own thought is philosophically deficient because it fails to acknowledge the unity of experience and the metaphysical insight into the primordial unity of being and from these basic insights to proceed to think all things together as a unified whole. Because of his starting point in the human person as individual and in the fact of freedom as possibility, Kierkegaard tends in a direction that neglects to account for the oneness of God that is at the origin of all that is and for the relation of the infinite and the finite that is the condition of the possibility of religion at all. Despite the power and insight of Kierkegaard's thought, his presentation of the Christian religion has displaced divine truth with the idol of subjectivity and has left the way open for any belief, no matter how irrational.

## The Infinite and the Finite as Paradigmatic for the Relation of Religion and Philosophy

*The Spurious Infinite*

If we are to think the whole as unity-in-difference and to make precise the meaning of the sublation of religion in philosophy, we need to reflect briefly on the relation of the infinite and the finite. In Hegelian fashion we proceed to the formulation of the true conception of the infinite by first opposing it to the false conception of infinity that is characteristic of thought at the level of the understanding. Because its categories are not dialectical but fixed, the understanding thinks infinity in opposition to finitude as a mutually exclusive relation.

When on first thought the finite is taken as a determinate existent, then that which is not-finite is simply empty and indeterminate (cf. SL, 139; W5, 152). When the infinite is set over against the finite as qualitatively other, then we have what Hegel terms the "bad infinite" [*Schlecht-Unendliche*] (SL, 139; W5, 152). In effect, this conception finitizes the infinite because "the infinite is only the *limit* [*Grenze*] of the finite," and this way of thinking ends in contradiction (SL, 140; W5, 152), as will be clear.

Along with his treatment of the bad infinity in logic, Hegel treats the formulation of the bad infinity as it manifests itself in reflection upon experience. At the level of sensation, the finite is the transient, the succession of drives and desires, and when one desire is satisfied, it is followed by another, hence both the desire and its satisfaction are finite (LPR I, 290; V3, 193–94).

In reflection we set a totality of knowing over against an endless manifold of information, and at the level of appetite, complete satisfaction over against an endless desiring. The aim of both is to subsume the multiplicity into unity, but the opposition of complete unity and endless multiplicity at both the level of knowledge and of appetite is thought as interminable. "The goal ... is set up in such a way as to be unattainable" because the multiplicity of the elements must always remain an *Aussereinander* (LPR I, 292; V3, 196). When we abstractly think this opposition of complete unity over against a self-subsistent multiplicity; the infinite and finite "mutually exclude one another." The finite is the realm of what is limited, which has its limit at the realm of the infinite. When thought in this way, Hegel points out, the infinite has its limit in the finite since it is defined by what it is not, viz., the finite (LPR I, 293; V3, 197). In this way Hegel has formulated the important insight that brings into relief the inherent contradiction that characterizes any religious thinking that sets God in opposition to his creation as utterly transcendent to creation. This insight into the contradiction of the infinite and finite, which in religion is thought of as the opposition of God and world as exclusive of one another, is the necessary step toward achieving the true conception of infinite and finite.

*The True Infinite*

In the true conception of infinite and finite "the infinite *in itself* includes the finite" (SL, 154; W5, 171) as the concrete, determinate unity of both. Infinite and finite are in a dialectical movement of self-mediation. The finite is not true in itself but is a "*transition*" [*Übergehen*] and "an *emergence into something higher*" [*Übersichhinausgehen*], which is to say that in itself the finite is null, and the infinite, which is spirit, is the nullification of this nullity (*Vernichtigen des Nichtigen*) (Enc § 386, R). This nullity of the finite is found in strikingly concise terms when Hegel points out that because the infinite is the absolute and necessary ground of all that is finite and contingent, we do not properly proceed from finite to infinite being as though the finite and contingent were the ground of the absolute, but that the true inference is that "the *non-being* of the finite is the *being* of the absolute" (SL, 443; W6, 80). We see then how finite, determinate being arises through the dialectic's moving force of negation. The negation of the finite, which is the infinite, is the negation of the non-being of *Dasein* (that is, the negation of the negating activity that brought about the determination of *Dasein* from indeterminate *Sein*). The result is not two mutually exclusive determinately existing sides but one movement by which each side sublates itself in its opposite. Thus the finite sublates itself in its own negation with the result that the infinite is not an "empty beyond" but a dialectical interrelation of finite and infinite through the activity of negation. The infinite does not sublate the finite from outside the finite, but the infinite sublates itself in the inclusion of the finite (SL, 146–47; W5, 160–62). The true conception of the infinite is not thought as an interminable line but a circle wherein the infinite is wholly present in the inclusion of all finite moments (SL, 149; W5, 164).

When the infinite and finite are conceived in dialectical relation we see that the question of how the infinite becomes finite is badly posed because it implies an already existing infinite that is separate from the finite. The truth is that the infinite and the finite are distinguished but inseparable. Their comprehension — i.e., their concept — is their inseparability (SL, 153; W5, 170).

> The answer, therefore, to the question: *how does the infinite become finite?* is this: that *there is not* an infinite which is *first of all* infinite and only subsequently has need to become finite; ... on the contrary, it is on its own account just as much finite as infinite. The question assumes that the infinite, on the one side, exists by itself, and that the finite which has gone forth from it into a separate existence — or from whatever source it might have come — is in its separation from the infinite truly real; but it should rather be said that this separation is *incomprehensible* [*unbegreiflich*]. (SL, 153; W5, 170)

This logical explication of the true conception of the infinite provides the means by which we can think the relation of God and world, which in traditional metaphysics is explained by God's creation-preservation of the world. We cannot grasp the relation of God and world from the standpoint of the finite unless we recognize that the finite must first sublate or negate itself and become "an essential moment of the infinite in the nature of God" (LPR I, 307; V3, 211–12). "God creates, he is active: therein lies the distinguishing, and with distinction the moment of finitude is posited. This subsistence of the finite, however, must be sublated once more" (LPR I, 308; V3, 212). The finite cannot be conceived as existing on its own but as sublated in the infinite activity of spirit. In its concrete actuality the infinite spirit is an internal dialectical movement that sets a barrier (*Schranke*) for itself in the finite and sublates this barrier in order to be itself as spirit (Enc § 386). To return to the image of a circle, we can say that God is the circle without beginning or end in time or being, which includes the coming to be of all its moments as points on the circle, points which are themselves, each in its own way, momentary totalities. Infinite and finite must be grasped as moments of the process that is spirit (LPR I, 309; V3, 213). We cannot think God apart from the world nor the world apart from God, hence the infinite and the finite become conjointly because the infinite is "as much finite as infinite" (SL, 153; W5, 170), or as Hotho strikingly renders Hegel's thought at this point, "without world God is not God" (LPR I, 308; V3, 213).

## The Sublation of Religion as Preservation

Infinite and finite cannot be thought outside one another but as a distinguishing within their unity. Each side of the dialectical opposition sublates itself into the process that is spirit.

> Each is in its own self this unity, and this [unity] only as a *sublating* of its own self in which neither would have the advantage over the other of having being in-itself and affirmative determinate being [*Dasein*]. (SL, 145; W5, 160)

Each side is self-sublating. Neither absorbs the other, but the two sides are united in their opposition.

If sublation as unification without loss of differentiation still appears impossible to Mure, on the one hand, because the empirical and contingent resist inclusion within thought, or to Kierkegaard, on the other hand, because infinite and finite are absolutely opposed, it is because they fail to accept that reality is thought. Dialectic is entirely an activity of thought, so that when we think the finite and infinite at the conceptual level, we think them together as negating and sublating one another. It is only in the same way according to Hegel that we can think together God and world. Logic is metaphysics (Enc § 24). From the insight that only thought can unite all reality, we are led to the more basic insight that it can only do so if reality is thought or, more specifically, constituted by thought. Hegel says,

> Every philosophy is essentially an idealism or at least has idealism for its principle, and the question then is only how far this principle is actually carried out. This is as true of philosophy as of religion. (SL, 154–55; W5, 172)

The infinite whole is the process of spirit thinking itself. Nothing stands apart from thought as somehow real in itself. What is real is determination as a self-sublating moment of the inclusive whole. The finite exists and has meaning only within the concrete process of the dialectical whole. Ultimately for Hegel, it is not the infinite but the finite that must be accounted for.

If religion opposes Hegelian philosophy, it does so at the cost of being self-contradictory because, in its denial that the finite has "veritable being" [*wahrhaft Seiende*], it does not recognize its idealistic principle. Philosophy makes explicit the content of religion, viz., that everything has its being in God and is in relation to God. "The task of philosophy is to show forth the rationality of religion" (LPR III, 247; V5, 175). Philosophy makes clear then the idealistic principle of religion. It is a false idea that sets religion apart from thought as something irrational and thus places religion and philosophy in irreconcilable opposition. "Religion is completed in thought without ceasing to be religion, because only in thought can human finitude raise itself to infinity."[27]

Throughout this chapter we have sought to clarify the movement of sublation. In regard to the problem of religion's relation to philosophy, we can say that religion is sublated in philosophy by a movement interior to religion itself that cancels the external and contingent elements of religious representation and brings into relief the true content of religious expression. Philosophy does not subsume religion as a finite moment except as religious awareness is focused and fixed upon its finite modes. If religion understands itself by finite ways of thinking, it is its own enemy. In its principle, religion is idealistic since religion already has God and God's relation to humanity as its content. Philosophy does not absorb religion but is "its confirmation and achievement in an intimate union with the trinitarian God."[28] Hegel sets forth the absolute logic, i.e., God who reveals himself. In this view, the Christian revelation is absolute philosophy in germ, and because it is the revelation of the absolute it must sublate itself into absolute form. We are now in a position to discern more clearly the dialectical relation of religion and philosophy. We see that religion cannot ultimately ground itself because it is essentially representational, yet we see as well that philosophy can only be itself when it provides the foundation in reason for what is revealed in representation. Philosophy is above religion in the sense that it succeeds revealed religion as its more mature form within the single unifying activity of absolute spirit. Succession, however, is not the same as replacement. We agree with Lauer's interpretation of Hegel's thought that "religion itself is perfected in philosophy in such a way that the two are no longer distinct; religion is now philosophical religion."[29]

The sublation of religion in philosophy is only the negation of a religion that essentially defines itself in terms of subjective feelings, nonrational commitment, and historical events. But the sublation of religion as defined by its divine content — i.e., its dogmas — is the explicit recognition of the dialectical identity-in-difference of revealed religion and speculative philosophy in the inclusive activity of absolute subjectivity or spirit.

> Philosophy no longer has to face the reproach that it devalues [*herabsetze*] the dogmas. Instead it suffers the reproach of containing within itself too much of the teaching of the church, more than the generally prevailing theology of our time. (LPR I, 159; V3, 69)

When theology abdicates its proper task of knowing God, and formulates its reflections instead from subjective feelings and the finite categories of the understanding, it is ironically philosophy that "saves" religion from becoming meaningless and irrelevant by bringing forth the rational ground of the truth that religion expresses. "The reinstatement of the authentic doctrine of the church must emanate from philosophy, for philosophy is what guides that vacuous [*fade*] reflective activity back to its ground" (LPR I, 159; V3, 69). Religion's sublation within philosophy is religion's own truth, i.e., religion's conceptualization. Hegel is clear that the essential content of the consummate religion is preserved in philosophy. "The basic truths of Christianity are maintained and preserved by it [philosophy]" (LPR III, 262; V5, 188). What is not clear in Hegel is the status of religion as such from the standpoint of its speculative comprehension.

Does the religious form of life and expression vanish in philosophy when sublated in the pure form of thought? We will return to this question in the last chapter, but from our investigation of the dialectic and the nature of sublation we can tentatively argue at this point that religion as a life practice is preserved because by itself philosophy is less than religion.[30] Philosophy cannot be philosophy in the Hegelian sense — namely, the activity of absolute spirit — unless it includes its concrete forms. Philosophy is merely the mediation of what is, the recapitulation and elucidation of its own path. Religion too, to be authentic, is the recapitulation and elucidation of human experience in relation to what is absolute — it has no subsistence outside the human condition. Philosophy then, we would argue on Hegelian grounds, does not replace religion but only completes it. Inadequate and untrue forms must vanish as the human spirit matures, but human sensibility, emotion, and will must continually be informed and made whole through reason. In this view religious life and reason should form an integrated unity. It would be a misreading of Hegel's dialectic to think that absolute knowledge could be a form of life transcendent to the concrete modes of human existence (at least in this life). Man cannot live on thought alone. Like the man in Isaac Singer's story "The Spinoza of Marketstreet," who through the concrete experience of being loved comes to appreciate the intrinsic value of human existence here and now, without which his contemplation of the absolute and eternal is deficient, we must recognize that philosophy is true only within concrete life that comprehends religious life as its highest moment, while religion yet remains an "existential communication," or way of being, as Kierkegaard would have it. Hegel has shown us this truth at its foundational level through the description of the dialectic. Can we not say of the relation of philosophy to religion and to all the dimensions of life what Hegel says of the relation of infinite and finite?

> Each is in its own self this unity, and this [unity] only as a *sublating* of its own self in which neither would have the advantage over the other of having being in-itself and affirmative determinate being [*Dasein*]. (SL, 145; W5, 160)

Hegel's own words are well known as to what philosophy accomplishes in actual life.

> [Philosophy] appears only in time after actuality completes its process of formation and has made itself ready. What the concept teaches, and history

necessarily indicates as well, is that it is only when actuality is mature that the ideal first appears over against the real and that the ideal grasps this same real world in its substance and builds it up for itself into the shape of an intellectual realm. (PR, 12–13; W7, 28)

Philosophy is nothing apart from actuality. Its task is to reveal the incarnate *logos*. In doing so philosophy consummates religion and is itself the highest moment of revelation, but this consummation is dead apart from its concrete process. "The matter [*die Sache*] is not exhausted by stating it as an *aim*, but by *carrying it out*, nor is the *result* the *actual* whole, but rather the result together with its becoming" (PS, 2; W3, 13).

Philosophy brings forth the self-conscious unity of the otherwise disparate elements of religion (cf. Enc § 572). It is God as the activity of self-revelation that is the content of revelatory religion. Philosophy does not blindly affirm this content but demonstrates its rational necessity, and this necessity as absolute subjectivity is free (Enc § 573). In philosophy, the content has the form of self-conscious activity, and without this explicitly rational form the historical course of religions can only appear as arbitrary and contingent.

Philosophy's sublation of religion is the "loop" by which religion completes itself, grasping itself by becoming explicitly what it is implicitly (cf. Enc § 573). Its purely contingent and external elements are annulled, and its rational truth is brought forth.

# 5
# Truth

## Introductory Remarks

Throughout the previous chapters, in order to show how Hegel's claim is valid that absolute religion and absolute knowledge are identical in content, we have set forth the relation of form and content in Hegel's philosophy and the dialectical nature of the identity in content of religion and philosophy, as well as the specifically representational form by which religion's absolute content is given, and the meaning of the sublation of that content in speculative philosophy. These successive presentations are intended as a spiraling developmental presentation of Hegel's overall view of the philosophy of religion. Such a presentation is required by the systematic nature of Hegel's philosophy, which invites an "unpacking" of Hegel's system of thought if we are to analyze and appraise its pertinent elements. It is impossible to say everything at once, so that we must successively focus our presentation on one or another dimension of Hegel's thought. Nonetheless, each element must imply the wider view of the entire system, and we cannot speak about content, form, identity, dialectic, religion, philosophy, or truth exclusively of each other.

The inappropriateness of any exclusive focus on one or another element of Hegel's thought applies *a fortiori* to the Hegelian conception of truth to which this chapter is devoted because for Hegel the truth is the whole and hence entails the consideration of all the elements of his system. This consideration of truth is important from the religious standpoint if religion is to have grounding. If religion is only meaningful, emotionally satisfying, and culturally useful, then it cannot claim allegiance nor perdure. This consideration is important from the philosophical standpoint because of Hegel's claim that absolute religion and absolute knowing are identical in content — both express absolute truth. Religion is true because its content is divine; but because it is true, religion has its perfection when its content is given in the form of thought. Our comparison of religious and philosophical truth will further clarify the relation of religion and philosophy in the Hegelian system. We will argue that absolute religion expresses the truth, but only the purely rational expression of religion's content is the knowledge of this truth; furthermore, we will argue that this knowledge turns back upon religion in order to direct and purify our relation to God.

## The Logical Exposition

*God is Truth*

Hegel begins his *Encyclopaedia of the Philosophical Sciences* logic by stating that philosophy and religion "have the *truth* as their object, and indeed in that supreme sense in which *God* and God *alone* is the truth" (Enc § 1). In the present day, such an initial statement may appear striking, but the assertion expresses an idea integral to the Western intellectual tradition. Aquinas, for example, had argued that God is truth because "his very act of knowing is his being, and his act of knowing is the measure and cause of all other being and all other intellect, and he himself is his own being and his act of knowing" (*Summa Theologiae* Ia, 16, 5). As we continue, further comparison will be made to Aquinas's exposition of truth in order to highlight Hegel's conception, but for now we note that Hegel's philosophy stands in agreement with this identification of God and truth, and in fact finds this longstanding identification to express, in its most radical sense, absolute idealism.

Though religion and philosophy share as their object God and truth, philosophy differentiates itself from religion by "indicating the *necessity* of its content" (Enc § 1), by which Hegel means the scientific and systematic exposition of the whole as a dialectical unity of thought. "Philosophy should understand that its content is no other than the region of living spirit originally having brought forth and bringing itself forth as *world*" (Enc § 6). This bringing forth of the world from spirit is "the reconciliation of self-conscious reason with actuality" (Enc § 6), which, as we shall see, is in Hegel's meaning the truth as the agreement of concept and actuality in a processional whole.

## The Agreement of Thought and Object

Truth is the overcoming of the dichotomy of subject and object, which in its fullness is absolute knowing as "pure self-consciousness in its self-development" (SL, 49; W5, 43). Over against the view that there is a "ready-made world" [*fertige Welt*] external to thought, which thinking as a form receives from outside itself (SL, 44; W5, 36–37), absolute knowing is the overcoming of this separation of content and form by which thought is one with its subject matter (*Sache*) (cf. SL, 49; W5, 43). By arguing that thought is constitutive of all that is, that ultimately the form and content of thought coincide in the absolute, Hegel gives new meaning to the notion of truth as "the agreement [*Übereinstimmung*] of thought with the object." Ordinarily, we suppose that thinking adapts itself to the object in order to bring about this agreement (SL, 44; W5, 37), but for Hegel thought is the process that constitutes this agreement. Truth is the result of the whole process that is absolute spirit (cf. PS, 11; W3, 24), and every agreement of thought with its object — short of the infinite, absolute whole — is a moment within the life of absolute spirit. Hence, the notion that truth is "the agreement of thought with the object" is not incorrect, but it is a vague expression that as commonly understood does not make clear its idealistic principle. Each particular agreement of thought with its object is only a momentary self-determination of the entire process of the activity of spirit.[1]

## The Agreement of Concept and Actuality

We have indicated that the idea of truth as "the agreement of thought with the object" is imprecise, if not misleading, because it does not indicate the idealistic principle of the agreement. Hegel makes the same point when he notes that the usual meaning of truth as the "agreement of an object with its representation" is deceptive because it supposes an already existing object to which our representation must conform (*gemäss sein*) (Enc § 24, Zusatz 2, p. 86).[2] The more philosophically adequate idea of truth has a wholly conceptual meaning and even shows itself to have a basis in ordinary experience and everyday speech. "When we speak of a *true* friend," Hegel notes, "we mean one whose manner of conduct accords with [*gemäss ist*] the concept of friendship" (Enc § 24, Zusatz 2, p. 86).[3] This content is, of course, a thought-content because, as Hegel states, "logic and metaphysics fall together" — "*things* [*Dinge*] are held in *thoughts*" and "thoughts express the *essential natures of things*" (Enc § 24). To be true is to be grasped fully in thought. Truth, then, is the unity of that which is explained and that by which it is explained. As such, truth in its pure form is achieved only in philosophy, as will become clear.

Truth is the absolute form which has itself as its content (SL, 592; W6, 265). Pure truth, then, is logical truth, the science of the form of thinking in which there is brought about the perfect adequation of content and form, or more simply, the final phase of dialectical development in which the content is the form (cf. SL, 594; W6, 267). Kant had recognized that truth is the "agreement of cognition[4] with its object" but was unable to see the supreme value of this definition (SL, 593; W6, 266) and to carry out its implications because the forms of thought in Kantian epistemology are merely subjective and unrelated (and unrelatable) to the real (i.e., the noumena). On the one hand, Hegel points out, it is commonly understood that what immediately appears in sensation is mediated by thought, and in its concept the given of sensation emerges as what it is "in and for itself." In other words, what appears is merely contingent until mediated by thought that brings forth the essential nature of the object. Kant's philosophy, on the other hand, asserts that things as they are in and for themselves are inaccessible (*unzugänglich*) to reason. Hence, the unity of object and concept is for Kant only an appearance (SL, 590–91; W6, 262–63). The contradiction should be apparent. There cannot be truth in any meaningful sense for Kant if the essential nature of things is inaccessible to the mind. Hegel's correction of Kant is to argue that "the appearance is not merely something devoid of essence [*ein Wesenloses*], but a manifestation of essence" and "through the concept the object is brought back to its non-contingent, essential nature" (SL, 591; W6, 263). Had Kant accepted the implications of truth as the agreement of thought and its object, he would have recognized that reality (for Kant, the noumenal) that is not in agreement with the concept, and the "concept" (as Kant means it) that is not in agreement with reality, are untrue representations (SL, 593; W6, 266).

Truth is brought about when content is suited to its form, or reality to its concept (cf. SL, 593; W6, 265). We have continually to keep in mind that by truth Hegel does not mean the correspondence of cognition with an object independent of the mind, but that truth, as Mure explains, "is the whole concrete of knowing and known in relation. The term 'content' then means the object *qua* the 'filling' of the cognition."[5] This way of speaking may suggest Husserl's explanation of truth as "the agreement of what is meant with what is given as such,"[6] so that the object is present to cognition as intended. There are notable similarities between the two thinkers. As with Husserl, Hegel is describing the fulfillment of a meaning intention and is not implying any extramental "thing" beyond the cognized object. However, unlike Husserl, Hegel is not merely describing the acts of human cognition as such but is describing the determinations of thought that as a unified process are ultimately logic, ontology, and theology in one. Over against a merely formal logic that attempts to understand thought without regard to its content, Hegel's logic is the movement of the concept itself in which actuality is preserved and the whole process is implicitly present in each moment, so that the content of thought is not foreign to the form of thought, and not only not foreign, but that the form of thought is itself the content. The concept "through its own immanent [*gegründete*] dialectic passes over into reality" (SL, 591; W6, 264). The concept is the unified activity of thought that brings about the agreement of concept and reality.

We must keep in mind that logic for Hegel is the movement or activity by which thought explicates itself as a systematic whole. Within this activity of logic or pure thought, the movement by which the concept specifies itself is judgement (*Urteil*). Judgement then is the process by which the concept determines or specifies itself — *ein Fortbestimmen des Begriffs* (Enc § 171, R). It is, as the etymology of the German term indicates, a "partition from the source." That source is the concept. The judgement, for example, that a certain painting is beautiful, makes explicit that this painting is a determination of the concept of beauty. The whole of logic is a progressive determination of, and from within, being, which as the wholly indeterminate beginning contains *an sich* the entire development of the system of logic. Judgement belongs to that phase of the logic in which the concept, as the unity of being and essence, further differentiates itself. Judgement is not a subjective act of joining two independent concepts but is the activity by which the concept as such determines its object to itself. "To conceive an object means therefore to become conscious of its concept" (Enc § 166, *Zusatz*). To return to the example above, when a work of art is judged to be beautiful, a comparison is made between the object and what it should be, i.e., the object's concept (Enc § 171, *Zusatz*). Judgement for Hegel then belongs to the activity of truth, which is the actualization of the concept.

A true judgement expresses the form of the agreement of an object with itself, whereas a finite judgement of quality can only be correct (*richtig*) (Enc § 172, R and *Zusatz*). Here we encounter an important distinction in Hegel's thought between truth and correctness. In a merely correct judgement, subject and predicate are not identical, as the "is" of the judgement asserts. By contrast with correctness, truth is the full agreement of subject and predicate in which the subject realizes its concept, i.e., realizes itself in a form correspondent with its content. In a correct judgement, the truth has not been fully developed from the concept of the subject. Subject and predicate have merely a contingent connection, that is, they "touch together," but "they do not cover one another" (Enc § 172, *Zusatz*). In a true judgement, by contrast, the predicate is wholly contained in the subject. It may be correct to say that someone is sick, but this statement cannot be a true judgement because "a sick body is not in agreement with the concept of life" (Enc § 172, *Zusatz*).

*Truth as Idea*

The concept has its higher logical phase in the idea that Hegel calls "the *true as such*" or the "*adequate concept*" (SL, 755; W6, 462), in which the concept possesses externality as a self-determining identity (SL, 754; W6, 461). The concept is sublated and perfected in the idea in which the concept has become fully objective, and "everything actual *is* only in so far as it has the idea in itself and expresses it" (SL, 756; W6, 464). In another way of expressing the same point, the inner determinations of the concept are externally presented in determinate being as a unity of inner and outer determination (cf. Enc § 213). In the idea there is no longer a difference between what ought to be and what is, and the real is perfectly congruent with its concept (SL, 756; W6, 464), as, for example, a state exists in the measure that it is the concept of the state, and the perfect state — i.e., the true state — would be the perfect realization of the concept of the state (cf. SL, 757–58; W6, 465–66). Truth is the achievement of the correspondence of the ideal and the real "so that what now *is* is only what is idea" (SL, 757; W6, 465). The "proof" of the idea is the entire course of the dialectic as an achieved or sublated process (cf. Enc § 213, *Zusatz*), for the idea is essentially a process of infinite, subjective, thought that overreaches (*greift ... über*) finitude, objectivity, and being; that is, the infinite transcends the finite and yet is immanent in the finite (and so with the oppositions of subjective and objective, thought and being) (cf. Enc § 215, R). The full realization of the idea is the absolute idea, and that is absolute truth. It is important to keep in mind as we proceed that this logical exposition of the idea and its identification with truth is as well its identification with God (cf. Enc § 1), and, as Hegel makes clear, the idea is the speculative translation of what religion represents to itself as God's creation and providential care of the world (Enc § 213, *Zusatz*).

*The Unity of Subject and Object*

We have said that for Hegel in truth the dichotomy of subject and object is overcome, but we need to make this subject-object relation more precise. In the act of cognition the object is other than the subject and identical with it. They are distinct but not separate or separable. Cognition in general, as Mure states, "is at once this recognition of the opposition of subject and object and the certainty of their ultimate identity."[7] If on one side we take the cognizing subject as positing (*setzen*) or constituting its object, we have subjective idealism. On the other side, if we take the cognizing subject as an empty form that passively receives its object from outside, we have realism. Both views of cognition are one-sided and are resolved in the unity of both as "a *positing [Setzen]* that no less immediately determines itself as a *presupposing [Voraussetzen]*" (SL, 788; W6, 503–4). The object is within the cognizing subject. There is at once an acceptance of the world and a construction of the world, and each attitude is only meaningful in relation to the other. Truth then is "the relating comparison of the concept of the thing [*Sache*] and its actuality" (SL, 784; W6, 499) or, more simply stated, "the unity of concept and reality [*Realität*]" (SL, 785; W6, 499). Hence, truth is the realization of the activity of the concept in and through the cognizing subject and the cognized object. Through the cognizing subject, the concept posits the concrete content of the world for the subject as identical with the concept (cf. SL, 783; W6, 497). What the concept posits, however, is already presupposed as an object over against the subject. The actualization of the concept, which is truth, comes about through the self-negating activity of the concept, "holding itself back and making itself passive towards what confronts it, in order that the latter [the object] may be able *to show* [*zeigen*] itself, not as determined by the subject, but as it is in its own self" (SL, 786; W6, 501). The reception of the object by the passive subject and the constitution of the object by the active subject are united as opposing moments in the activity of the concept as it pushes toward self-realization.

In the absolute idea, the dichotomy of subject and object is completely overcome, or sublated, in the eternal moment in which the subject is object to itself in the pure activity that is spirit. The absolute idea is the *noēsis noēseōs* of Aristotle (Enc § 236, *Zusatz*). It is pure self-thinking whose content is itself, and as the concrete subject that unites all the diverse elements of its becoming, comprehending these elements as the moments of its *decursus vitae* (Enc § 237, *Zusatz*), Hegel calls it "person" or "personality" (SL, 824; W6, 549; SL, 841; W6, 570).[8] As the full actualization of the concept, it is "*self-knowing truth*" (SL, 824; W6, 549). In order to grasp the absolute idea, which grasping is to be one with it in its own activity of thinking, we must think in one consummate moment the tension of all its oppositions and all its thought determinations as a unified process.

We may say that Absolute Idea as object is the whole content of the Logic, the whole dialectic of categories — that is what as subject it thinks or knows. But equally then we must say that this whole dialectic is that thinking or knowing, is Absolute Idea as subject.[9]

Opposition remains within the absolute idea, for there cannot be thinking that is not discursive or, in Hegel's terminology, dialectical, and that does not suppose the oscillation of subject and object; but in the absolute, that inherent opposition is sublated as pure, infinite activity. This pure activity of thought is truth — "the necessary forms and self-determinations [*eigenen Bestimmungen*] of thought are the content and the highest truth itself" (SL, 40; W5, 44). Because, as we have indicated, God and truth are one (Enc § 1) and the idea is the logical exposition of the religious representation — God — we may say then that the pure activity of thought as inclusive subjectivity is God which can also be expressed as the ontological proof in its speculative sense wherein the concept of God is the activity of self-concretion.

## Error and Evil

If the highest truth is the culmination of the dialectical process and the unity of the process itself, how can error — and what is the same from the standpoint of will, evil — be included within the absolute truth without being, to use a word borrowed from Mure, "tainted"? Or, from the perspective of pure truth, we ask, Can there be the complete agreement of concept and actuality that gives due regard to error and evil and does not overlook the fact of their presence in the world?

To answer this question we need to turn to Hegel's insight and insistence that negation, division, and opposition are essential to the dialectical process of the totality. At every phase short of the absolute correspondence of ideal and real, error and evil are present, but they are not, from the viewpoint of the result of the entire process, self-subsistent. Rather, they are moments in the struggle to bring about the coincidence of ideal and real in the culmination of the absolute idea that sublates all its phases. We must keep in mind that the finite apart from the whole "*is not*" (Enc § 386, R). The finite subsists and has meaning only as sublated in the infinite. Error and evil are incident upon the finite moments of negation within the dialectic, but they are not "real" or actual in the sense that they are not the realized result of the self-activity of the concept. "Finite things [*Dinge*] are finite in so far as they do not completely have in themselves the reality of their concept" (SL, 757; W6, 465). Lacking the achievement of the absolute idea, any phase is untrue — "tainted" by error and evil. But what is actual is the result of the activity of the concept. Even the worst state, Hegel notes, "in so far as it exists [*existiert*] is still idea" (SL, 758; W6, 465–66), otherwise it would not exist at all. We are constantly in a struggle with error and evil because the concept has not been fully actualized.

> That the idea has not fully worked through its reality, has imperfectly subdued [*unterworfen*] it to the concept, this is a possibility arising from the fact that the idea itself has a *restricted* [*beschränkten*] *content*, that though it is essentially the unity of concept and reality, it is no less essentially their distinction. (SL, 757; W6, 465)

Error and evil as the moments of difference have only a finite status as sublated within the result of absolute spirit. The unity of the idea is a negative unity in which the infinite "overreaches" the finite (Enc § 215, R). In the absolute idea, where concept and actuality perfectly coincide, the finite moments of the process of the dialectic, which is the process of the world, are lifted up from their isolation and are made, so to speak, to contribute to the life of absolute spirit and thence to fall away in the eternal moment of reconciliation.

## Truth is the Whole

Until this point we have given a largely logical exposition of the truth, though inevitably we have been speaking metaphysically as well because of the correspondence in Hegel's thought of logic and metaphysics. It will now be of some benefit to see the meaning of Hegel's theory of truth and its relevance to our topic by looking more widely and generally at Hegel's theory. In order to do so we will first look at Hegel's statements about truth in the preface to his *Phenomenology of Spirit*.[10]

We have already noted that in the achievement of truth the dichotomy between the cognizing subject and the cognized object is sublated into a unity-in-difference. This unity is brought about through negative movement that constitutes the opposition of subject and object. In the phenomenological order this opposition appears as the unlikeness of the I (or subject-pole) and substance (or the objective world) which is overcome when substance shows itself to be subject (PS, 21; W3, 39). In knowledge, knowing and known are found to be identical as the activity of spirit. When in the history of consciousness this level is reached, it then becomes possible to set forth the unity of being and knowing as a logical movement, as a movement of the structures of thought (cf. PS, 22; W6, 39).

The unity of being and knowing, which is truth, cannot be the starting point of science without first comprehending the process that brings it about (except as being is the first moment in the movement of pure thought). Hegel points out that the comprehension of this process comes about through the negativity inherent in it. Falsity appears in the process toward truth not as something in simple opposition to what is true but as the partiality of any standpoint of knowledge short of the absolute. *In concreto* true and false appear together in the movement toward absolute truth. "One can know falsely," Hegel says, by which he means that there can be an inadequate knowing in which the knowing is unlike what is known. However, this unlikeness is the moment of distinguishing that is essential to the process of achieving the unity-in-difference that is truth (PS, 22–23; W3, 40–41). Truth includes the negative within its own organic movement; hence, what is commonly called false is a finite moment of knowing isolated from the process of absolute knowing. The individual shapes of spirit and determinations of thought do not persist (*bestehen*) (PS, 28; W3, 46). It is the movement itself that persists and constitutes the moments of its own appearing. In striking imagery Hegel compares truth to a "Bacchanalian revel" in which the drunken members together constitute one movement, but apart from this unified movement each collapses (PS, 27–28; W3, 46). It seems a strange metaphor for truth, as Loewenberg notes, that "the sobriety of ultimate truth, so to speak, thus depends on the toxic condition with which all proximate truth is infected," as though an integrated series of errors would constitute the truth.[11] The metaphor is apt, however, when we conceive the truth as a circular dance in which the individual members can only move when joined to the circle and apart from which each collapses. For Hegel, the truth appears, i.e., it constitutes its own appearance. Each individual appearance arises and passes away, but the movement of truth — i.e., its own activity of appearing — does not arise or pass away (PS, 27; W3, 46). The truth cannot be fixed upon this or that appearance, such as a particular and contingent fact. Truth, rather, constitutes itself as the result of its own necessary[12] process of manifestation.

We are now in a position to see why Hegel says, "The true is the whole" — "the essence that fulfills itself through its development" (PS, 11; W3, 24). Truth is the systematic exposition of knowledge. This systematic exposition is speculative philosophy that has for its content the actualization of the concept as it "engenders and moves through its own moments" (PS, 27; W3, 47). This systematic exposition of knowledge is not a static whole but a dynamic, self-articulating process that in achieving itself turns back upon its own process of achievement. It is simply dialectical movement, the pure form of thought — "the true shape [*Gestalt*] in which the truth exists" (PS, 3; W3, 14).

We should note that this process of development is not a temporal process since as a whole it is eternal or transtemporal. "It is the perpetual and unremitting activity of thought as it grasps instantaneously and without lapse the nexus between distinct yet mutually implicated elements."[13] Ironically, though, truth has its "time" — "it appears only when this [its] time has come, and therefore never appears prematurely, nor finds an unripe public" (PS, 44; W3, 66). Hegel's talk of "time" here has the sense of the biblical *kairos*, the appropriate moment, the hour of fulfillment that Hegel echoes in his famous words in the *Philosophy of Right* about the appearance of philosophical thought after the concept has carried through a certain phase of its actualization (cf. PR, 12–13; W7, 27–28). Philosophy, however, is not outside this process but is its fulfillment, the self-conscious moment of the entire movement of spirit, wherein substance reveals itself as subject. The moment of the self-consciousness of the whole is the completion of the circle as a scientific system whose content is truth in the form of truth.

To say "the true is the whole" is to say then that any particular element or part as isolated is false because it is fragmentary, not united with what is universal. But when a particular is cognized *as* particular, then it is beyond itself as what it is within the whole. Truth then is spirit, for spirit is the self-consciousness of the whole in which there is the achievement of a unity-in-difference, an integration of parts into the whole by a process of self-diremption and return. No particular thing is simply true or false. When I recognize something as false, I recognize that it is not as it should be, that knowing and known are in some degree disparate, and yet in that recognition its falsity is already transcended into the larger view. Similarly, if a particular claim is true, and I fix it at that level (as does the understanding), then I fail to see it as a moment within the process of coming to total truth, and it remains external to mind, fixed, and finite. Philosophic truth is the goal of the grasping of everything without loss or separation of its essential being. In short, truth is absolute spirit.

We can perhaps make Hegel's meaning clearer by indicating how his philosophy of truth resonates with our experience. When artists and writers of genius realize that, as good as their work is, it is still less than what it should be, they recognize the inadequacy and fragmentary character of what they have made in relation to the whole. Similarly, when great thinkers in their wisdom realize how little they know in relation to what is knowable, they see the "untruth" of their work as it falls short of the whole. Or, when holy men and women have the acute sense of their own sinfulness in relation to perfect holiness, the sense of limitation becomes more pronounced. It is this recognition of the *excessus* of all our art, science, and spiritual striving that indicates Hegel's meaning of truth as the goal of the totality.

When we recognize all our truths as partial, at the same time we nonetheless recognize them as truths, as immanent within the striving. The goal does not transcend our process of achievement but overreaches or consummates it, and so every actuality in its way is true as part of the immanent process of spirit. Truth is only reached by the labor of traversing its path. Though the path is winding and full of impediments, it is nonetheless the pathway that must be travelled because, as Hegel is famous for saying, reason is cunning (Enc § 209, *Zusatz*), and thus every seeming failure ultimately transcends its partiality, its "falsity," in view of the whole.

To say that truth is the whole or absolute spirit is another way of expressing the metaphysics of absolute idealism, which is the source and foundation by which we can declare that truth as the agreement of thought with the object has a wholly conceptual meaning. In order to understand the meaning of truth in Hegel's philosophy, we have always to realize that Hegel has brought philosophy to its full idealistic development. Aristotle has said that through knowledge "the soul is in a certain way all things" (*De Anima* III, 8. 431b21), and this statement of the conformity of intellect and reality has a radicalized meaning in Hegel. In truth, the mind (or spirit or intellect) conforms to things, which means for Hegel that ultimately the form of mind is the form of reality as an entire process at work in every particular act of knowing. The mind does not impose an order on the world apart from which the world would lack intelligible order, as in Kant, rather scientific cognition surrenders to "the life of the object," which is the object's "inner necessity" (PS, 32; W3, 52). The mind's becoming the reality it knows is possible because "being is thinking" [*das Sein Denken ist*] (PS, 33; W3, 53). By conforming to the object, object and mind unite, the mind finds its own inner content in the content of the known object, and the activity of knowing "is totally absorbed [*versenkt*] in the content, for it [the activity of knowing] is the immanent self of the content" (PS, 33; W3, 53). Hence, knowing is an activity, being known is an activity, and at the absolute level, knowing is the recognition that knowing and being known are one activity and one being.

Hegel makes the same point about the oneness of activity in knowing and being known in the introduction to the *Phenomenology of Spirit* when he shows the absurdities that result from supposing the separation of thinking and being. If cognition is active and instrumental in attaining what is in truth — i.e., the absolute — then cognition changes the *Sache* and "does not let it be as it is for itself." On the other hand, if cognition is "a passive medium," then we still only attain the truth as through the medium and not the truth in itself (PS, 46; W3, 68). If cognition is an instrument or means for reaching the real, then it filters the real, and we are ever obstructed from the thing itself because what we cognize is necessarily a distortion of what is. The mistake is in supposing that cognition is an instrument or means and hence in supposing "a *distinction between ourselves and this cognition*" (PS, 47; W3, 70). To avoid the absurdities inherent in supposing an original separation between cognition and that which is in itself that is not contingent upon any act of cognition — i.e., the absolute — the correct assumption is that "the absolute alone is true or the true alone is absolute" (PS, 47; W3, 70). Whether we show that the object corresponds to the concept or the concept, to the object, from the point of view of absolute knowing or philosophy, in the end both procedures are the same because the distinction of consciousness, or the for-itself, from what exists, or the in-itself, is a distinction within consciousness itself (PS, 53; W3, 76–77). The import of Hegel's analysis of consciousness in the *Phenomenology of Spirit* is to show the agreement of concept and reality. When given its logical and ontological foundation, we see that what is is what appears as a total process of spirit appearing to spirit.

Hegel demonstrates not only that if reality is intelligible it must be thought, but more fundamentally that there must be an ontological identity of thought and the object of thought if we are to explain truth.[14] Whereas truth for the understanding concerns the union of two disparate elements — viz., thought and the extramentally real object — so that some instrument or means must exist to bring them together, from the standpoint of reason, thought and reality are, in the fullest and most fundamental sense, one. The distinction of thought and reality is contained in their unity.

## Religious Truth

Because truth is the agreement of concept and reality, the truth of religion is found by grasping the activity of the concept in (i.e., grasping the inner rationality of) actual religion over against an empirical study of religion (cf. LPR I, 198; V3, 107–8). Hence, Hegel's philosophy of religion is a comprehension of religion as a movement of inclusive and absolute subjectivity. It follows as well that the true religion is the religion that perfectly actualizes the concept of religion. Hegel's approach to religion as a philosopher is new in the history of philosophy because the concept of God is made explicit by thinking the inner rationality of actual religion as God's activity and revelation of self. Philosophy of religion, then, for Hegel is philosophy of God. Through the comprehension of the inner principle of religion we find that God is spirit, which means that "God is essentially in his community" (LPR I, 186; V3, 96). In logical terms, "the concept of God is his idea" (ibid.), which is to say that concept and objectivity are one, or that the concept "gives itself in the form of external existence [*Dasein*]," and this correspondence of concept and objectivity is "truth *in and for itself*" (Enc § 213). Hence Hegel can say, "God ... has truth for the first time and is so only as absolute idea, when the side of his reality is posited for itself and in identity with the concept" (LPR I, 187; V3, 96). We see then that actual religion is not incidental to the knowledge of God (which is our knowledge of God and God's self-knowledge), but that actual religion, in however inadequate form, is the necessary self-objectification of God. We might think that philosophy would understand religion as the attempt of a human community to relate itself to God, but Hegel's insight is that, when speculatively comprehended, religion reveals itself as God's constituting by his own inner dynamism this relationship of a human community to himself.

This speculative comprehension of religion is obviously not religion's own understanding but a rational explication of what is found in actual religion. However, religion has a content that it represents to itself as doctrine or truth (LPR I, 239; V3, 148). As has been explained above in the chapters on form and content and on representation, this content is not given according to the form of its inner, rational necessity but is represented. The truth as represented in religion is not yet perfected because it is not thought of as the perfect coincidence of concept and reality. The elements of the content of religion as represented have only an external and contingent mode of connection, whereas speculative thought brings forth the inner, necessary connections of the religious content. "Because this content is the truth, and thus is in and for itself speculative and mystical in nature, it is merely the form that is stripped away [by philosophy]" (LPR I, 249; V3, 158). By saying that speculative thought brings forth the truth of religion in the form of truth by removing the representational form, Hegel is not downplaying (at least in his Berlin lectures) religion's role in revealing this truth but is only indicating that its representational form, as he says, "dissolves itself into the form of thought" (LPR I, 251; V3, 159). Because it is the truth, its content is already implicitly speculative.

Only the whole of speculative philosophy is capable of doing this [that is, rationally cognizing religion's content], and simultaneously that nothing is further from its intention than to overthrow religion, i.e., to assert that the content of religion cannot for itself be the truth. On the contrary, religion is precisely the true content but in the form of representation, and philosophy is not the first to offer the substantive truth. Humanity has not had to await philosophy in order to receive for the first time the consciousness or cognition of the truth. (LPR I, 251; V3, 159)

Philosophy in Hegel's way of thinking does not oppose religion but only opposes the fixation of some religious thinkers upon religion's representational form. This fixation upon representation constricts and, in effect, denies religion's speculative truth. If religion mistakenly seeks to "defend" itself against philosophy, it has already lost the battle because religion's truth has its destiny in thought, from which it receives its grounding. Hence Hegel explicitly opposes any way of thinking that assumes that "the religious ceases to be religious when it is made comprehensible [*begreiflich*]" (LPR I, 254; V3, 162). On the contrary, religion is perfected when made conceptual because its content is the truth.

## The Theoretical and Practical Elements of Religious Truth

The impulse of the concept of religion to actualize fully or objectivize itself — in other words, to be true — has two aspects: the theoretical and the practical. These two aspects are developed in the 1824 and 1827 *Lectures on the Philosophy of Religion*, although Hegel employs different material in the respective developments of these two aspects. The theoretical aspect concerns religious consciousness, or the knowledge of God by which God sunders himself in revealing himself so as to become objective to human consciousness. The practical aspect concerns the cultus by which God is reconciled to himself through humanity's participation in the divine life. The practical aspect of the concept of religion is the moment of subjective self-consciousness in the spiritual awareness of the community.

### THE THEORETICAL ELEMENT

In the theoretical aspect in the 1824 lectures, Hegel offers a kind of phenomenology of the concept of religion by which the concept is actualized. Because truth is the actualization of the concept, it follows that the true religion is the one by which the concept of religion — i.e., the self-consciousness of God — is fully actualized. Because God is spirit, the true religion is Christianity, in which God is represented as spirit. "In this religion the reality is equal to the concept, the content presents the nature of spirit" (LPR I, 333; V3, 234). Another way of expressing the same point is that "its appearance is equal to its essence" (LPR I, 332; V3, 234), and here we recall Hegel's statement about truth in the *Science of Logic* that the concept is one with its object in appearance so that the appearance of the concept is not a *Wesenloses* but is "the completely liberated manifestation of essence" (SL, 591; W6, 263). The true religion, then, is the one in which its appearance is completely one with its essence. We quote the entire paragraph in the *Lectures on the Philosophy of Religion* in which we see a clearly presented application of Hegel's general understanding of truth to his philosophy of religion.

> The authentic [*wahrhafte*] religion corresponds to its content; in it we have the ultimate and highest that the content raises itself to itself — that the appearance of spirit is, in and for itself, how the content is in accord with the concept of spirit. Here in this mode God is manifest [*offenbar*] to himself or quite generally has become manifest, then there is no longer anything hidden in him. His appearance is equal to his essence. He is still not manifest as long as the mode of his appearance is unequal to his concept. His concept is still locked up, unfulfilled. (LPR I, 332; V3, 234)

The true religion is the one which fully accords with its concept; however, it is not yet the full truth itself until the truth appears in the form of truth, i.e., until philosophically expressed. Hence, as Hegel states, "the proper task of philosophy is to transmute the content that is in the representation of religion into the form of thought" (LPR I, 333; V3, 235).

In the theoretical aspect of religion in the 1827 lectures, Hegel includes the proofs for God's existence as they express the elevation of the finite spirit to infinite spirit. We will mention only the ontological proof because it most clearly manifests the truth as the agreement of concept and reality and is for Hegel the proof characteristic of Christianity. The ontological proof in Hegel's rendering is another way of expressing the logic of the concept. "The *concept* is the *truth of being and essence*" (Enc § 159) and as such is "an infinite and creative form, which includes, but at the same time releases from itself, the fullness of all content" (Enc § 160, *Zusatz*, p. 307). In line with, and parallel to, this notion of truth, the concept of God in its speculative sense is the self-actualization of the entire dialectical process. "The concept is ... what mediates itself with itself; one of its determinations is also being" (LPR I, 436; V3, 325). "Through the negation of the particularization ... the concept [comes] to be identical with itself or to relate itself to itself" (LPR I, 437; V3, 326). In contrast with the understanding that views the concept as a mere form of thought or an abstraction, the concept in speculative philosophy is self-determining activity. Hence the ontological proof in speculative philosophy is God's self-proof. We do not prove God, but we come to think what God is — the infinite movement of diremption and reconciliation. This concretion and actualization of the concept of God is the same as what is meant by truth.

As Hegel makes clear, the truth is in God in whom the order of thinking and the order of being are one. Human spirits have finite concepts that are true. The truth of these concepts is not in their finitude but in the conceptual unity of thought and reality that can only be grounded ultimately in infinite thought's determining itself to being. Lauer points out that the ontological proof, as Hegel explicates it, demonstrates the nature of truth itself because the order of thinking is the same as the order of being. Our conception of God remains merely subjective unless God is thinking in our thinking.[15] We see then that the identification of God and truth (Enc § 1) is the unity of concept and reality, and is, in the theoretical consideration of religion, God's activity, which raises finite spirit to the infinite and thereby brings finite spirit to fulfillment in thought.

THE PRACTICAL ELEMENT

The practical aspect of the concept of religion concerns the cultus.[16] By contrast with the theoretical relation to God, in which God as object stands over against the I, in the practical relation to God,

> I have not only to know the object, to be filled, but to know myself as filled by this object, to know it as within me and likewise myself as within this object that is the truth — and so to know myself in the truth. (LPR I, 442; V3, 330)

This relationship of God and the human subject is in truth because the dichotomy of subject and object is overcome and the concept of religion has arrived full circle in the reconciliation of God and oneself. Hegel says that the foundation of the cultus is that "since God alone is actuality, I should have my truth and actuality in God" (LPR I, 444; V3, 332). Through the life of the religious community the believer shares interiorly in the divine life. The believer is in the truth because the concept of God is actualized in the human spirit. On the practical, communitarian level, this moment of truth corresponds to the moment of reconciliation in revealed religion, where the essence "through this mediation [of God and the human person] brings about [*bewirkt*] its own indwelling in self-consciousness and is the actual presence of the essential and self-subsisting [*an und für sich seienden*] spirit as the universal" (Enc § 570).

By way of the cultus, the alienation of God and world is overcome and "God is in his community" (cf. LPR I, 186; V3, 96).

*The Religion of Truth*

We should briefly consider some of Hegel's comments on truth in his lectures on the consummate religion so as to augment and further to clarify his presentation of truth in regard to religion, even though his exposition of the concept of religion already contains the substance of his thinking on this matter.

Hegel states that the Christian religion is the religion of revelation, truth, and freedom (cf. LPR III, 63–65, 170–73; V5, 2–5, 105–8). These three characteristics are mutually implicative and constitute a single process. Because the content of the Christian religion is spirit, "it is the concept, which is absolute reality, existence, appearance, outgoing [movement] [*Heraus*]" (LPR III, 64; V5, 4). Because concept and reality are in accord, God shows forth his essential nature, and divine and human nature are reconciled. The opposition of the human subject and divine object is overcome in the activity of absolute spirit. "Truth consists in the being adequate to each other of what we have characterized as subject and object. That spirit as object to itself constitutes the reality, the concept, the idea: this is the truth" (LPR III, 171; V5, 106). This movement of spirit that is truth can as well be expressed as freedom because the alienation of God and world is negated and their opposition becomes a self-conscious unity through spirit's inner movement of self-determination. We must bear in mind that the object of the consummate religion is the absolute subject, knowing and differentiating itself, so that for Hegel the transition from the absolute religion to philosophy is the identification of the absolute subjectivity of the Christian religion with the concept of speculative philosophy. In philosophy, the content of the Christian religion reveals its truth, for it has "the *shape* of the certainty of itself" (PS, 485; W3, 582).

## Religion and Philosophy:
## United and Distinguished within the Truth

We have already shown that religion and philosophy share the same object (God who is truth), and that philosophy distinguishes itself from religion by having as its task to demonstrate the rational necessity of its object (cf. Enc § 1). There can be for Hegel no thought of religious truth and philosophical truth in opposition with one another. Moreover, the truth is concrete activity that entails a theoretical and a practical aspect, so that both religion and philosophy share the task of bringing humanity into relation with the divine. Religion and philosophy, however, are in principle distinct, and that distinction lies within the unity of the truth as the whole. It is now our purpose to clarify the relation of religion and philosophy according to the idea of truth as the whole.

*Truth as a Unitary Movement in Religion and Philosophy*

For Hegel, neither religion nor philosophy can be defined or appraised according to empirical criteria but only according to the concept, that is, according to the inner principle of rationality at work in each. Truth belongs to the inner content of religion and philosophy. We cannot be satisfied with merely studying the various forms of religion and philosophy but must comprehend these forms as a systematic unity as they, with varying degrees of adequacy, express a single truth, or rather, the truth. This task of systematic comprehension is, of course, properly philosophical — it is an activity of reason. Its goal, however, is the same as religion's — the fulfillment of the human spirit in the perfect reconciliation of God and humanity. Because this reconciliation is the work of spirit — or, simply stated, is spirit — religion cannot accomplish this reconciliation unless it allows free run to the activity of spirit to move through the subjective, particular, and external forms so as to arrive at what is wholly universal and interior. Philosophy, Hegel says, is *Erkenntnis durch Vernunft* and as such is common to the cognition of all human beings (LPR I, 126; V3, 42). Philosophy cannot rest upon what is subjective or particular, such as feeling or opinion, but must push toward the grasp of what is objectively true for all rational creatures. Philosophy then for Hegel is the perfection of religion, which, we would argue, means philosophical religion. We correctly distinguish religion and philosophy, but they are part of the same process; and, from the standpoint of the result of the process, religion and philosophy are redefined in the light of their speculative comprehension. Religion and philosophy as actually found in human history are the highest manifestations of the activity of spirit, and they unite in the goal of truth. Throughout the preceding pages we have been at pains to show that truth is not a treasure that lies waiting to be discovered but is the activity of its own realization as the immanent movement of the whole. We can as well call truth "God," and, as we have seen, Hegel has no reserve about equating truth and God. God is the source, goal, and immanent activity of the whole of reality. While we may (perhaps, must) in a certain phase of history oppose religion and philosophy, they are not in principle opposed but are ultimately the confluence of one movement of truth. This confluence is the activity of the divine at work within the human spirit. The human spirit, Hegel says, is driven (*getrieben*) to seek truth in the measure that it recognizes the dignity of its own spirit (LPR I, 128; V3, 44). Fidelity to this drive means that any attachment to external and contingent connections must be avoided and that the expression of the relation of God and world must be supposed to have an inner unity that can be discovered. The quest for this unity must characterize religion and philosophy.

As a matter of observable fact, philosophy does not appear to attain a single comprehension of the whole, yet Hegel argues

> truth is one and one only. As a formula this belongs to our conscious thinking as such, but, in a deeper sense, the starting-point and aim [*Ziel*] of philosophy is to know this one truth as at the same time the source from which everything else flows, all laws of nature, all phenomena of life and consciousness.... Philosophy's aim is to bring back all these laws and phenomena by an apparently reverse way to that single source, but in such a way as to grasp [*begreifen*] them as issuing from it. (ILHP, 18; H, 29)

When understood in this way, philosophy, like religion, is not merely a human endeavor but is the result of divine activity. Philosophy has a history that in complex ways expresses the history of the spiritual maturation of peoples and cultures. Hegel's aim is not to show one philosophical view as false or true against another but to conceive the variety of philosophical systems "as the progressive development of the truth," so that, as the succession itself of philosophical systems, "their fluid nature makes them at the same time moments of an organic unity" (PS, 2; W3, 12). Hegel's frequent use of organic imagery indicates that truth is to be conceived as a process of growth according to an inner teleology. At the end of his *Lectures on the History of Philosophy,* Hegel states his aim in the study of the history of philosophy, and (whatever may be our appraisal of Hegel's reading of one or another philosopher) it is this aim that is all-important to Hegel's insight on truth.

> I wish that you should learn ... that the history of philosophy is not a blind collection of fanciful ideas, nor a fortuitous progression.... The general result of the history of philosophy is this: 1. that throughout all time there has been only one philosophy, the contemporary differences of which constitute the necessary aspects of the one principle; 2. that the succession of philosophic systems is not due to chance but presents the necessary succession of stages of this science. (LHP III, 552; W20, 461)

Truth is not a simply already existing reality that one or another finite subject discovers; nor can it be constituted *ex nihilo* by any finite subject. The truth must be achieved.

*Philosophical Religion*

How do religion and philosophy unite and differ in this quest of discovery that is as well the constitution of truth? We have considered what it means to say that religion and philosophy are one in content but different in form. Unlike religion, philosophy relates itself to its subject matter by thought. Yet, even in making this distinction Hegel is careful to qualify his statement, for "religion too has general thoughts," which sometimes are found "in the form of thoughts.... Moreover, we encounter within religion philosophies directly expressed, e.g., the philosophy of the Fathers and the Schoolmen" (ILHP, 125; H, 168–69). In our chapter on representation, above, we argued that all religious representations are not on one level and that doctrinal expressions of religion's content manifest the effort to give rational expression to what is, or should be, believed. Nonetheless, doctrine as religiously expressed retains some degree of externality, and the connection of the elements is not completely demonstrated. Yet, even here, as Hegel notes, we find "within religion philosophies directly expressed" (ILHP, 125; H, 169). It is this fact, as well as our reasoning about the relation of religion and philosophy, that has led us to argue, in agreement with such interpreters of Hegel as Lauer and Ricoeur, that philosophy as a purely conceptual grasp of the truth turns back upon religion and informs religious doctrine and praxis, purifying it of the elements that hamper its development in the truth.

Hegel's philosophy of religion has in part the object of criticizing a religious outlook that opposes itself to reason or that is satisfied with a separate peace, which is, for Hegel, no peace (cf. FK, 55; W2, 288; ILHP, 145; H, 196; F-L, 225; F-M, 227–28; W11, 42–43). There cannot be a religious satisfaction in separation from philosophical satisfaction because "there can only be one 'most inward,' and so the satisfaction of this innermost self by its own means can also be one only" (ILHP, 145; H, 197). At the level of what is "most inward," religion and philosophy unite, and that in which they unite is the quest of the truth as absolute, eternal, infinite. Religion and philosophy for Hegel differ within the unity of this quest, and they do so not only in their respective *modi operandi* but in their achievement, for only pure thought for Hegel can achieve truth in its pure form. Pure thought, however, is not an ethereal realm in separation from the productions and activities of the human spirit.

> Thought is the universal substance of the spirit; from it everything else develops. In everything human it is thinking, thought, which is the effective thing [*das Wirksame*].... An animal has sensuous feelings, desires etc., but no religion, science, art, imagination; in all these thought is at work [*ist wirksame*]. (ILHP, 55; H, 82)

The achievement of the truth as the goal of the endeavor of philosophy, we would argue, informs religion and brings it to its perfection so that religion may bring about the reconciliation of the divine and the human, at least in the measure that is possible in this life.

## Philosophy's Destiny as Rational Religion

If the perfection of religion is its total agreement with the concept of religion by which in the practical order the human self finds its self-conscious unity in God (cf. LPR I, 442–43; V3, 330–32), and if philosophy has the proper task of explicating the truth in wholly rational form, do not religion and philosophy unite in their goal in such a way that philosophy's sublation of religion is the elucidation of religion according to philosophy's proper form? There are some texts in Hegel that may suggest how we are to proceed in clarifying the relation of religion and philosophy.

In the 1827 lectures on the concept of religion, Hegel compares one's activity within the religious cultus to one's activity within philosophy. To the extent that the highest form of the cultus is to renounce all that is external to one's inmost self so as to purify one's heart and "raise oneself up to the realm of the purely spiritual," Hegel says "philosophy is a continual cultus" (LPR I, 446; V3, 335). Philosophy, like religious life, demands the renunciation of external attachments so as to be freely united with God.

> It is part of knowing the true that one should dismiss one's subjectivity, the subjective fancies of personal vanity, and concern oneself with the true purely in thought, conducting oneself solely in accordance with objective thought. (LPR I, 447; V3, 335)

Hegel's statement that "philosophy is a continual cultus" is not merely a metaphor but expresses in speculative form what in religious terms is the *unio mystica,* which he describes as "the feeling of this enjoyment that I am with God in his grace, ... the consciousness of my union and reconciliation with God" (LPR I, 445; V3, 333). Hence can we not say that the highest goal of religious life is identical with the object of philosophy, viz., the free, spiritual union with God that has transcended all external means so as to achieve a wholly interior relation with God that is recognized as God's activity within the deepest self?

We would add that this "mystical union" is not present *ab initio*, and if it is achieved at all, the human subject must ascend by means of the ladder of intuition, representation, and life within a spiritual community. We are already familiar with Hegel's assertion that "religion is the truth *for all*" (Enc § 573, R, p. 373) or "religion is that form of the consciousness of truth which is available to all" (ILHP, 142; H, 192). We would argue that Hegel's assertion is not a concession to the fact that the mass of humanity is incapable of speculative thought, but that truth in its pure form has its concretion and practical actualization in rational religion wherein the spiritual and mundane realm are brought into harmony according to the truth (cf. ILHP, 149; H, 200). In the ontological proof according to the 1831 *Lectures on the Philosophy of Religion,* Hegel makes the statement that

> religion must be for all humanity as a whole — for those who have so purified their thinking that they know what is in the pure element of thinking, [i.e., for] those who have attained to speculative cognition of what God is, as well as for those who have not advanced beyond feeling and representation. (LPR III, 357; V5, 275–76)

It seems that "those who have attained to the speculative cognition of what God is" are not apart from the less enlightened, but that those who know in pure thinking, like the disciples in their descent from the mount of transfiguration (Mt. 17:1–9), must actualize this knowledge in concrete life and in *Gottesdienst* that humanity may perfect its relation to God. Simply stated, "religion is relationship to God" [*ist Beziehung auf Gott*] (LPR I, 448; V3, 336).

In this perspective — namely, that religion is relationship to God — philosophy is "higher" than religion but is equally "within" religion as "the leaven that makes the whole mass rise." In this perspective, religion and philosophy are not separable, at least not ultimately, but they are united and distinguished as forms of thought.

> Humanity does not exist as pure thinking; instead, thinking itself is manifested as intuiting, as representing.... Philosophy thinks what otherwise only is for representation and intuition. In representing, human beings are also thinking, and the content of truth comes to them as thinking beings. Only what thinks can have religion; and thinking is also representation but it is only thinking that is the free form of truth. (LPR III, 357; V5, 276)

It may be, as we indicated earlier in the chapter on representation, that in his later years Hegel came to be more at ease with truth as expressed in religious form and that he no longer needed to denigrate (if this term is not too strong) the religious forms of expression in his effort to establish absolute knowledge as the summit of knowledge and the pure form of truth. We must remember that Hegel is often at pains to demonstrate that religion's content is rational over against those who would place intuition or representation above rational thought, and that this polemic is often present in his philosophy of religion. But once it is established that religion is rational, what then is the continuing status of religion so conceived? Hegel's admission that "humanity does not exist as pure thinking" may allow us to interpret Hegel as saying that philosophy is "within" religion, not as subordinate to it but as its higher, animating principle, analogous to the way the soul exists in its body, and that religion is the concrete means by which philosophy actualizes the truth for all humanity. If we are correct in saying, as we did in the last chapter, that philosophy has no subsistence outside concrete human life, then philosophy, as the pure expression of absolute knowledge, is, as Ricoeur says, "the thoughtfulness of all the modes that generate it."[17] Thus philosophy is the guiding principle and the ground of religion.

It is impossible to think of truth as other than self-revealing; hence, it must actualize itself, incarnate itself, in such a way that the infinite overreaches the finite (Enc § 215, R). The finite is essential to the actualization of the truth. "That which is in and for itself, and that which is finite and temporal — these are the two fundamental determinations [*Grundbestimmungen*] which must be found in a doctrine of truth" (F-L, 252; F-M, 234; W11, 52). The truth is eternal, but it is not outside time. Time is a characteristic of the natural world insofar as it is finite; "the true, on the other hand, the idea, spirit, is *eternal*. But the concept of eternity must not be grasped negatively as abstraction from time, as existing, as it were, outside of time" (Enc § 258, R, p. 50). Infinite, eternal truth has its concretion, its essential determination, in, by, and through what is finite and temporal. Because the eternal nature of truth is to appear, "the absolute truth itself assumes its appearance in temporal shape and in its external conditions, relationships, and circumstances" (F-L, 247; F-M, 230; W11, 45). It is the achievement of philosophy to conceive the relation of truth and its appearance in such a way that the essential, eternal truth is found in its appearance.

> The aspect of the momentary, local, external non-essential element [*Beiwesens*] must be clearly distinguished from the eternal appearance which is inherent in the essence [*Wesen*] of truth so as not to confuse the finite with the infinite, the indifferent with the substantial. (F-L, 247; F-M, 230; W11, 46)

We often characterize the religious, as opposed to the secular, outlook as finding God within the ephemeral and phenomenal. As William Blake wrote,

> To see a World in a Grain of Sand
> And a Heaven in a Wild Flower,
> Hold Infinity in the palm of your hand
> And Eternity in an hour.
>
> ("Augeries of Innocence")

This outlook is essentially religious, even mystical. Spirit appears. It is for the human spirit to see God in and through the phenomenal surface. The understanding focuses upon the empirical and finite elements of the world and possesses only the surface, or *Beiwesen,* of the appearance. Philosophy, as the activity of reason in systematic form, separates the *Wesen* from the *Beiwesen* of the appearance. By so doing, philosophy restores religion's essential content, and religion, as the concrete means by which the human community relates itself to God, is preserved by philosophy. A new phase in the history of spirit has been accomplished in Hegel's elucidation of the goal of absolute knowledge, and we cannot turn back from this stage without regressing from the truth, but we need not conclude on Hegelian grounds that religion has come to an end with the rise of speculative philosophy.

*The Concrete, Immanent Activity of the Truth*

Because the truth for Hegel is the agreement of concept and reality, truth is essentially "incarnational" — the divine must become concrete and by so doing reconcile the ideal and the real. The achievement of truth is not an eternal immobility but is the eternal activity of the reconciliation of ideal and real. The following reflections, which help indicate the immanent and active character of truth, are drawn from an article by Théodore Geraets in which he compares Hegel's notion of truth with the Judaic, Hellenistic, and Christian notions of truth as fidelity, substance, and revelation, respectively.[18] As with the notion of truth in Judaism — namely, God's fidelity to his people — the Hegelian notion of truth has an irreducibly historical and dynamic character. However, there is as well in Hegel's notion the Hellenistic idea of truth as a purely eternal, spiritual vision. Both notions are one-sided and inadequate. For Hegel, the truth is spiritual and eternal as well as moving and immanent in history. In the Christian sense of truth as revelation, the truth is not a "landscape," as in the Greek conception, but a "face."[19] It is the revelation of God as subject but no longer with the externality that characterizes the religious mode of expression. In absolute knowing, the content of truth "has received the shape of the self" (PS, 485; W3, 583). The concept that has come to fulfillment, which is the truth, contains "the *acting* [*handelnden*], self-assured spirit" (PS, 484; W3, 581). Hegel's philosophy entails a dynamic sense of truth as a process of realization through our activity. This process in not accomplished by God from outside, but from within, humanity. Truth is revealed to us not as what is transcendent and immutable but as "unending articulation, in thought and in reality, of a living totality, one, without a higher instance which would itself be 'wholly other' in relation to this totality."[20]

The truth then is not a static achievement beyond the so-called "real world" but is spirit active in the world. It is the activity of reconciling the human and divine as a "continual cultus" (cf. LPR I, 446; V3, 335) by which the human spirit is brought into relation with the divine. This relation is what we call religion, which, as Hegel shows, has its source and goal in thought (cf. LPR I, 448; V3, 336).

If truth in the pure form of truth has its definitive articulation in Hegel's system, it does not follow that truth has fully actualized itself in the world. Only when all disparity between ideal and real has been completely sublated "so that God may be all in all" (I Cor. 15:28) is the concept wholly in accord with reality. At that point, religion falls away in the perfect reconciliation of God and world in which all humanity is in "mystical union" with God and all external means of relation to the divine have fallen away. Obviously this state of affairs exists only in seed.

Humanity's continuing task is *Gottesdienst*, and that task is properly religious. Hegel is careful to distinguish, but not to separate, religion and philosophy. His intention is to overcome the antipathy of religion and philosophy and to reunite them. We interpret this unification to mean that religion must be rational so that the eternal truth, which is the common object of religion and philosophy (LPR I, 152; V3, 63), may be actualized in humanity's full reconciliation with God.

> Religion and philosophy coincide in one. In fact philosophy is itself *Gottesdienst*; it is religion, because it involves the same renunciation of subjective fancies and opinions in its concern [or "occupation," *Beschäftigung*] with God. Thus philosophy is identical with religion, and the distinction is that philosophy is [identical with it] in a mode peculiar to itself, that is distinguished from the mode we are accustomed to call religion as such. Their common element is to be religion [*Ihr Gemeinsames ist, Religion zu sein*], what distinguishes them consists only in the type and mode of religion. Both differ from one another in the peculiar character of their concern with God. (LPR I, 152; V3, 63)

When Hegel equates philosophy with *Gottesdienst* and "religion," does this not mean that philosophy has a specifically intellectual task that has its embodiment in practices that we would recognize as distinctively "religious"? From our investigation of the nature of truth we conclude that Hegel's philosophy implies the necessity of rational religion, grounded and guided wholly by the light of reason, that would exist through the employment of representational modes of expression and the activities of a faith community. In this sense religion as a way of life completes philosophy because "humanity does not exist as pure thinking" (LPR III, 357; V5, 276) and reason must have its embodiment.

# 6
# Hegel's Rational Religion:
# The Perdurance of Religion in Philosophy and the Actualization of Philosophy in Religion

## Preliminary Remarks

In the preceding chapters, we have sought to explicate the complex, dialectical character of the identity in content of absolute religion and absolute philosophy as well as to clarify and to make precise the relation of religion and philosophy as an interrelated dyad, or in a term adopted from biology, a symbiosis, in which each has its distinctive character but has its life only in relation with the other. We have shown as well that philosophy is religion's "higher" moment, which, in an interpretation of Hegel's system, we have argued, sublates religion in such a way that it preserves religion. This preservation of religion (although not without purifying change by philosophy) is also philosophy's concretion and "incarnation." This last argument has been presented skeletally and has now to be "fleshed out" so that the argument is seen to be coherent and integrative of Hegel's philosophy. This "fleshing out" will answer questions that yet remain from the Hegelian standpoint and advance the argument of the inherent coherence of Christianity and philosophy.

## Religion's Essential Role in the Life of Absolute Spirit

As we have seen, Hegel argues that religion is "the self-consciousness of absolute spirit" (LPR I, 318; V3, 222), which, in Hotho's rendering, means "the self-knowing of divine spirit through the mediation of finite spirit" (LPR I, 318; V3, 222). Religion, then, is not merely the effort of human consciousness to relate itself to the divine but is God's activity mediated through human spirits. This speculative comprehension of religion supposes, of course, that the philosophical standpoint is a higher standpoint than religion *per se* because it knows religion according to religion's inner necessity. Religion has the essential role, historically and speculatively, in humanity's coming to the truth, but only philosophy can comprehend this essential role, because philosophy, in contrast with religion, is the scientific system of truth (PS, 3; W3, 14), "an objective science of truth, a science of its necessity, of conceptual cognizing" (ILHP, 17; H, 27) whose "ultimate aim and interest ... is to reconcile thought, the concept, with actuality" (LHP III, 545; W20, 455).

Even though philosophy has a higher position in the dialectical development of absolute spirit as it comprehends and grounds the truth content of religion in the form of truth, there is a genetic priority of religious revelation to philosophical knowing because it is the nature of consciousness first to know objective truth as external to itself by means of sensuous apprehension (cf. ILHP, 130; H, 174). Religion has the essential role (and we would argue, always retains this role) of revealing the absolute to human consciousness because religion is the "form of the consciousness of truth which is available to all" (ILHP, 142; H, 192). However, a pictorial and historical presentation of the objective truth of the absolute is the presentation of spiritual truths in nonspiritual form. If we are to know God in spirit and in truth (Jn. 4:24), there must be a unity of the human spirit and the divine spirit, in other words, an overcoming of the human spirit's externality and contingency to the spiritual truth revealed to it in religion (ILHP, 130; H, 175). In short, spirit is not at home in nonspiritual modes. That an individual, human spirit appropriates and comprehends the divine spirit is not, as we have shown for Hegel, the activity of individual, human consciousness as individual and as human but is universal, absolute spirit's own activity of self-appropriation and self-comprehension (ILHP, 132; H, 177). The substantive unity of absolute spirit is the foundation for revelation and for the ability of the human spirit to rise above its finitude and to know and to enjoy God.[1] For Hegel, the possibility of religion's claim to reveal truth rests upon the human spirit's being *capax dei*. The "thrust" of the human spirit toward God is God's own activity within the human spirit, which mediates the unity-in-difference of infinite and finite spirit. Philosophy shares, and completes, religion's aim to reconcile God and humanity through uniting the finite spirit with the movement of the inclusive subjectivity of absolute self-consciousness, which is the common content of absolute religion and absolute philosophy. The process of this reconciliation Hegel expresses as a struggle of the finite self-consciousness with the absolute self-consciousness that has its end when "finite self-consciousness has ceased to be finite; and in this way absolute self-consciousness has, on the other hand, attained the actuality it lacked before" (LHP III, 551; W20, 460).[2]

Hegel traces in the history of philosophy the struggle of spirit to come into its own. At first, divine truth is given inwardly and immediately to the human spirit in the form of doctrines to be accepted on faith. Later thinking opposes faith so as to free the human consciousness from what this later thinking (wrongly) perceives to be external and alien. For Hegel the merit of the phase of "free thinking" of the Enlightenment is to bring consciousness to a realization of its own freedom. Yet the finite categories of the understanding, as characterized in Enlightenment thought, oppose religious faith only because they are incapable of grasping the divine truths revealed in religious form. The true relation of faith and thought enshrines the freedom from external constraint that is appropriate to spirit yet recognizes for itself the absolute and universal truths contained in religion. This last position is the perfection of thinking that yet does justice to the content of religion (ILHP, 140; H, 190).

Although philosophy and religion may seem for a time to go their independent ways, they share the same need — the discovery of truth — so there cannot be independent satisfactions of this same need (ILHP, 145; H, 197). The satisfaction of this shared need to discover the truth, which is the reconciliation of philosophy and religion, "must issue [*herbeiführen*] from philosophy" (ILHP, 145; H, 196).

## The Continuation of Religion

*The Close of the Four-Lecture Series on Religion and the Implications of Hegel's Thinking for the Future of Religion*

At the close of his *Lectures on the Philosophy of Religion* Hegel treats the realization of the spiritual community, and by so doing offers further reflection upon the relation of religion and philosophy. Hegel's treatment of the subject is not identical among the four lecture series. This fact demonstrates that Hegel was not firmly settled in his thinking and continued a process of nuancing and refinement in quest of an exact formulation. Vis-à-vis philosophy, the future status of religion is not fully clear. In fact, in 1821 he avoids the issue of the future of religion by stating flatly, "How things turn out is not our [the philosophers'] affair [*Sache*]"

(LPR III, 162; V5, 97). We will look at Hegel's statements about the relation of the Christian religion and philosophy in these various lectures and offer an interpretation of what it can mean that religion "takes flight" in philosophy or in the concept. Despite the ambiguity of Hegel's thinking about the future status of religion, complicated by textual variations, the material at the end of these various lectures is richly suggestive.

After speaking of the community of faith as the indwelling of the holy spirit (LPR III, 149; V5, 85), of the church as an enduring institution of the life of the spirit (LPR III, 151; V5, 87), and of the spirit's presence in the cultus with a comparison of various interpretations of the Eucharist (LPR III, 152–56; V5, 88–91), Hegel then speaks of a "going under" or "perishing" [*Untergehen*] of the faith community that is at once a transition (*Übergang*) of the community into the kingdom of heaven because "the holy spirit has eternal life in its community" (LPR III, 158; V5, 93–94). Hegel is speaking of a process of change in what we have known as the church and of the culture as a whole because all things historical pass away. The future of organized religion, however, is unclear. Bauer's 1840 edition speaks of the transition of the Christian faith community as its fulfillment that is only apparently a passing-away. The community's "realization appears to be at the same time its passing away" [*so scheint diese Realisierung zugleich ihr Vergehen zu sein*], and the question is posed whether we can speak of *Untergang* when the holy spirit lives eternally in its community (LPR III, 158; V5, 93). The fact of the eventual death of all temporal things is, Hegel says, the wrong note (*Misston*) (LPR III, 158 and 161; V5, 94 and 96) with which to leave his hearers. After criticizing teachers of religion who by their employment of reflective understanding leave the ordinary mass of humanity without the true content of religion, Hegel says that instead of opposing reason and religion, as is characteristic of the present, the discord (*Misston*) should be resolved in philosophy (LPR III, 161; V5, 96) (in the 1840 edition, philosophy has already resolved the conflict [LPR III, 162; V5, 97]). Then follows the significant phrase, whose meaning we will shortly consider, that religion will or must flee into philosophy for refuge: "Religion in die Philosophie sich flüchten" (LPR III, 162; V5, 96).

At the close of the 1824 lectures, Hegel states that his aim has been to reconcile reason with religion in its manifold forms and to cognize (*erkennen*) these forms as at least necessary (LPR III, 247; V5, 175). Similarly, at the end of the 1827 lectures Hegel says he has sought to exhibit "the rational cognition [*Erkennen*] of religion" (LPR III, 347; V5, 270).

In an explanation not given in the 1821 manuscript — namely, that the realization of the community involves its transformation (LPR III, 237;

V5, 167) — Hegel shows in 1824 that philosophy must, on the one hand, seemingly oppose the church by removing its objective content from the external form of representation and, on the other hand, oppose the reflective thinking of the Enlightenment that in opposing the authoritarian form of religion also eschews its content (LPR III, 245–47; V5, 174–75). Philosophy reconciles these oppositions by combining the unfettered, inner form of the thinking characteristic of the Enlightenment with the immediately given content of religion. Only as concerns form, Hegel makes clear, does philosophy oppose religion, because "the truth in its all-embracing meaning is set down in religion" (LPR III, 247; V5, 175), and it is for philosophy to bring forth this truth. Rather than philosophical thought opposing religion, religion's content "flüchtet sich dann in den Begriff" against the attacks of the Enlightenment thinking (LPR III, 245; V5, 174).

In the 1827 lectures Hegel repeats a theme of the 1824 lectures that the realization of the spiritual community is also its transformation (LPR III, 339; V5, 262), but he develops this theme in a threefold logical-historical structure by which the spiritual community relates itself to the world. The first moment of reconciliation of the spiritual and the worldly is in life. Hegel distinguishes three stages within this first moment of the realization of the spiritual community. The first is the community's reconciliation with God over against the world as exemplified by the early church. The second continues the unreconciled stance of the community with the world but this time in a state of domination of the worldly realm as exemplified by the medieval church. The third is the reconciliation of the community and the world in ethical life (*Sittlichkeit*) by which reason, eternal truth, and freedom are embodied in the state (LPR III, 339–42; V5, 262–65).

The second moment of the community's realization is in thought in contrast with the first moment of realization in life. This moment is characterized by Enlightenment thought which develops the freedom of reason for its own sake, at the expense, so to speak, of the content of reason, viz., the idea of God (cf. LPR III, 343; V5, 265). This removal of the idea of God from knowledge has the result of making religion a matter of subjective feeling because, it is argued, "'we cannot know [*erkennen*] God'" (LPR III, 343; V5, 266). Hegel is, of course, criticizing Kantian thinking and the natural outcome of such thought in the religion of Pietism (LPR III, 344; V5, 266–67).

The third moment of the spiritual community's realization is the reconciliation of the content of the Christian religion with the form of thought by the conceptualization of this content in speculative thought. The content of religion "in den Begriff flüchtet" and thereby is justified

(LPR III, 345; V5, 267). With a play on his terms, Hegel states that "the Enlightenment of the understanding and Pietism volatalize [*verflüchtigen*] all content" (LPR III, 345; V5, 267). Hegel has, of course, frequently criticized Enlightenment thinking and subjective spiritualities (deriving in part from Kant and Jacobi) for stating that knowledge of God is impossible. If the knowledge of God is impossible, then religion is devoid of content and hence devoid of truth. Against this ignorance of God found in Enlightenment thinking and in contemporary theology and spirituality Hegel argues that only philosophy can safeguard religion and give it refuge. The concept, Hegel says, is "the justification of religion, in particular of the Christian religion, the true [*wahrhaften*] religion; it cognizes this content according to its necessity, according to its reason" (LPR III, 345; V5, 268).

The 1831 transcript contains added material that defends philosophy against the attack that philosophy rejects what is given in religious feeling and representation. Hegel (according to student notes) makes clear that the content of faith in whatever form it is given is not rejected but, on the contrary, is verified in thought.

> Philosophy has been reproached for placing itself above religion. But as a matter of fact this is surely false because philosophy has only this and no other content, although it gives it in the form of thinking.... The form of the subject as one who feels, etc., concerns the subject as an individual; but feeling as such is not eliminated [*ausgestossen*] by philosophy. The question is only whether the content of feeling is the truth and can prove itself to be true [*wahrhafte*] in thought. Philosophy thinks what the subject as such feels, and leaves it to the latter to come to terms with [*abzufinden*] its feeling. Thus feeling is not rejected by philosophy but rather receives its true [*wahrhafte*] content through philosophy. (LPR III, 346; V5, 269)

Hegel also states (according to student notes) in 1831 that while philosophy's achievement is to render the content of faith in the form of thought, it does not thereby "place itself above religion but only above the form of faith as representation" (LPR III, 374; V5, 289).

In these passages, which close his *Lectures on the Philosophy of Religion,* Hegel presents the realization of the spiritual community as the indwelling presence of the spirit in *Sittlichkeit* that overcomes the externality of the relationship of church and world characteristic of earlier eras.

Alongside his defense of the content of faith against the attacks of reflective thinking, Hegel criticizes subjectivistically grounded belief. Clearly Hegel shows that the search for truth cannot stop short at religious belief's meaningfulness or its mere subjective relevance but must find the rational grounding from which religious claims can be evaluated. Hegel recognizes clearly that, on the one hand, if philosophy abandons the knowledge of God then it abandons its proper task and becomes sterile, and on the other hand, if religion separates itself from *Wissenschaft*, then religion has no claim to truth and is ultimately lost. Although from the religious standpoint some may find disconcerting Hegel's speculative reading of the religious traditions, Hegel nonetheless argues clearly that religion's content has no choice but to flee to, and take refuge in, conceptual thinking. *Reflexion*, the philosophy of the understanding as epitomized in Enlightenment thinking, has "broken into" religion and has taken a "hostile stance" [*feindliche Stellung*] toward religious expression (LPR III, 245; V5, 174). Without rational defense, religion appears as a vanishing superstition when face to face with the scientific worldview (as is amply demonstrated since Hegel's time). If religious need (*Bedürfnis*), which means for Hegel the desire for absolute spirit, takes refuge (*Zuflucht nehmen*) in feeling, then there can be no church or spiritual community because there develops a divisive multiplication of *Weltanschauungen* according to the subjective feelings of individuals (LPR III, 246; V5, 174). More fundamentally, religion based on feeling abdicates any claim to truth. Without its foundation and justification in speculative philosophy, religion has no future. This negative conclusion about religion's future can be drawn clearly from Hegel's exposition, but what can be positively said about the future of religion and its form derives from our reasoned interpretation of Hegel's work.

In the 1821 manuscript, as we have seen, Hegel avoids any predictions (cf. LPR III, 162; V5, 97). He does, however, speak of the passing away of the community, though as a description of its transformation (LPR III, 158; V5, 93–94). In the 1824 lectures Hegel distinguishes three stages in the "Rücksicht auf das Reich des Gottes," the last of which is "the community of philosophy." In Hotho's version of this lecture, "the community of philosophy" is rendered as "the philosophizing community" [*philosophierender Gemeinde*] (LPR III, 247; V5, 176). As in 1821, there is no talk of religion's future but only a *Rücksicht* over the stages of spiritual ascent to philosophy. What can "the community of philosophy" mean? Surely it is not a community of philosophers, unless "philosopher" is to be defined so widely as to include all human beings as rational.[3] Here we find that Hotho's "philosophizing community" is suggestive. Can we not say that this community is the community in quest of God that seeks the reconciliation of the divine and human spirit in love and truth by the incorporation of the achievements of reason? "The community of philosophy," then, is, in representational language, "the kingdom of God," actually incipient, not yet realized in full.

In 1827 Hegel develops more fully the logical and historical progression of the realization of the spiritual community by which philosophy reconciles the "real" and "ideal" moments, and, as this reconciliation of the divine and worldly realms, philosophy is, Hegel says, theology (LPR III, 347; V5, 269). Moreover, against the vain, empty criticisms of Enlightenment thinking, philosophy "demonstrates [*aufzeigt und nachweist*] that reason resides within" religion (LPR III, 347; V5, 269). In this sense philosophy sustains (*erhält, empfängt*) and justifies religion (LPR III, 346; V5, 268).

In general, by 1827, and more clearly in 1831, Hegel presents the movement of the reconciliation of God and world in three dimensions, viz., within (1) the church, (2) the ethical life of the state, and (3) philosophy.[4] To our thinking, this logical-historical movement is not a succession of stages by which a latter stage replaces a former, but an intensification of the life of absolute spirit in its own movement toward absolute and inclusive self-consciousness. Religion's "flight into the concept," then, is religion's sublation as its justification and the "passing away" of its hostile stance toward the world that is at once the transformation of the world according to the concept of ethical life. "The true realization of religion in the worldly sphere is the inward realization, namely, that an ethical [*sittliches*] and just civil life should be instituted [*organisiere*]" (LPR III, 373–74; V5, 289).

From the standpoint of the Christian faith community, God and world are conceived horizontally — not, however, as the secularization of the world, but rather as its divination (cf. LPR III, 342; V5, 264), the world's inward realization. In our interpretation of Hegel's dialectical movement, the church is the means by which "the whole mass of dough is leavened." In this interpretation we distinguish means and end. The end is, in parabolic terms, "the kingdom of God," "'like yeast which a woman took and kneaded into three measures of flour. Eventually the whole mass of dough began to rise'" (Mt. 13:33). The means to this end is the Christian faith community, the church, which is not the kingdom of God but is rather the yeast that passes into the flour.[5] From a Hegelian standpoint, can we not speak of a move toward the faith community's greater transforming reconciliation with the world, hostile only toward error, evil, and finitude and directed toward the world's inward realization, whose final goal is "God all in all things," or spirit? The faith community, then, we would argue, has a future. As long as the discrepancy of real and ideal remains, as long as the concept is not yet actualized, then, we would argue, religion perdures (evolving, of course) as it works the reconciliation of the divine and human through *Gottesdienst* by and toward absolute reason. Absolute spirit is the goal drawing forth the process of its own realization toward "new heavens and a new earth" in which the infinite overreaches the finite.

When we say that the church is not the kingdom of God, we are nuancing, and even altering, some of Hegel's statements, for he does say, "The church is the kingdom of God" (LPR III, 151; V5, 87), and

> the church is, by and large, the institution whereby subjects come to the truth, appropriate the truth to themselves, so that the holy spirit becomes real, actual and present within them and has its abode in them, whereby the truth can be within them and they can enjoy and give expression to the truth of the spirit; it is the means whereby they as subjects *are* the active expression of the spirit. (LPR III, 333; V5, 256)

Here is further support for our argument that religion in its Hegelian sublation does continue, for Hegel speaks of the subsistence of the church wherein human subjects live in the truth, are reconciled with God, and enjoy the presence of the spirit (cf. LPR III, 333; V5, 256). However, we would be clear that the kingdom of God cannot be equated without qualification with any actual manifestation of the presence of the spirit in the here and now. The qualification is this: The kingdom is wherever people live inwardly reconciled with the divine, but nowhere is this presence of the spirit complete. The church as the community of spirit is rather the inbreaking of the spirit that has yet to reconcile fully the world with itself.

> The developed community is a *church*, which as an existing community undergoes expansion, but is fixed as far as its determinate being in the actual world is concerned; it is inwardly at peace and endures through time.... The church is the kingdom of God, the achieved presence, life, preservation, and enjoyment of the spirit. (LPR III, 151; V5, 87)

The presence of the spirit is achieved, with its meaning given figurative and somewhat vague expression in the realized eschatology of the gospels, but this presence is obviously not fully achieved (and we find it incumbent to qualify Hegel's statements in this way), for even our highest experiences of love, peace, and spiritual union are imperfect — infected with finitude and contingency. All the same there is no contradiction in saying, "The kingdom of God is within you" (Lk. 17:21; LPR III, 144; V5, 80), for it is only the full actualization, the reconciliation of all the elements of the world and of our experience, that is not yet.

*The Argument from Hinrichs's* Die Religion im inneren Verhältnisse zur Wissenschaft

We have argued that the identity in content of absolute religion and absolute philosophy entails, on the grounds of Hegel's system, the preservation of absolute religion as sublated in this religion's own higher moment, which is absolute knowledge. Religion and philosophy, in a way of speaking, are symbiotically related. We find this argument buttressed by the thinking of Herman Hinrichs's 1822 *Die Religion im inneren Verhältnisse zur Wissenschaft,* for which Hegel wrote a foreword. Eric von der Luft, in *Hegel, Hinrichs, and Schleiermacher on Feeling and Reason in Religion,*[6] to which we shall make reference in further developing our own argument, has given a scholarly translation of this work of Hinrichs's as well as an introduction to its argument and a commentary on Hegel's foreword.

In the foreword to Hinrichs's book Hegel praises Hinrichs's speculative treatment of religion in contrast with the contemporary, subjectivistic climate in theology and the nonspeculative character of philosophy. It is significant to note that here Hegel places Hinrichs in association with the "right-wing Hegelians" Daub and Marheineke, who (in an indication of Hegel's own thinking)

> still preserve Christian doctrine and the right and honor of thought, and writings in which the principles of reason and ethical life [*Sittlichkeit*] are grounded through the concept and defended against those doctrines destructive of the substantial ethical ties of men and of the state and of religion. (F-M, 244; F-L, 267–68; W11, 66)

Hegel then closes his foreword by quoting from a letter of Hinrichs to him (which Hegel has actually reworded but without altering its content)[7] in which Hinrichs expresses his personal difficulty with any conflict between religion and *Wissenschaft* and his need to reconcile religion and *Wissenschaft.* Hinrichs says (in Hegel's wording),

> Science [*die Wissenschaft*], however, had deprived me of the element of representation [*das vorstellende Element*] in which I had been accustomed to see the truth, and what was more natural than that I should strive to sublate the extreme disharmony [*Entzweiung*] and extreme despair produced in me by science and so win a reconciliation in the element of knowledge [*des Wissens*]. (F-M, 244; F-L, 268; W11, 66)

In commenting on Hinrichs's position as regards the reconciliation of religion and reason, von der Luft says,

> The relationship between Christianity and philosophy which Hinrichs professes is not one in which either reason sits in judgment of faith or faith sits in judgment of reason, but rather one in which each simultaneously sits in judgment of the other.[8]

Is this Hegel's own position on the relation of Christianity and philosophy? The fact that Hegel quotes Hinrichs as saying he would eschew philosophy if it could not grasp the absolute truth of Christianity (but happily Hinrichs finds modern "Christian philosophy" to be "the supreme product of Christianity" [F-M, 244; F-L, 268; W11, 66–67]), and the fact that Hegel wrote a foreword to this book, which he did for no other author, indicating at least his *nihil obstat* for Hinrichs's work, would incline us to answer our question in the affirmative.[9] At this point our argument is historical and hence external to Hegel's thought. Our argument must be demonstrated on purely rational grounds, internal to systematic thinking, for it is possible that a philosopher might affirm one or another position that is not sufficiently grounded in, or congruent with, his philosophy as a whole; moreover, in this case the external evidence is not sufficient to establish that Hegel accepted Hinrichs's position *in toto*.

We have argued on the basis of the Hegelian meaning of truth that philosophy's sublation of religion is religion's preservation as rationally purified. Let us briefly consider Hinrichs, who as a disciple of Hegel moved to a similar conclusion out of Hegel's system of thought. We will take some direct quotations from Hinrichs himself but will more often draw upon von der Luft's excellent introduction to Hinrichs's philosophy of religion because it condenses in more readable form the detailed, dull, and turgid expression of Hinrichs's argument. Despite his style, Hinrichs is a rigorous thinker who merits some brief consideration because he has developed in a thorough and systematic way an application of Hegel's logic to the philosophy of religion.

According to Hinrichs, systematic thought and revealed religion (i.e., Christianity) are two interrelated modes of expression of the one movement of absolute spirit, so that the content of revealed religion as mediated by thought is, in Hinrichs's terminology, "absolute religion," or what we are terming "rational religion." Absolute spirit has its concrete manifestation as religion sublated by systematic knowledge.

> Without the guidance and life provided only by religion, philosophy, however exact, rigorous, or productive it may be, is meaningless; and, without the introspection, analysis, and common sense provided only by philosophy, religion, however sincere, profound, or widespread it may be, is mere superstition.[10]

The mediation in thought of the content of revealed religion is the movement of reconciliation of the division between God and creation in such a way that the self-manifestation of absolute spirit is rational religion.

> Reason must expand to have no limits at all if it is to be adequate to the absolute truth of religion — and eventually, religion itself becomes this reason which has no limits. In a similar way, the content of religion must grow to allow itself to be known by reason and conceived by systematic knowledge, so that systematic knowledge itself becomes the content of the absolute religion, i.e., the revealed religion which has become this knowledge's own religion. Only when this twofold goal has been achieved will the form (systematic knowledge) be identical with the content (religion), and vice versa.[11]

For Hinrichs, the final stage of the dialectical process of absolute spirit is absolute knowledge as shared by the Christian religious community. Hinrichs expresses this culmination of the dialectic in the form of a judgement.

> *Absolute spirit is absolute spirit* — which is why the self-manifestation of absolute spirit, as *revelation* in the religion of spirit and as *a process of manifesting* in the systematic knowledge [von der Luft's rendering of *Wissenschaft*] of absolute knowledge, the revealing and manifesting which are *knowledge* in general, constitutes *one and the same manifestation*.[12]

We see that in Hinrichs's argument the identity in content of absolute religion and absolute knowledge means that the Christian religion and philosophy together constitute the movement of self-manifestation that is absolute spirit. In his explanation of the passage quoted above from Hinrichs, von der Luft says:

> Absolute spirit qua absolute truth, absolute spirit qua absolute religion, absolute spirit qua absolute knowledge, etc., are all ultimately one and the same thing in different manifestations. We understand absolute spirit only to the extent that we understand its manifestations and their interrelationships — and this can be accomplished only through systematic knowledge mediated through feeling, belief, critical reason, love, etc.[13]

In drawing upon Hinrichs's philosophy of religion and in indicating the fact that at least in general Hegel approved of Hinrichs's efforts, we develop and deepen our own thesis that the identity in content of absolute religion and absolute philosophy as well as the meaning of sublation as preservation and of truth as the whole process of the actualization of the concept imply and demand that absolute knowledge by which God and creation are reconciled find their embodiment in concrete religious life and practice. Rather than the disappearance of religion in pure thought, the final stage of the dialectic of absolute spirit has its truth only in its concrete realization in the spiritual community whose proper activity is *Gottesdienst* (cf. LPR I, 152; V3, 63), and this activity of a spiritual community by which humanity is related to God is properly termed "religion." This "religion," however, no longer opposes reason but finds its higher moment and ground in speculative thought. In Hinrichs's terminology "revealed religion" as mediated by, and identical with, *Wissenschaft* becomes "absolute religion."[14] As stated within the closing sentence of Hinrichs's book, "the *self-manifestation of absolute spirit as absolute religion* is the *divine life of absolute spirit*."[15] In other words, absolute spirit, whose essence is to appear, has its life and concretion in religion as sublated in *Wissenschaft*.

*Response to the Secularizing Interpretation of Hegel's Thought*

Following upon our consideration of Hegel's somewhat enigmatic reflections at the close of his *Lectures on the Philosophy of Religion*, and Hinrichs's interpretation of Hegel's logic with regard to the place and status of revealed religion in the Hegelian system, we continue with some opposing comments of Pierre-Jean Labarrière and Charles Taylor on the future of religion.

In comments made at a conference on "The Meaning of Absolute Spirit" at the University of Ottawa in 1981, Labarrière says,

> It seems to me there clearly remains in the Hegelian world and even at the level of its full elaboration a place, and that is badly said, for God and for religion as such. At the summit of his system ... Hegel includes the totality of the process which opens itself and will pass through art, religion and philosophy, under the global term or global signification of religion. (Enc § 554; cf. § 63, R)

> If one suppresses this existence of religion or of the religious form in arguing that Hegel had happily attained to the domain of absolute spirit, absolute spirit itself would disappear, because it [spirit] is only an interpretation of historical forms.[16]

In reply to Labarrière, Charles Taylor argues for the secular interpretation of Hegel's philosophy whereby philosophy replaces religion both as a belief and as a cultus.

It seems to me that the secularizing interpretation should say, on the one hand, that philosophy entirely replaces, and renders ineffective, the representative form and that, on the other hand, moral and political practice also completely replaces the religious cultus. M. Labarrière said there is that recapitulative aspect, that genuine philosophy should take in charge all that has existed as practice but this in no way necessitates that the practices thus recapitulated be actual. It can be retrospective in this respect as well, as is the case with the entire practice of the Greek city state. Thus it is not at all necessary that the modern era have churches and a religion.[17]

Taylor incisively states the interpretation of the sublation of religion in philosophy as the vanishing of the religious form of life and practice into the ethical life of the state. That religion has had an essential role in the dialectical life of absolute spirit does not entail its continuation from the standpoint of the present achievement of the Hegelian dialectic. Taylor's argument has cogency.

We have argued in chapter 4 on sublation and chapter 5 on truth that the highest achievement of the dialectical process as pure thought redounds and has its embodiment in the whole of reality as comprehended in thought. The question is whether this comprehension of absolute spirit can be accomplished in the ethical life of the state without religion's cultus and representational forms of expression. In response, we must note that by the state Hegel does not mean any present social and communitarian life but the concept of the state that is to be actualized. "The state is the actuality of the ethical idea" (PR § 257). Moreover, the eternal goal of the dialectic is the indwelling presence of the spirit for which Hegel uses the biblical term "kingdom of God." We have argued that the "kingdom of God," which "is the spirit" (LPR III, 142; V5, 78), is eschatologically imminent in time and realized in eternity. Further, we have argued that religion is the "leaven" (the means); and "the kingdom of God" is "the risen mass" (the end), so that religion and religious community drop away in the kingdom of God. In fact, the church is the means by which human beings enjoy and express the truth of spirit (LPR III, 333; V5, 256). The world, however, is in the "leavening" stage — obviously, the concept of the state is not anywhere actualized, and "the kingdom of God" is breaking into the world but is not yet fully realized. To suppose, as Taylor does, a secular world in which the spirit is indwelling without the specifically and explicitly divine forms of thought and expression that we term "religious," appears unrealistic. It seems to us that Taylor's secularized interpretation of the future process of the realization of spirit would be the world's forgetfulness of, if not antipathy to, the content of religion, in other words, a world that would look very much like that characteristic of the Enlightenment rather than a world in the process of its divinization. Without specific focus upon the divine, and without the symbolisms and myths that speak deeply everywhere to the human heart, how can humanity be awakened to its divine destiny? Moreover, we have argued that this destiny for its achievement requires a transformation of our present human condition more than an endless process of improvement toward a goal that is never achievable. Hegel describes the *unio mystica* as "the feeling of this enjoyment that I am with God in his grace, ... the consciousness of my union and reconciliation with God" (LPR I, 445; V3, 333). In the religious tradition from which Hegel draws this notion of "mystical union," it was thought that in this life one's union with God was at best partial and that eternal life could not be fully achieved in this life. Our point is that what Hegel describes as the spirit is not on the level of endless temporal succession but is a final moment that overreaches the finite, and in so doing, transcends it. We are at this point adapting Hegel's philosophy, though in a way consistent with the inner meaning of spirit. "Reason is spirit when its certainty of being all reality has been raised to truth, and it is conscious of itself as its own world, and of the world as itself" (PS, 263; W3, 324). Spirit is not another world but this world brought to fulfillment from within as perfected unity-in-difference without disparity between real and ideal. But exactly because it is the perfection of this world, it is "another" world, "the kingdom of God," "God all in all things," as speculatively explained. Spirit is for Hegel the goal (*Ziel*) of perfect self-revelation, the absolute concept (PS, 492; W3, 591). "*The goal*, absolute knowing, or spirit knowing itself as spirit, has for its path the *Erinnerung* of spirits as they are in themselves and as they accomplish the organization of their realm" (PS, 493; W3, 591). The recollecting, that is at once the interiorizing, of all the elements that constitute the path of its self-becoming is, as we have argued, an eternal "already" and a temporal "not yet" that seems to us best expressed in eschatological terms. Religion perdures in the future as the means of reconciling humanity and God. However, the goal of this process of reconciliation is not in the future since the goal, spirit, is not temporal. As achieved in eternity, the goal is religionless. It is secular as much as sacred since the basis of the distinction no longer has meaning in "the kingdom of God."

## The Relation of Religion and Philosophy in Hegel's Thought

*The Compatibility of Christianity and Hegelianism*

In order to make more incisive our argument that Christianity and philosophy possess the same content and, moreover, that the Christian religion has not only its fulfillment and warranty in philosophy but its preservation, and, moreover yet, that philosophy has its concretion in religious, spiritual community, we will respond to certain denials of the compatibility of Christianity and philosophy and challenges to the continuation of religious life and practice in the light of Hegel's philosophy.

J. M. E. McTaggart's argument against the compatibility and congruence of Christianity and Hegel's philosophy is longstanding in the field of Hegel scholarship. Against its attackers, McTaggart says, Hegel is an ally of Christianity, though ironically this "ally"

> proves to be an enemy in disguise — the least evident but the most dangerous. The doctrines which have been protected from external refutation are found to be transforming themselves till they are on the point of melting away, and orthodoxy finds it necessary to separate itself from so insidious an ally.[18]

Hegelianism, McTaggart continues, is "an antagonist all the more deadly because it works not by denial but by completion."[19]

F. Copleston concurs with McTaggart's assessment.

> Hegel gives philosophical proofs of such doctrines as the Trinity, the Fall and the Incarnation. But when he has finished with stating them in the form of pure thought, they are obviously something very different from the doctrines which the Church believes to be the correct statement of the truth in human language. In other words, Hegel makes speculative philosophy the final arbiter of the inner meaning of Christian revelation. Absolute idealism is presented as esoteric Christianity and Christianity as exoteric Hegelianism; and the mystery insisted on by theology is subordinated to a philosophical clarification which amounts in fact to a transformation.[20]

It is true that for Hegel speculative philosophy is "the final arbiter of the inner meaning of Christian revelation," but as we have established, rather than "obviously something very different," the doctrines of the church are only apparently different from their philosophical exposition because doctrine by its nature has its destiny and proper form in rational thought.

McTaggart's and Copleston's statements as given without their reasoned argumentation are, of course, merely dogmatic assertions. When examined, we find their arguments to lack penetration because they fail to demonstrate what can be the grounds of Christian revelation and doctrine, if not the truth that can only be established by reason. Precisely, it is the inner criterion by which one assesses the truth claims of any religion that must be evaluated.

The faultiness and lack of incision that underlie McTaggart's conclusions about the relation of Christianity and Hegel's philosophy can be seen and presented in his reasoning that for Hegel Christianity is not only as adequate as religion can be among past religions but as any religions to appear in the future as well.[21] McTaggart is correct in reasoning that, for Hegel, Christianity is the definitive religion and that no new, more adequate religion can arise. McTaggart questions this Hegelian position by saying it is "impossible to be certain that no religion will arise in the future which will express the truth more adequately than Christianity" (249) because we cannot on Hegelian grounds have an *a priori* knowledge of empirical elements of reality, and the symbolism of a particular religion is empirical, hence we cannot conclude, according to McTaggart, on Hegelian grounds that a more adequate religious symbolism other than Christianity's might arise (ibid.). We draw upon this criticism of Hegel's claim that Christianity is the consummate religion and McTaggart's claim that a more adequate religious symbolism other than the Christian is at least conceivable in order to show that his argument is only apparently convincing and leaves untouched a more substantive issue. On Hegelian grounds it would make more sense to say that a more adequate religious expression of the absolute would be a more rationally purified Christianity — i.e., a religion of identical content — and not a new religion. The real issue, of course, is what one understands to be Christianity. Hegel's argument that Christianity is the absolute, consummate religion is a purely rational argument to be evaluated according to its inner criteria and is not dependent for its validity upon historical and empirical details. As Hegel has shown, the story of Jesus (*die Geschichte Jesu*) is

> not only this external history [*Geschichte*] ... but also it has the divine for its content.... This absolute divine action is the inward, the true [*Wahrhafte*], the substantial dimension of this history and this is just what is the object of reason. (LPR I, 399; V3, 294)

Reason for Hegel adjudicates the symbols, myths, and scriptures of religion, and not conversely.

> The words of the Bible constitute an unsystematic account.... [I]t is spirit that grasps [or "interprets," *auffasst*] the content.... This true spirit can only be the

one that proceeds within itself according to necessity, not according to assumptions [*Voraussetzungen*]. (LPR I, 168; V3, 77–78)

McTaggart and others cannot claim Hegel has distorted the doctrines of Christianity unless they explicate the grounds by which to judge what are and are not the doctrines of Christianity.

Charles Taylor's claims of the incompatibility of Christianity and Hegelianism similarly suppose the very matter that needs to be demonstrated, viz., the essential content of the Christian religion. Taylor argues that Hegel's philosophy, though it fully apprehends the historical life of Jesus and the church's doctrines of the Fall, Incarnation, and Trinity, is, nonetheless, "ultimately incompatible with Christian faith."[22] Taylor argues that because Hegel's God acts according to rational necessity, it is not the Christian God of free and gracious love to whom one responds in prayer (493–94). Furthermore, Hegel has changed the essence of the Incarnation in the Christian faith because it cannot be said of Jesus "that he was God in any sense other than that in which we all are identical with God" (495; cf. 208–10).

In response we must ask, what do divine freedom and its related theological notion, grace, mean? If, as Hegel says, love is "a distinguishing of two, who nevertheless are absolutely not distinguished for each other" (LPR III, 276; V5, 201), then we have the speculative meaning of the Trinity. If God is love, then God has the inner "necessity" to be absolute unity-in-distinction. Rather than a denial by Hegel of divine freedom and grace, we find in Hegel the need to rethink radically our ordinary conceptions of "necessity" and "freedom" when applied to God. Following upon the notion of divine necessity, Taylor asks, "How does a Hegelian philosopher *pray*? Certainly the prayer of petition has no meaning for him" (494). Would Taylor require the religious person always to retain anthropomorphic, even manipulative, conceptions of one's relation to God? If prayer is the activity of uniting finite with infinite spirit, then cannot Hegel's philosophy as a whole better account for the asking and granting of petitions than the irrational conception of God implied by Taylor's notion of what is essentially Christian prayer? As with doctrine, can one claim it is impossible for a Hegelian to pray without first rationally explaining the meaning and nature of prayer?

As for Taylor's claim that in Hegel's philosophy Jesus was not uniquely God, we have Hegel's own argument in response.

> The unity of divine and human nature must appear in one human being [*in einem Menschen*].... [This] substantial unity is what humanity implicitly is.... Hence it must stand over against subjective consciousness, which relates to itself as ordinary consciousness and is defined [*bestimmt ist*] as such. That is

exactly why the unity in question must appear for others as a single human being set apart. (LPR III, 313; V5, 238)

In short, "God can appear as spirit on only one unique occasion because uniqueness is a moment of spirit" (LPR III, 366; V5, 283). In other words, God cannot become man *in abstracto*. If, from the religious standpoint, one objects that Hegel has changed the content of the Incarnation, then one is forced to define the doctrine of the Incarnation in an alternative intelligible form; otherwise, one is simply opining what is the doctrine. At the most fundamental level, the Christian theologian, or anyone interested in explaining the content of the Incarnation, must address the question, What must be the order of reality for the Incarnation to occur?[23] To this question Hegel, at least, gives a systematic answer.

The theologian Karl Barth also finds Hegelianism incompatible with the Christian religion principally because of the necessitarian God that results from the identification of God with the dialectical method. "Hegel, in making the dialectical method of logic the essential nature of God, made impossible the knowledge of the actual dialectic of grace, which has its foundation in the freedom of God."[24] According to Barth, Hegel's God is subordinated to, and limited by, human thought, for

> everything God is and does will be and is understood from the point of view of man, as God's own necessity. Revelation can now no longer be a free act of God; God rather, *must* function as we see him function in revelation. It is necessary to him to reveal himself.[25]

With Barth's statements as such we have no disagreement, but the question of the compatibility of Christianity and Hegel's philosophy goes begging. It is precisely the ground of revelation, and more generally, the relation of the human and divine, that must be explained. By emphasizing the sovereignty of God and the doctrine of grace, does Barth imply a bad infinity? If the infinite does not include the finite, then it is limited by what it opposes, and the relation of God to the world becomes problematic. The relation of the divine and human requires delicate exposition. In response to Barth, the theological task is to establish the elevation of the human to the divine without thereby subordinating the divine to the human.[26]

In general, we find that the arguments for the incompatibility of Hegel's philosophy and the Christian religion (e.g., of Kierkegaard, Ping, McTaggart, Copleston, Taylor, Barth) suppose the very matter that needs to be demonstrated, namely, the intelligible content of what is believed (since it is impossible to believe what is absurd). The criticisms fail to deal with the radical implications of the intelligibility of reality, the claim to truth of the Christian religion, and the meaning of necessity when applied to the absolute. On what basis can one claim that one or another doctrine is essential to Christianity if it has not its basis in reason? If tradition is the basis, then what validates one's interpretation of the tradition if not reason? Without rational justification, one is asserting subjective opinion. Only the truth can found one's claims. As Hegel has shown, what is given in representation must have its rational elucidation if one is to separate the essential from the nonessential. If the matter is decided by authority (e.g., church, tradition, scripture), then this authority, to be genuine, cannot be other than the divine spirit at work within the rational quest for truth. If we accept that reality is open to being known and (what is the same) that God is revealing, then the human spirit in rising from its limitations can know the whole of reality, at least in principle. If one claims that reality is not fully intelligible, then the providence and wisdom of God are denied and, further, the condition of the possibility of revelation is lost.

*The Concretion of Christian Faith and Reason in Hegel's Thought*

As we noted in chapter 1, there is in Hegel's philosophy a rethinking of the relation of religion and philosophy. Philosophy is not the handmaid of religious faith, as for Aquinas; nor is religion simply an incidental object, even an impediment, in philosophy's independent quest for the truth, as in Enlightenment philosophy; nor are religion and philosophy in separate compartments, dwelling in an uneasy truce where knowledge belongs to the empirical, finite realm and faith to the supersensible, infinite realm, as in Kant's philosophy (cf. FK, 55; W2, 288). For Hegel, religion is "the relation [*Beziehung*] of human consciousness to God" (LPR I, 150; V3, 61), in which humanity finds "the thought, the consciousness of God" (LPR I, 150; V3, 61). However, to say no more of Hegel's philosophical consideration of religion than that it studies humanity's consciousness of, and relationship to, God would leave out of focus what is singularly striking in this consideration, namely, that religion is not only our consciousness of God, but God's consciousness of self. Hence, in contrast with what one customarily thinks of as philosophy, wherein God receives an abstract and purely logical treatment, in the philosophy of religion, Hegel considers "God as the utterly concrete idea together with its infinite appearance" (LPR I, 120; V3, 37). Religion for Hegel has a privileged place within philosophy, for it is religion's content that is God's "infinite appearance as spirit" (LPR I, 120; V3, 37). In a way of speaking, God "needs" religion. As spirit, God cannot remain "shut up in himself" but must manifest himself in ever-more-adequate modes, the most adequate of which for Hegel, as we have explained, is in the form of pure thought as the absolute idea wherein the content, or what appears, is its form, or its appearing. "That God is spirit consists in this: that he is not only the essence that maintains itself in thought but also the essence that appears, the essence that endows itself with revelation and objectivity" (LPR I, 119; V3, 35).

As we have argued, however, pure thought, thought in the form of thought, is the comprehension of all the stages of its realization, which rather than being abstract, is what is most concrete. Thus it seems to us that philosophy's relation to religion is not a final achievement of spirit as pure thought separated in its realization from religion but the turning back of thought into the concrete spiritual community.

> God can only be genuinely conceived [*wahrhaft begriffen*] as he is as spirit and so makes himself into the counterpart [*Gegenbild*] of a community and brings about the activity of a community in relation [*Beziehung*] to him, and thus the doctrine of God is to be grasped and taught only as the doctrine of religion. (LPR I, 116; V3, 33)

Thus it seems to us that philosophy serves religion, yet not, as in the scholastic era as religion's servant, but as its master "that comes not to be served but to serve." Philosophy has privileged status as the elucidation and purification of representative modes of religious thought, but philosophy only has its meaning and place within a spiritual community in its relation to God. This community is the faith community that is "the certainty of the truth of the intrinsic connectedness [*an sich seienden Zusammenhangs*] of spirit within itself and in its community" (LPR I, 342; V3, 242), not based upon external authority but upon the inner witness and attestation of the spirit that dwells within it. Here in the community of faith we find the bringing together of thought and belief as the concretion (literally, "the growing together") of the divine spirit in the human spirit.

> Everything spiritual is concrete; here we have the spiritual in its deepest determination for us, namely, spirit as the concretion of believing and thinking [*als das Konkrete des Glaubens und Denkens*]; both are not only intermixed in the most manifold ways, in an immediate crossing over from one to the other, but rather are so intimately bound together with one another, that there is no believing which is not reflecting, reasoning, or thinking as such, just as there is no thinking which does not contain in itself, if only momentarily, believing. (From lecture I, "On the Proofs for God's Existence," in W17, 352)

Religion and reason, the believing acceptance of what is immediately given and free thinking, the reception of revelation and a reasoned reflection upon that revelation, are the activities of a single human consciousness that is driven to hold its various thoughts together without contradiction. In order to be received, the content of revelation must be intelligible. Revelation and reason are not separate modes of truth but are found to be one in the movement of spirit. Reason, then, not only sheds light on revelation already given but is the condition and constitutive means for the content and the form of revelation.

## Concluding Remarks

A conclusion on a work of Hegelian philosophy appears to demand a "closing together" of the constitutive elements of the presentation toward a summation that is the dialectical upthrust of the whole. In order to close together our thoughts, we would say that the end of this study is in its beginning, namely, in the validity of Hegel's argument for the identity in content of absolute religion and absolute knowledge. As established in the preceding chapters, the innermost core of the Christian religion — i.e., its content — is absolute subjectivity as a movement of self-diremption and return to its goal of absolute unity-in-difference, or in a word, spirit. This thought-content has its actualization in the dialectical movement of the real, for in describing the movement of thought we are describing the movement of actuality. The unity of this movement of thought and actuality as a whole is the truth. From the eternal standpoint, what is conceived is achieved, but from the temporal standpoint, the truth as the entire movement of the correspondence of thought and actuality is not achieved until eternity fully overreaches the process of actual things, which is time. Within the temporal world, we argue, religion continues as the means of the actualization of the concept in the spiritual community toward its realization in the "kingdom of God," which is spirit.

Religion and philosophy, then, are distinct but not separable. Philosophy sublates religion by the mediation in thought of the content of religion. By its speculative exposition, the truth content of religion is revealed in a form adequate to its truth. By its translation into scientific form, the content of religion is given firm foundation and thereby finds refuge from attacks based on the finite categories of the understanding. At the same time, we argue, religion in conformity with reason works the actualization of the concept in the concrete life of humankind. In fact, the achievement of speculative philosophy would be sterile without its embodiment in religious symbol, myth, worship and community life by which the human spirit is brought to explicit awareness of the presence and activity of the divine spirit.

The history of the relation of religion and philosophy in the Christian West has, from the Hegelian standpoint, entered a new phase. From the religious standpoint, the history of this relation has exhibited two main tendencies: a fideistic attitude and a rational attitude. From the philosophical standpoint the history of this relation has also exhibited two main tendencies: an antagonistic attitude and a synthetic attitude. A "middle" course of mutual exclusion and delimitation of separate realms has also exhibited itself. The tracing of the emergence of these various attitudes and approaches is itself a study in the history of thought. Clearly, Hegel has penetrated the latent meanings of these attitudes and approaches and has revealed the deep divisions engendered in the human spirit by the opposition or separation of religion and reason. No one can serve two masters. The desire to know, the courage of cognition, the quest of truth is the innermost drive of spirit and cannot be subordinated without grave damage to the human spirit and all the products of the human spirit. Hegel realized in his own time, even with a prescience beyond his time, that the opposition of "faith" and "pure insight" is a false opposition, and more importantly, he worked out the means by which to extricate them from their one-sidedness and bring about their reconciliation in the truth — not an imposed reconciliation, but an explication of their own implicit unity. Only reason can save religion. This fact should be eminently clear, but it is not only religion and its self-reflection in theology that have to heed the demands of reason but philosophy as well, at least what often is called philosophy. As Hegel has noted, a nation without metaphysics is a temple without a sanctum (SL, 25; W5, 14). Philosophy cannot base itself upon the method of a lower science or upon external reflection (SL, 27; W5, 16), nor yet can it take intuition or common sense in place of the labor of the concept any more than, as Hegel says, chicory can substitute for coffee (PS, 42–43; W3, 63–65). The study of the relation of religion and philosophy has implications far beyond the religious realm. It extends to all the sciences and to social life. These implications are beyond this study. But we can conclude our study of Hegel's philosophy of religion by way of reflection upon some possible implications of this study for religion.

First of all, philosophical truth must not only prove itself in rigorous thinking but "prove" itself in lived, human experience. No one will be convinced by Hegel's argument, whatever its brilliance and internal coherence, unless he or she finds its resonance in personal experience. For example, Hegel claimed to translate the religious notion of providence into purely rational terms. The fact is, people do not believe in providence — i.e., that the course of world events serves a good purpose — only, or primarily, because it has been philosophically demonstrated, but because in their own lives they find the footsteps of a benevolent and loving God, and they then incline to believe the history of the world to be guided by benevolence and love. This is so because in their own lives they discern and experience the provident hand of God. We are not stepping away from the systematic integration of Hegel's philosophy to focus upon one or another fact in isolation, since to isolate is to falsify, and only the whole is true, but we are making clear that the whole must also find its exemplification in particular events. When Hegel speaks of the absolute idea as the whole system of its development by way of comparison to the *decursus vitae* of an individual life and to a childhood faith enriched by the experience of a lifetime (Enc § 237, *Zusatz*), we can as well reverse the order and say that Hegel's philosophy manifests its insight and truth in common experience. The mediation in thought of a religious content parallels the mediation of a religious creed in the life of an individual and of a people. Another fact of human experience that exemplifies Hegel's philosophy is the *unio mystica* — "the feeling of the enjoyment that I am with God in his grace and that God's spirit is alive within me" (LPR I, 445; V3, 333). The awareness of being reconciled with God in the privileged moments of religious experience inclines one to a serious consideration of its explanation in Hegel's philosophy.

What continuing evolution should one expect in religion in the light of Hegel's philosophy? We have spoken of "rational religion" but have not said much about its shape in detail. Specific applications of philosophy to religion may be moot, but some suggestions can be made. For one, ecclesiastical authority, to be genuine, must be wholly founded upon spirit, upon truth. On the one hand Hegel warns against the subjectivistic splintering of the church that results from following one's feelings in place of doctrine (LPR III, 246; V5, 174–75); on the other hand he makes clear there can be no legitimate authority that is external to the human spirit — spirit "calls to *every* consciousness: *be for yourselves*, what you all *are in yourselves — rational*" (PS, 328; W3, 398). When understood correctly, obedience to God is obedience to oneself. Furthermore, religion must have a clear recognition of the divine dignity of thought. Anti-intellectualism in religion that glorifies "faith" in opposition to systematic rational thought is implicitly contrary to religion. Also, Hegel's philosophy engenders a natural reticence in the religious mind about ever saying We cannot know God or All is mystery, for the natural outcome of such expressions, as shown by Hegel, is not piety but agnosticism; moreover, such expressions mask intellectual laziness, a recoil from the *Anstrengung des Begriffs*. At the same time it must be recognized that the method of the sciences based upon the static, finite categories of the understanding is unsuited to the truth of religion. This recognition is necessary in order to understand correctly the place and role of exegesis and history in theology. A factual understanding of the Scriptures does not of itself touch upon the truth of the Scriptures and of the religious tradition in general. Spiritual truth must be uncovered by spiritual means. We are acquainted with Hegel's severe criticisms of the theologians of his time who adopted the mode of thought characteristic of the Enlightenment (e.g., "theology is reduced to historical erudition and then to the meagre exposition of some subjective feelings" [F-M, 233; F-L, 251; W11, 50]). Such criticism may have application today as well. Also, Hegel's philosophy has value in ecumenical dialog and in dialog with nonbelievers. Such dialog is possible because of the universality of reason and must proceed on the basis of the truth as the whole by sublating the one-sidedness of an initial position toward reconciliation that is not reduction but enrichment. Finally, Hegel's philosophy demonstrates that negation is radically built into the order of the real so that we realize clearly no spiritual progress can occur on the individual or community level except through self-denial and sacrifice.

This study has sought to bring forth the validity of Hegel's argument for religion's and philosophy's identity in content and the manner in which this argument indicates the inherent rationality of the Christian religion as grounded in Hegel's philosophy. It is incumbent that the student of Hegel's philosophy forego any suppositions about the content of the Christian religion and its relation to philosophy and instead think, rigorously and systematically, the *Sache* from within itself as it manifests itself. Only by following the course of dialectical reason are we able to grasp the true content of religion as it unfolds itself to and by spirit. Dialectical thought seeks to be, and claims to be, infinite and comprehensive, to be nothing less than the exposition of God. If such thinking appears as hubris, it is no less a sin than the false humility that does not possess the courage of knowing or, what is the same, the courage of the truth. It is to Hegel's enduring credit that he has provided a synthesis of religion and philosophy that can in principle assimilate every element of the history of religions and religious experience from within. Whatever one's evaluation of this synthesis, it stands on reasoned argumentation and cannot be ignored by the serious student of religion and of philosophy. It may be that Hegel is fundamentally wrong, that there is no immanent principle that organizes the diversity of phenomena, and that Hegel has only spun an elaborate web from his own entrails. But if such is the case then the endeavor of all science is futile, and ultimately God, as the common object of religion and philosophy, is unknowable, or else there is no God to know. But then there is no spirit, human or divine, and religion and philosophy are at an end, for if there is no spirit then the history of religion and of philosophy is of no philosophical significance. Such is obviously not our conclusion. On the contrary, Hegel has opened to us a way of thinking that challenges the human spirit to develop its latent, unbounded capacities while yet doing justice to the frailty, ignorance, and error that everywhere infect the human condition. One may argue with one or another element of Hegel's philosophy of religion from the philosophical or religious standpoint, but the basic inner coherence of Hegel's philosophy of religion and its fruitfulness in various areas of human reflection witness to its power. Hegel has left us a formidable achievement and a potent challenge for further study and reflection. By explicating and developing the manner in which Hegel demonstrates the Christian religion and philosophy to be identical in content, this study has limited itself primarily to the concept of religion and has not dealt extensively with specific Christian doctrines. Hegel himself, of course, has provided a speculative translation of many Christian doctrines, such as the Trinity, the Incarnation, the Eucharist, and the Fall. Study has been done,[27] and more study needs to be done, with regard to the correspondence of the content of specific doctrines with specific elements within Hegel's philosophy. Such study can help in clarifying and evaluating Hegel's basic claim to identify the Christian religion's and speculative philosophy's content.

# List of Abbreviations

Enc   *Encyclopaedia of the Philosophical Sciences* (1830). Part 1, *Hegel's Logic*, translated by William Wallace. Oxford: Clarendon Press, 1975. Part 2, *Hegel's Philosophy of Nature*, translated by William Wallace. Oxford: Clarendon Press, 1970. Part 3, *Hegel's Philosophy of Mind*, translated by William Wallace, with *Zusätze* translated by A. V. Miller. Oxford: Clarendon Press, 1971. § = section. R = "Remark." For longer segments of the *Encyclopaedia of the Philosophical Sciences,* page numbers are given from the *Werke in zwanzig Bänden* (see below). I have altered translations where I thought it appropriate.

FK   *Faith and Knowledge*. Translated by Walter Cerf and H. S. Harris. Albany: State University of New York Press, 1977.

H   *Einleitung in die Geschichte der Philosophie*. Edited by Johannes Hoffmeister. Hamburg: Felix Meiner, 1940.

F-L   "Hegel's Foreword to Hinrichs's *Die Religion im inneren Verhältnisse zur Wissenschaft*." Translated by Eric von der Luft. In *Hegel, Hinrichs, and Schleiermacher on Feeling and Reason in Religion*. Lewiston, New York: Edwin Mellen Press, 1987.

F-M   "Hegel's Foreword to Hinrichs's *Die Religion im inneren Verhältnisse zur Wissenschaft*." Translated by A. V. Miller. In *Beyond Epistemology*, edited by Frederick Weiss. The Hague: Martinus Nijhoff, 1974.

ILHP   *Introduction to the Lectures on the History of Philosophy*. Translated by T. M. Knox and A. V. Miller. Oxford: Clarendon Press, 1985.

LHP   *Hegel's Lectures on the History of Philosophy*. 3 vols. Vol. I translated by E. S. Haldane. Vols. II and III translated by E. S. Haldane and Frances Simson. London: Kegan Paul, Trench, Trübner, 1892 (vol. I); 1894 (vol. II); 1896 (vol. III); reprint, London: Routledge and Kegan Paul, 1963.

| | |
|---|---|
| LPR | *Lectures on the Philosophy of Religion.* 3 vols. Edited and translated by Peter Hodgson et al. Berkeley: University of California Press, 1984 (vol. I); 1987 (vol. II); 1985 (vol. III). |
| PR | *Hegel's Philosophy of Right.* Translated by T. M. Knox. Oxford: Oxford University Press, 1967. § = section. |
| PS | The *Phenomenology of Spirit.* Translated by A. V. Miller. Oxford: Clarendon Press, 1977. |
| SL | *Hegel's Science of Logic.* Translated by A. V. Miller. London: George Allen and Unwin, 1969. |
| V | *Vorlesungen: Ausgewählte Nachschriften und Manuskripte.* Volumes 3–5: *Vorlesungen über die Philosophie der Religion.* Part 1: *Einleitung. Der Begriff der Religion.* Edited by Walter Jaeschke. Hamburg: Felix Meiner, 1983. Part 2: *Die bestimmte Religion,* 1985. Part 3: *Die vollendete Religion,* 1984. Number with letter indicates volume. |
| W | *Werke in zwanzig Bänden.* Frankfurt am Main: Suhrkamp Verlag, 1969. Number with letter indicates volume. |

# Notes

## Chapter 1
## The Religious-Philosophical Context of the Problem

1. In the *Summa Theologiae* Ia, 19, 3, Aquinas distinguishes and explicates in relation to God two kinds of necessity — absolute and hypothetical. Absolute necessity derives from the implication of the terms (*ex habitudine terminorum*), as a predicate is contained in the definition of a subject. In Kantian terminology we think here of an analytic judgement that is *a priori* necessary. Aquinas gives as an example of absolute necessity the truth that man must be an animal.

Hypothetical necessity, by contrast, is the necessity that follows from a supposition. The supposition is not necessary but only what follows from it, as it is necessary for Socrates to sit while seated, though it is not necessary that Socrates be seated. As an absolute necessity God must will his own goodness, but of things other than himself God wills them hypothetically; in other words, as given, God must will them.

The reason that creation is hypothetically necessary but not absolutely necessary is that God's goodness is complete without other things. Aquinas notes as well that there is necessity in God's will to be self-determining. In other words, God's will is not contingent upon, or constrained by, anything outside itself. We can say, then, that God's will has the absolute necessity to be self-determining. In the passages quoted, in which Aquinas argues God must create intellectual beings, the necessity is hypothetical.

2. Quentin Lauer, *A Reading of Hegel's* Phenomenology of Spirit (New York: Fordham University Press, 1976), 200, n. 37.

3. Quentin Lauer describes the *Science of Logic* as "the prolonged account of what thought inevitably finds when it examines itself conscientiously." Quentin Lauer, "Is Absolute Spirit God?" in *Hegel: le Sens de l'Esprit absolu/The Meaning of Absolute Spirit: Proceedings of the International Symposium on the Meaning of Absolute Spirit Held at the University of Ottawa November 6–8, 1981,* ed. Théodore Geraets (Ottawa: University of Ottawa Press, 1984), 93.

Dale Schlitt describes Hegel's logic as "the speculative dialectical method in and through which the Concept determines itself as a non-temporal movement of thought categories." Dale Schlitt, *Hegel's Trinitarian Claim* (Leiden: E. J. Brill, 1984), 17–18.

4. By being is meant the whole of reality as thought, and thought in its first moment without distinction — absolute, simple, indeterminate, immediate. This beginning may be termed God, though God *a se* in his absolute simplicity, empty of determinate content.

5. Hegel's use of the terms "abstract" and "concrete" is not the same as ordinary usage, but the terms must be understood in the context of his philosophy. In ordinary usage what is immediately present to sensation is termed concrete, but for Hegel what is immediately present to perception is abstract because it is unmediated by thought and is one-sided. "Concrete" for Hegel means adequately mediated by, or more fully articulated in, thought.

6. The relation of phenomenology and logic in Hegel's philosophy is a matter of much discussion and was a matter of ongoing reflection in Hegel's life. For a brief discussion of the matter and references to the problem, refer to Schlitt, *Hegel's Trinitarian Claim*, 128–31.

7. Küng compares the *Phenomenology of Spirit* and the *Science of Logic* by saying,

> The path of the *Phenomenology* is experience's stren[u]ous uphill climb to the level of absolute knowledge; the *Logic* is the mountain path of absolute knowledge *qua* truth itself.... The *Phenomenology* considers conceptual definitions in the order in which they appear in the individual subject or in the universal Spirit, while the *Logic* considers them in their own right as pure essences in their relationship to pure knowledge. Even so, the *Phenomenology* and the *Logic* are not mere parts but rather moments of the one system; each in its own way contains the whole: the same content, first as forms of consciousness and secondly as forms of the Notion. (Hans Küng, *The Incarnation of God*, trans. J. R. Stephenson [New York: Crossroad, 1987], 251)

8. Copleston, adopting McTaggart's terminology, says Hegel attempts to show that Christianity is exoteric Hegelianism and that absolute idealism is esoteric Christianity. Frederick Copleston, "Hegel and the Rationalization of Mystery," in *New Studies in Hegel's Philosophy*, ed. Warren Steinkraus (New York: Holt, Rinehart, and Winston, 1971), 193; also *Fichte to Nietzsche*, vol. 7 of *A History of Philosophy* (Westminster: Newman Press, 1963), 241.

9. Théodore Geraets, "The End of the History of Religions 'Grasped in Thought'," *Hegel-Studien* 24 (1989): 70–71.

10. *Vorstellung* has been variously rendered in English as "figurative thought," "pictorial" or "imaginative presentation," "pictorial thought," or "picture thinking." It seems best to render this term in English as "representation."

## Chapter 2
## The Argument for the Identity in Content
## of Religion and Philosophy

1. Quentin Lauer makes the same point when he says that Hegel's philosophy of religion is not philosophizing about religion but is "thinking philosophically what religion thinks religiously." Quentin Lauer, "Hegel on the Identity of Content in Religion and Philosophy," in *Hegel and the Philosophy of Religion*, ed. Darrel Christensen (The Hague: Martinus Nijhoff, 1970), 273. There is of course much debate whether Hegel's formulation of God is the same in content as the God of Christianity. We conclude that it is, but this conclusion can only be stated at this point in anticipation of its argument.

2. Ibid., 261.

3. Here Hegel expresses the central difficulty. The original is,

wenn die Philosophie das, was in Form der Vorstellung ist, in die Form des Begriffs umwandelt, so kommt freilich die Schwierigkeit hervor, an einem Inhalt zu trennen, was Inhalt als solcher, der Gedanke ist, von dem, was der Vorstellung als solcher angehört. (V3, 299).

Virtually the same wording is found in the 1832 version some pages earlier. LPR I, 397; V3, 292. The point of precisely explaining how a content can be transposed is ambiguous in the whole of Hegel's philosophy of religion. Does the content itself divide, and if so, how is it identical?

4. Cf. Edward Black, "Religion and Philosophy in Hegel's Philosophy of Religion," *The Monist* 60, 2 (1977): 207. Frederick Copleston, *Fichte to Nietzsche*, 240–41. J. M. E. McTaggart, *Studies in Hegelian Cosmology* (Cambridge: Cambridge University Press, 1901), 197–251.

5. Charles Ping, *The Genius of the Christian Religion: A Study in the Religious Thought of Georg Wilhelm Friedrich Hegel* (Ann Arbor: University Microfilms, 1961), 273.

6. This formulation of the concept of religion is only explicitly worked out in the 1827 *Lectures on the Philosophy of Religion*.

7. Refer to Geraets, "The End of the History of Religions."

8. Cf. Peter Ely, *Hegel's Version of the Ontological Proof: Key to the Reconciliation of Religion and Philosophy* (Ann Arbor: University Microfilms, 1974), 264.

9. Cf. Walter Jaeschke, *Reason in Religion: The Foundations of Hegel's Philosophy of Religion*, trans. J. Michael Stewart and Peter C. Hodgson (Berkeley: University of California Press, 1990), 288–92.

10. Interestingly, Hegel seems not to use the precise distinction he makes between sensation and feeling in Enc § 402–3, in which feeling ranks above sensation because feeling is the subjective integration of sensations that are merely given. By this distinction in meaning, animals would have sensations but not feelings. In any case, it is clear that because religion is essentially a human

phenomenon, and the specific difference of the human is rational thought, then rational thought cannot be anything foreign to religious awareness. (LPR I, 209-10; V3, 118).

11. The *Zusätze* in the *Encyclopaedia of the Philosophical Sciences* are compilations of the notes of Hegel's students: von Henning and his fellow students Hotho, Michelet, and Geyer for Part I; Michelet, for Part II; and Boumann, for Part III. Even though the *Zusätze* have not the weight of the written text, they do contain Hegel's *ipsissima verba* as well as student interpretations and interpolations. Although they are fairly reliable, they must be assigned a "deutero-canonical," and in some cases, apocryphal, status. Nonetheless, the *Zusätze* are invaluable to an understanding of Hegel's philosophy, and as J. N. Findlay has said of them,

> They at least bring us into touch with the spoken element which is quite essential in a philosophy like Hegel's, and they invariably illuminate and assist understanding, rather than confuse and complicate it. (J. N. Findlay, Foreword to *Hegel's Logic* [Oxford: Clarendon Press, 1975], viii)

It is with this outlook that use will be made of the *Zusätze* in bringing Hegel's thought to light.

12. Emil Fackenheim, *The Religious Dimension in Hegel's Thought* (Bloomington: Indiana University Press, 1967), 162.

13. Walter Jaeschke, "Speculative and Anthropological Criticism of Religion: A Theological Orientation to Hegel and Feuerbach," *Journal of the American Academy of Religion* 48 (September 1980): 354.

14. W. T. Stace, *The Philosophy of Hegel: A Systematic Exposition* (New York: Dover, 1955), 177.

15. John Burbidge, *On Hegel's Logic* (Atlantic Highlands, N.J.: Humanities Press, 1981), 74. Burbidge uses "difference" for *Unterschied*, although we find "distinction" the more appropriate translation in the *Logic* and reserve "difference" for *Unterschied* in the *Realphilosophie*.

16. Errol Harris, *An Interpretation of the Logic of Hegel* (Lanham, Md.: University Press of America, 1983), 182.

17. Ibid., 183.

18. André Léonard, *Commentaire littéral de la logique de Hegel* (Louvain: Editions de l'Institut Supérieur de Philosophie, 1974), 214.

19. G. R. G. Mure, *A Study of Hegel's Logic* (Oxford: Clarendon Press, 1950), 83.

20. The placement of these subcategories differs somewhat in the two *Logics* because, as Errol Harris notes, "all categories of Essence have this dual aspect of inner and outer, content and form, essential and inessential." E. Harris, *An Interpretation*, 172.

Because the science of logic is the science of form, Peter Rohs notes that it is difficult to determine precisely where form should be treated within logic — hence the difference in treatment and placement of form and content in the two

*Logics*. In the 1817 *Encyclopaedia* the relation of form and content receives only a brief treatment. The fuller treatment of form and content in the later editions occurs in "the world of appearance," and the form-content relation is not treated in relation to the problem of ground as in the *Science of Logic*. Cf. Peter Rohs, *Form and Grund: Interpretation eines Kapitels der Hegelschen Wissenschaft der Logik* (Bonn: Bouvier, 1969), 181–95.

For a concise statement of Rohs's observations on this subject, cf. Schlitt, *Hegel's Trinitarian Claim*, 16, n. 33.

21. Stace, *The Philosophy of Hegel*, 190.
22. Mure, *A Study*, 113.
23. Ibid., 118.
24. Stace, *The Philosophy of Hegel*, 202.
25. Peter Rohs, in his study of form and ground, notes that "the content has a determination within itself and another outside itself or from without, through the form. The first is its own determination, the content-determination — the other is foreign to it, the form-determination." In general for Hegel, Rohs notes, the preposition "in" corresponds to "unity" or "identity," and "outside" corresponds to "distinction." Rohs, *Form und Grund*, 182.
26. Falk Wagner, "Die Aufhebung der religiösen Vorstellung in den philosophischen Begriff," *Neue Zeitschrift für Systematische Theologie und Religionsphilosophie* 18 (1976): 67.
27. Ibid., 67.
28. Ibid., 69.

## Chapter 3
## Representation

1. Anselm Min, "Hegel's Absolute: Transcendent or Immanent?" *Journal of Religion* 56 (1976): 86. Also cf. Anselm Min, "Hegel's Retention of Mystery as a Theological Category," *Clio* 12 (1983): 333–53.
2. Copleston, "Hegel and the Rationalization of Mystery," 200.
3. David Tracy, *Blessed Rage for Order* (New York: Seabury Press, 1975), 108.
4. Pure being — which equally is nothing because it is utterly "absence of determination (*Bestimmungslosigkeit*)" and hence is thought as the "*movement of the immediate vanishing of one into the other*" (SL, 82–83; W5, 83), which is becoming — is highly problematic as the starting point of logic. How can one think what is wholly unmediated by thought? It seems to us that being/nothing/becoming can only be pointed to retrospectively from the standpoint of the thought of determinate being as within being. Perhaps we could say that, because being is not grasped in thought, it is not a concept but a representation,

although Hegel cannot develop his starting point of logic in this way because, as beginning, being must be pure thought without qualification. Hegel himself notes that "*being* is simple, as *unmediated*; hence it is only a *Gemeintes* and we cannot say of it what it is." (SL, 601; W6, 275; also cf. Enc § 87, *Zusatz*).

5. Lauer, *A Reading of Hegel's* Phenomenology of Spirit, 232.

6. Malcolm Clark, *Logic and System: A Study of the Transition from "Vorstellung" to Thought in the Philosophy of Hegel* (The Hague: Martinus Nijhoff, 1971), 205.

7. For Hegel, ineffability is a kind of intellectual laziness since things have an inner rationality by which they reveal themselves to spirit. A romanticist glorification of ineffability is implicitly a denial of the intelligibility of the real and a refusal to follow spirit's thrust toward the perfect adequation of knower and known. Daniel Cook, in commenting on the relation of ineffability and knowledge, notes that for Hegel ineffability is a momentary inadequacy of our power of expression and not an expression of the nature of the real.

> For Hegel anything that does not find its effect, its truth expressed elsewhere, beyond its own isolated existence, does not really exist. This is one meaning which can be given to Hegel's famous dictum about the real (*wirklich*) being rational and *vice versa*: what "works" or has an effect upon others (*es wirkt*, *Wirkung, Wirklichkeit*) can ultimately be expressed and conceptualized. To be sure, each form of expression or language is eventually seen somehow to be inadequate, just as various gradations of conscious experience are evoked and then transcended, but ultimately truth and the possibility of its adequate expression coalesce in the realm of absolute knowledge. {Daniel Cook, *Language in the Philosophy of Hegel* [The Hague: Mouton, 1973], 158)

8. Cf. Clark, *Logic and System,* 85.

9. Similarly, Hegel notes that when philosophy draws from the representations of ordinary language to express its concepts, it also recognizes that some representations correspond to concepts more closely than others.

> It must suffice therefore if representation in the use of its expressions that are employed for philosophical determinations has before it some vague idea of their distinctive meaning, as it may be the case that in these expressions one cognizes shades of representation that are more closely related to the corresponding concepts. (SL, 708; W6, 407)

10. Dominique Dubarle, "Révélation de dieu et manifestation de l'esprit dans la philosophie de Hegel," in *Manifestation et révélation* (Paris: Editions Beauchesne, 1976), 121–22.

11. William Desmond, *Art and the Absolute* (Albany: State University of New York Press, 1986), 41.

12. Dale Schlitt, "Feature Book Review: Hegel's Berlin Lectures: The Consummate Religion," *The Owl of Minerva* 19, 1 (1987): 70.

13. William Desmond, "Hegel and the Problem of Religious Representation," *Philosophical Studies* 30 (1984): 13.

14. Refer to Schlitt, who notes with particular reference to revelatory religion in the *Phenomenology of Spirit* that the representational form of the content of the Christian religion "inhibits" and "facilitates progression to absolute knowledge"; in other words, through the Christian religion's representations, spirit progresses to its final shape as absolute knowing. *Hegel's Trinitarian Claim*, 125, n. 139.

15. Desmond, "Hegel and the Problem of Religious Representation," 17.

16. Paul Ricoeur, "The Status of *Vorstellung* in Hegel's Philosophy of Religion," in *Meaning, Truth and God*, ed. Leroy Rouner (Notre Dame: University of Notre Dame Press, 1982), 73.

17. "Although the language of religion and philosophy may correspond and each have absolute truth as its object, philosophic thinking alone can guarantee that the various *Vorstellungen* invoked by theological formulations are appropriate and do not pervert the speculative role for which they are intended." Cook, *Language in the Philosophy of Hegel*, 154.

18. Raymond Williamson, *Introduction to Hegel's Philosophy of Religion* (Albany: State University of New York Press, 1984), 375, n. 16. Desmond makes a similar point without expatiating. "The Thomist doctrine of analogy might be seen as responding to this dilemma forced on us by the tension between the finite and the infinite in religious representation." Desmond, "Hegel and the Problem of Religious Representation," 12.

19. In answer to these questions, Hampus Lyttkens's study on Thomistic analogy has been valuable as a basis for the following reflections. Hampus Lyttkens, *The Analogy between God and the World* (Uppsala: Almqvist and Wicksells Boktryckeri, 1952).

20. "When the name 'wise' is said of a man, in a certain way it circumscribes and comprehends the thing signified, but not however when said of God; when said of God the name leaves behind the thing signified as not comprehended by, and as exceeding, the signification of the name." *Summa Theologiae* Ia, 13, 5.

21. Unfortunately for his students, Aquinas never wrote a general treatise on analogy as such but rather treated analogy throughout his works as a means of dealing with specific problems. Moreover, Aquinas's doctrine of analogy developed and shifted as he developed his philosophical insights and metaphysical principles out of the theological and philosophical tradition that he inherited. A thorough exposition of Thomistic analogy is obviously beyond the scope of this study. Our concern here is how we are to speak of God and God's relation to the created order. We agree with George Klubertanz that the analogy between God and creation for Aquinas's philosophy is best explained by causal participation.

> Since whatever is intrinsically in God is identical with His essence and with Him as well as with His existence, these perfections are predicated of God by nature, essentially. On the other hand, in creatures these perfections are possessed as limited by the subject in which they are received, as partial, and

as multiple. Hence between God and creatures there is an analogy of participation of all the perfections mentioned (being, goodness, and so on). If we add to this our previous consideration of God's total causality, we can most adequately name the analogy between God and creatures as an analogy of causal participation. Implicit in this description are further qualifications: God is the cause of the world by intellect and will, and so as an intelligent efficient cause He is both the primary exemplar and the ultimate goal of all creatures, and they exist as images, made to the likeness (in imitation) of their Creator. (George Klubertanz, *St. Thomas Aquinas on Analogy* [Chicago: Loyola University Press, 1960], 134–35)

22. Desmond, "Hegel and the Problem of Religious Representation," 18.

23. Ibid., 19.

24. Ricoeur, "The Status of *Vorstellung*," 80–81.

25. Walter Jaeschke, *Die Religionsphilosophie Hegels* (Darmstadt: Wissenschaftliche Buchgesellschaft, 1983), 116.

26. "In terms of the relation between philosophy and religion, Hegel suggests that religion must be formally present in order to give to philosophy its flesh and bones. And in fact Hegel himself uses religious conceptions such as God, reconciliation, ... as abbreviations [*Abbreviaturen*] that can immediately communicate a meaning which still remains naive." Vitor Westhelle, *Religion and Representation: A Study of Hegel's Critical Theories of "Vorstellung" and Their Relevance for Hegelianism and Theology* (Ann Arbor: University Microfilms, 1985), 348. Cf. Hegel's review of Göschel's *Aphorismen* (W11, 378).

27. Karl Rosenkranz, *Georg Wilhelm Friedrich Hegels Leben* (Darmstadt: Wissenschaftliche Buchgesellschaft, 1963), 182–83. Cf. Karl Rosenkranz, "The Report of Rosenkranz about Hegel's Philosophy of Spirit in the Early Jena Period," in *Hegel's System of Ethical Life and First Philosophy of Spirit*, trans. and ed. H. S. Harris and T. M. Knox (Albany: State University of New York Press, 1979), 257.

28. The translation of this passage is largely that of Dale Schlitt.

29. Vitor Westhelle points out that

the main accomplishment of Goeschel was to avoid a static dualism that posits *Vorstellung* and concept as alternative modes of presenting the truth. In Hegel's view, this was certainly a reason for joy, and this is certainly the motif that elicited the praise that Goeschel's *Aphorismen* received from the master. (*Religion and Representation*, 467)

30. Dubarle, "Révélation de dieu," 124–26.

31. Williamson, *Introduction to Hegel's Philosophy of Religion*, 300.

32. Ibid., 303.

33. Min, "Hegel's Retention of Mystery," especially 343–51.

34. One might question that what is rational is logically necessary. Aquinas would argue that the Incarnation is rational but not necessary in logical priority to its occurrence. However, for Hegel, absolute knowledge grasps the absolute

according to its essence and internal relations, i.e., *an und für sich*. Ultimately the rational does not admit of contingency.

35. Min, "Hegel's Retention of Mystery," 350.
36. Mure, *A Study*, 22.
37. Ibid., 25.
38. What Hegel says of words and names applies to language in general.
39. Hegel's intention for his logic is that it be internally complete, without need of further development as to the articulation of the basic structure of thought, and that in the absolute idea there be a momentary grasp of the whole in the pure form of thought.

The movement from immediacy to mediation in terms of otherness and then to unity of the two was to be an exhaustive analysis and synthesis of reality as thought. In this sense and on this level there was to be no need of or possibility for a fourth, whether that be a presupposed substratum or a further synthetic moment. The triadically structured movement of pure thought was for Hegel to constitute the paradigmatic and constitutive structure of all reality as taken up in thought. (Schlitt, *Hegel's Trinitarian Claim*, 47)

40. Claude Bruaire, *Logique et religion chrétienne dans la philosophie de Hegel* (Paris: Editions du Seuil, 1964), 100.
41. Hans-Georg Gadamer, *Truth and Method*, trans. Garrett Barden and John Cumming (New York: Seabury Press, 1975), 318.
42. Ibid., 319.
43. Ibid., the section titled "Language as Horizon of a Hermeneutic Ontology," 397–447. "A thought first attains determinate existence in being formulated in words." Hans-Georg Gadamer, *Hegel's Dialectic; Five Hermeneutical Studies*, trans. P. Christopher Smith (New Haven: Yale University Press, 1976), 94.
44. Gadamer, *Truth and Method*, 422.
45. Gadamer, *Hegel's Dialectic*, 94. Against Hegel, Gadamer agrees with Heidegger, who

refers to language as the "house of being," in which we dwell with such ease. To be sure, there occurs in it, indeed precisely in it, the disconcealment of what is present to the point of the objectification of the latter in a statement. But being itself, which has its abode there, is not disconcealed as such, but keeps itself concealed in the midst of all disconcealment occurring in speaking; concealed as in speaking, language itself remains essentially concealed. (Ibid., 97)

46. In answer to the charge that Hegel's philosophy is culturally relative because its expression, if not bound up with the German language in particular, is bound up with language in general, John Burbidge argues that philosophy "sets its own vernacular in the context of a more universal comprehension of human culture. Therefore it can discriminate between the inherently universal validity of thought and the relative expressions of subjective psychology."

Burbidge, *On Hegel's Logic,* 33. The fact of the recognition of the limitations of linguistic expression is the transcending of those limitations. "Broadly speaking the instinctive act differentiates itself from the intelligent and free act in that the latter occurs with consciousness." SL, 37; W5, 27]; cf. Burbidge, *Hegel's Logic,* 242, n. 39. We should further note that the transcendence of the contingent and relative features of language is not a transcendence of language *tout court* for "there is no supra-linguistic realm of thought. Using a particular set of categories and grammatical structures, the philosopher distinguishes the essential universal concept from the contingent forms of its representations." Burbidge, *Hegel's Logic,* 33.

John McCumber argues that the movement from prephilosophical language to philosophical language is the movement of the realization of the concept through and in language that parallels the threefold mediation of philosophy in the *Encyclopaedia* § 575–77. John McCumber, "Hegel's Philosophical Languages," in *Hegel-Studien,* vol. 14, pp. 183–96 (Bonn: Bouvier, 1979).

47. Clark, *Logic and System,* 205. Similarly, Daniel Cook notes that speculative thought and language

> must lead consciousness ... from the exoteric to the esoteric. For this reason it cannot initially abandon the images and ideas of ordinary language and can never completely do away with them. Ordinary language and the consequent conflict between it and speculative thinking is essential to the philosophical endeavor itself and can never be utterly transcended. (Cook, *Language in the Philosophy of Hegel,* 172)

Cook's use of "transcended" here may be ambiguous. We would be clear that while language itself cannot be transcended as the necessary means of philosophical thinking, the limitations of the language employed can be transcended when one thinks speculatively.

48. Cf. Gadamer, *Truth and Method,* 405.

49. Merold Westphal, "Hegel and Gadamer," in *Hermeneutics and Modern Philosophy,* ed. Brice Wachterhauser (Albany: State University of New York Press, 1986), 79.

50. "End," "aim," "goal," or "purpose." We should not focus too much on the various connotations of these English terms. Hegel himself uses *Ende* in proximity with *Zweck.* Our task is to understand the category of teleology and to interpret it in answer to our problem.

51. This example comes from E. Harris, *An Interpretation,* 273.

52. Ibid., 271.

53. Ibid.

54. Ibid., 272. Mure also appears to take the view of teleology as continual development.

> Yet activity is always to some extent an end in itself, and the means in which it is expressed is, therefore, never quite a means. And equally ... teleological

activity is never completely self-realizing, and its means is, therefore, always a means to an end beyond it. (Mure, *A Study*, 256–57)

55. Refer to E. Harris, *An Interpretation*, 271.

56. "If absolute knowing has a finality at all, it is a finality related not to chronological succession, but to timelessness; it is the knowing of an exhaustively mediated present, and the suite of spiritual configurations which form this mediation are dialectically, and not chronologically constituted." Robert McRae, *Philosophy and the Absolute* (Dordrecht: Martinus Nijhoff, 1985), 116.

57. Théodore Geraets points out, with reference to *Encyclopaedia* § 553 and § 577, that the freedom which characterizes conceptual thought "cannot be found in a closed system, but only in sharing the essentially open, eternally producing activity, generation and fruition of eternal self-articulation ... as absolute spirit." Théodore Geraets, "The Impossibility of Philosophy ... and Its Realization," *The Owl of Minerva* 16, 1 (Fall 1984): 38. Moreover, Geraets points out that Hegel's dialectic is a dialogical, interrogative process (cf. Enc § 81, R) whose achievement in pure thought is the comprehension of this infinite, eternal process but not an end to the interrogative process itself.

The comprehension is thus *total*, because it is comprehension of the necessarily total interrogation, but this comprehension is *never achieved*, because the total and concrete interrogation, which is the dialectic of the thought-object and of subjective cognizing, does not cease. (Théodore Geraets, "Dialectique et interrogation," *Archives de Philosophie* 39 [1976]: 283)

We agree that to Hegel's thinking the achievement of the absolute idea is the full elucidation of the structure of the dialectic but that for him the dialectical process itself is unending. Our precise problem is in saying that the process of absolute spirit is ever progressing but never complete-able, that the eternal comprehension of the process is open-ended and hence never com-prehensible. It may be that when we conceive absolute unity-in-difference (which is absolute spirit in its fullness), one of us inevitably conceives *unity*-in-difference and another, unity-in-*difference*. Absolute unity suggests a still point "beyond which nothing greater can be conceived." Absolute difference suggests movement and further advance. We must attempt to think both, and the result, we suggest, is the conception of timeless movement in which all things are thought together without loss of singularity in a movement of fully achieved unification — in a movement beyond movement, in a paradoxical way of speaking.

58. E. Harris expounds Hegel's view by saying,

The end is in truth eternally realized in its perpetual struggle to realize itself. Sound moral theory finally recognizes the Good to be *the good life*, the constant endeavour of the good will, the unceasing striving to overcome evil, the continuing and unfailing love of one's neighbour, which does not consist in any single act or any final state of affairs but is an established disposition of mind and will and a persistent on-going activity. (E. Harris, *An Interpretation*, 286)

## Chapter 4
## Philosophy's Sublation of Religion

In the title to this chapter, I have translated *Aufhebung* as "sublation." "Suspension" and "supersession" have connotations that would make either an unacceptable translation in regard to the arguments of this thesis. "Sublation" is so uncommon a word in English that it appears neutral and hence can carry the multiple meanings that are laid upon it without needlessly prejudicing the reader. However, we should note that reading "sublation" has a different effect on the English reader than reading *Aufhebung* in its original context has on the German reader, because *Aufhebung* and its verb forms are everyday words with everyday uses in German. By contrast, the English "sublation" is rarely seen outside Hegel translations and commentaries.

1. Ibid., 41.

2. The teleological thrust of the dialectic is evident in both the active and the passive voices, since the *telos* is the agent and the opposing moments are the objects of the teleological activity.

3. Mure, *A Study*, 45.

4. Hegel speaks of becoming in which being and nothing are "vanishing, sublated moments" in "*determinate* unity." SL, 105; W5, 112. But there is a question whether Hegel can meaningfully speak of sublation prior to the first true determination in *Dasein*, since the "determination" of being/nothing/becoming is "absence of determination" prior to *Dasein*.

5. Cf. E. Harris, *An Interpretation*, 297; also cf. Schlitt, *Hegel's Trinitarian Claim*, 28, n. 95, where the author describes the quadraplicity as "immediacy, progression, result, and then renewed immediacy" and then in concise form refers to difficulties that may arise from a tetradic interpretation of Hegel's dialectic. We should be clear that the dialectic is movement and therefore resists any structural fixing.

6. Mure, *A Study*, 45.

7. Ibid., 38.

8. As the movement of cancellation, preservation, elevation, Schlitt notes that sublation for Hegel is "the key to an understanding of the relation between finite human thought and the one, infinite movement of pure thought," and therefore it is questionable whether we can think pure being as beginning without a prior movement from finite, determinate thought. Schlitt, *Hegel's Trinitarian Claim*, 75–76.

9. More precisely, absolute spirit is not actual prior to actual thinking. Absolute spirit is the single activity of self-thinking thought, implicit as a goal within each phase of its own actualization.

10. Ricoeur, "The Status of *Vorstellung*," 77.

11. Ibid., 88.

12. Quentin Lauer, "Hegel on Proofs for God's Existence," *Kant-Studien* 55 (1964): 445.

13. Ibid., 465.

14. E. Harris, *An Interpretation*, 293.

15. Mure, *A Study*, 301.

16. According to Robert McRae, the finality of Hegel's system is the dialectical and "timeless" constitution of all the shapes of spirit in and by absolute knowing. "This knowing is satisfied, and is in a sense final, when the fullness of its mediation accounts for, and is accounted for by, its subjective presentation," that is, when the empirical and *a posteriori* elements are mediated within the system of thought. McRae, *Philosophy and the Absolute*, 118.

17. E. Harris, *An Interpretation*, 293.

18. Søren Kierkegaard, *Concluding Unscientific Postscript*, trans. David Swenson (Princeton: Princeton University Press, 1968), 112.

19. Aquinas also had argued the superiority of faith to reason, but on the basis of the superiority of divine authority to human authority, not on the basis of faith *per se*. *Summa Theologiae* 2a2ae, 2, 10.

20. Ping, *The Genius of the Christian Religion*, 292.

21. Kierkegaard, *Concluding Unscientific Postscript*, 369; and Ping, *The Genius of the Christian Religion*, 307–8.

22. Kierkegaard, *Concluding Unscientific Postscript*, 195; cf. Ping, *The Genius of the Christian Religion*, 298.

23. "Kierkegaard rejects any objective foundation of faith." Louis Dupré, *Kierkegaard as Theologian* (London: Sheed and Ward, 1963), 123.

24. "Kierkegaard has lodged the Christian categories in a reflection so deep that no intellectual argument can ever again take hold of them. Henceforth, faith is only a matter of a choice: Do you wish to believe, or not." Ibid., 144.

25. Kierkegaard, *Concluding Unscientific Postscript*, 179–80.

26. Ibid., 182.

27. Lauer, "Hegel on Proofs for God's Existence," 459.

28. Bruaire, *Logique et religion chrétienne*, 100.

29. Lauer, "Hegel on the Identity of Content," 273.

30. Louis Dupré says there is a sense in which philosophy is subordinate to religion, viz., by connecting the realm of pure thought of Hegel's logic with the realm of nature in its otherness through the concept of spirit. "Faith shows how the Spirit connects the two by assuming the entire creation into the divine identity of the Word." Louis Dupré, *A Dubious Heritage* (New York: Paulist Press, 1977), 71. It is true that Hegel's philosophy has not only its initial *élan* from Christianity but also returns to the Christian representation of spirit for the all-important concept of spirit by which Hegel links the logic and the *Realphilosophie*. Cf. *A Dubious Heritage*, 70–71. We would add to Dupré's insights, however, that Hegel's philosophy, when fully developed, "stands on its

own"; it does not depend for its truth upon any representation. Our claim for the "subordination" of philosophy to religion is that spirit for its life, concretion, truth, and actualization needs religious life and practice so as to come to full fruition which it cannot do by philosophy alone, unless "philosophy" becomes so widely defined as to be indistinguishable from rational religion. This claim will be argued and developed at various places in the succeeding pages.

# Chapter 5
# Truth

1.  From one perspective, Hegel can be seen to carry through the condition of the possibility of truth to its idealistic foundation in the creative activity of absolute spirit. If there is truth, then in some fashion mind and being must be one. Aquinas had argued that truth in its primary meaning is in the intellect and in its secondary meaning is in things insofar as things are in relation to an intellect. The intellect "is true in so far as it has the likeness of the thing in thought, which is the form of the intellect in the act of knowing." *Summa Theologiae* Ia, 16, 2. Truth then is defined as "the conformity of the intellect and the thing" [*per conformitatem intellectus et rei veritas definitur*]. *Summa Theologiae* Ia, 16, 2. We note three things: (1) that for Aquinas truth is a likeness in form between intellect and thing and that Hegel's notion of truth agrees with Aquinas's notion on this point in that for Hegel the form of thought is the form of the world; (2) that for Aquinas we can speak of truth as one in the sense that "all things are true by virtue of one first truth to which their being gives them a likeness.... Truth is one in the divine intellect according to which all things are termed true" (*Summa Theologiae* Ia, 16, 6) and that Hegel's notion agrees with Aquinas's as well on this point; and (3) that the continuity and the difference of Aquinas and Hegel lies in the fact that Aquinas stresses being as the fundamental category and speaks of thought in relation to being, while Hegel stresses thought as the fundamental category and speaks of being in relation to thought.

It should be evident that Aquinas's notion of truth is closer to Hegel's than some more recent truth theories, e.g., that of empirical realism. Certainly Hegel would find Aquinas's explanation of truth "idealistic in principle." Does not the convertibility of being and truth imply the creative activity of one infinite mind? How else can intellect and thing conform unless they are implicitly one? If for Aquinas all things are true in reference to the divine intellect from which they have their being and intelligibility, and one were to develop this way of thinking as an immanent process of the divine, might not the systematic result resemble Hegelian metaphysics? As we will see, Hegel's idea of truth has a wholly active and historical character at variance with the medieval worldview, but Hegel's thinking is rooted in certain basic metaphysical insights on the relation of God and the created order. If we note a philosophical kinship between Aquinas and Hegel, it is indicated in Hegel's own feelings of estrangement in his own time that has regrettably lost scientific interest in metaphysics. Hegel's words in the preface to the first edition of his *Science of Logic* are both sad and condemnatory.

> The fact is that there no longer exists any interest either in the form or the content of the metaphysics of an earlier time or in both together. If it is remarkable when a nation has become indifferent to its constitutional theory, to its national sentiments, its ethical customs and virtues, it is certainly no less remarkable when a nation loses its metaphysics, when the spirit which employs itself with its own pure essence is no longer an actual existence in the life of the nation. (SL, 25; W5, 13)

2. Of course, this notion of truth would not be incorrect if it were understood and explained as the positing and presupposing activity of the self-determining activity of the concept, as will be explained, but obviously that is not how this idea of truth is commonly understood. We should note, however, that even this common notion of truth can be thus shown by Hegelian reasoning to have an idealistic foundation.

3. Within a more static and "realistic" framework we find Aquinas expressing the same point.

> Everything is said to be true without qualification according to its relation to the intellect on which it depends. Thus artificial things are said to be true by their relation to our intellect ... natural things are said to be true in so far as they bear a likeness to the types which are in the divine mind. (*Summa Theologiae* Ia, 16, 1]

> Artificial things are simply and in themselves false in so far as they are deficient in the form of their art; hence an artist is said to produce a false work when it is a deficient working of his art. (*Summa Theologiae* Ia, 17, 1)

4. In this study, *Erkenntnis* is translated as "cognition" so as to distinguish it from *Wissen*, even though the English "knowledge" would be a natural rendering for *Erkenntnis* in many contexts, were it not for the value of distinguishing *Erkenntnis* from *Wissen*.

5. G. R. G. Mure, *An Introduction to Hegel* (Oxford: Oxford University Press, 1940), 168.

6. Edmund Husserl, *Logical Investigations*, trans. J. N. Findlay, (New York: Humanities Press, 1970), vol. 2, investigation 6, p. 765.

7. Mure, *A Study*, 271.

8. "As subject ... since it [the absolute idea] synthesizes Life with Cognition, it is absolute personality; but again, as object it is its own personality which it knows." Ibid., 291.

9. Ibid.

10. The preface to the *Phenomenology of Spirit* is notorious. It attempts to do what it disclaims to do, viz., to state the result of the philosophical system before working through the process — "how and what can properly be said about philosophy in a preface ... cannot be accepted as the way and mode in which to

present the truth of philosophy." PS, 1; W3, 11. However, there is no contradiction in presenting the wide view before proceeding with the process even though it supposes what has yet to be established. It is like a statement of the plot. Even as an overview of Hegel's philosophy, the preface is "inadequate," as Loewenberg notes. Despite its inadequacies, however, the preface provides "a summary and vindication of the nature and function of philosophic knowledge." J. Loewenberg, *Hegel's Phenomenology: Dialogues on The Life of Mind* (LaSalle, Ill.: Open Court, 1965), 2–3. With the wide view provided by the preface and the force and insight of some of Hegel's comments, we will be better able to grasp and appraise Hegel's truth theory.

11. Loewenberg, *Hegel's Phenomenology*, 5.

12. We should be clear that necessity for Hegel has the same meaning as truth, i.e., the agreement of concept and reality through the actualization of the concept. Logical necessity, Hegel says, means that "what is, is in its being, its concept." PS, 34; W3, 54–55.

13. E. Harris, *An Interpretation*, 29.

14. Mure, *An Introduction*, 167.

15. Lauer, "Hegel on Proofs for God's Existence," 461.

16. For our purposes we need not differentiate the 1824 and 1827 lectures concerning the practical element of the concept of religion.

17. Ricoeur, "The Status of *Vorstellung*," 86.

18. Théodore Geraets, "La verité entre concept et récit," *Archivio di Filosofia* 53 (1985): 409–20.

19. Geraets, "La verité," 418.

20. Geraets, "La verité," 420, *pace* Geraets, however, we argue that the temporal process has an eternal end, which is a "conclusion" in its etymological sense and which contains and "transcends" its temporal process.

# Chapter 6
## Hegel's Rational Religion

1. We equate God with the absolute spirit of Hegel's philosophy. No one can doubt that in Hegel's philosophy God is spirit, but there is not the same universal agreement that spirit is God. It seems to us that to speak of the principle and goal of the entire movement of reality as the movement of one *Geist* in the process of thinking itself as infinite, eternal subject, *noēsis noēseōs*, and not to equate this absolute spirit with God is to say "God" is not God, i.e., to use the word "God" for what is not ultimate. If God and absolute spirit are not equated, how are they to be distinguished? When we say "yellow is a color," but "color is not yellow," we distinguish genus and species, but no such distinction between God and spirit can obtain here. Whatever in Hegel's thought is "that beyond which no greater can be thought" we term "God," and philosophically

we do not use the term "God" for any representation or any particular element described in Hegel's system. If the "absolute actual personality" (Enc § 147, *Zusatz*, p. 292), or the "absolute *person*" (Enc § 151, *Zusatz*, p. 295), is somehow to be conceived more narrowly than the "*identity* eternally returning and returned into itself ... the judgement [or "original partition," *Urteil*] *in itself* and *in one knowing*" (Enc § 554), we do not understand how such a distinction or specification is to be made in Hegel's thought. We agree with the arguments of Quentin Lauer on this matter in "Is Absolute Spirit God?" 89–99.

2. Mure says philosophy would not be possible if "there were not in every man, however intermittently he feels it, and however inadequately he interprets it, the nisus towards attaining a total and unreserved self-consciousness." Mure, *An Introduction*, 80. The élan of the movement of spirit is directed toward spirit knowing itself as spirit.

3. Hegel opposes any sort of philosophical elitism that would make philosophical knowledge a kind of *gnosis* of the few which deprives the common lot of humanity of philosophy's relevance and benefit. Rosenkranz records Hegel as saying, in an introduction to his lectures on the system of philosophy from his Jena period, that

> we must note briefly that philosophy as the science of reason is by its very nature meant for everyone because of its universal mode of being. Not everyone achieves it, but that is not to the point, any more than it is to the point that not every man gets to be a prince. The disturbing thing about some men being set over others only lies in this, that it might be assumed that they were distinct by nature and were essentially of another kind. (Rosenkranz, *Georg Wilhelm Friedrich Hegels Leben*, 186. Cf. "The Report of Rosenkranz about Hegel's Philosophy of Spirit," 260)

The import of the achievement of speculative philosophy is very clearly for Hegel not "aristocratic," but "democratic."

4. Dale Schlitt, "Hegel on the Kingdom of God," *Église et Théologie* 19 (1988): 63.

5. Hegel states clearly, "The church is the kingdom of God, *the achieved* presence, *life and preservation*, and enjoyment of the spirit." LPR III, 151; V5, 87. We are amending Hegel's thought at this point to argue that the church is the incipient realization of the kingdom of God, and that the kingdom will be realized in full when the world is wholly in accord with the concept of reason. See further on this question in the text.

6. Eric von der Luft, *Hegel, Hinrichs, and Schleiermacher on Feeling and Reason in Religion* (Lewiston, N.Y.: Edwin Mellen Press, 1987).

7. Cf. ibid., 16–17 and 165.

8. Ibid., 165.

9. In commenting on a draft of Hinrichs's work, Hegel did not suggest any change in content but only a change in style and presentation. Cf. ibid., 9–12.

10. Ibid., 28.

11. Ibid., 79.

12. Herman Hinrichs, *Religion in Its Internal Relationship to Systematic Knowledge*, trans. Eric von der Luft, in Luft, *Hegel, Hinrichs, and Schleiermacher*, 484.

13. Luft, *Hegel, Hinrichs, and Schleiermacher*, 113.

14. Cf. Hinrichs, *Religion in Its Internal Relationship,* 486.

15. Ibid.

16. Pierre-Jean Labarrière, recorded discussion comments, in *Hegel: le Sens de l'Esprit Absolu/The Meaning of Absolute Spirit: Proceedings of the International Symposium on the Meaning of Absolute Spirit Held at the University of Ottawa November 6–8, 1981,* ed. Théodore Geraets (Ottawa: University of Ottawa Press, 1984), 143.

17. Charles Taylor, recorded discussion comments, in *Hegel: le Sens de l'Esprit Absolu/The Meaning of Absolute Spirit: Proceedings of the International Symposium on the Meaning of Absolute Spirit Held at the University of Ottawa November 6–8, 1981,* edited by Théodore Geraets, (Ottawa: University of Ottawa Press, 1984), pp. 138–47.

18. J. M. E. McTaggart, *Studies in Hegelian Cosmology*, 250.

19. Ibid., 251.

20. Frederick Copleston, *Fichte to Nietzsche*, 240–41.

21. McTaggart, *Studies in Hegelian Cosmology*, 248–49.

22. Charles Taylor, *Hegel* (Cambridge: Cambridge University Press, 1975), 494.

23. "*After* the event of the Incarnation one can, and should, go on to ask about the conditions of its possibility, anthropological and ontological, and to make sense of it by mediating it.... [T]o leave the Incarnation as a brute fact and no more, would be to deprive it of its universal, salvific significance to mankind." Min, "Hegel's Retention of Mystery," 349.

24. Karl Barth, *Protestant Thought: From Rousseau to Ritschl*, trans. Brian Cozens (New York: Harper and Row, 1959), 304.

25. Ibid.

26. We should note that while theologically unable to accept Hegel's philosophy, Barth has evidently studied Hegel's thought with remarkable insight, deep appreciation, and even, perhaps, awe. When Barth poses the question why Hegel has not become for Protestantism what Aquinas has been for Catholicism (ibid., 268), the answer seems to entail not only theological objections to Hegel's thought, but, Barth suggests, humankind's loss of "self-confidence" in rationality in the time after Hegel.

> The attempt to make a key to every lock must itself have come under suspicion, a deep resignation must have been born not only as far as the How of the Hegelian method was concerned, but also as regards its That, as regards the possibility of such a universal method at all. There is no other way of explaining the retreats which now began in every sector of the front.

The natural scientists withdrew into their laboratories. The historians retired to a consideration of the none-too-subtle question: how was it in those days? The philosophers fell back upon psychology and the theory of knowledge, the theologians upon the historical Jesus and upon the history of religion in general. (Ibid., 291–92)

Barth points out that modern humanity's self-confidence in its rational powers reached its summit in the philosophy of Hegel, and all later intellectual developments are declines from that summit. Ibid., 292.

Barth acknowledges that Hegel's thought may yet assert itself more forcefully. "It may be that the dawn of the true age of Hegel is still something that will take place in the future" (ibid., 274), although Barth himself does not see this new age on the horizon, and unlike Moses, Barth himself seems not to hail this promised land with any confidence.

27. For example, Küng, *The Incarnation of God;* Schlitt, *Hegel's Trinitarian Claim;* James Yerkes, *The Christology of Hegel* (Missoula, Mont.: Scholars Press, 1978).

# Selected Bibliography

### Hegel's Works

Hegel, Georg W. F. *Einleitung in die Geschichte der Philosophie*. Edited by Johannes Hoffmeister. Hamburg: Felix Meiner, 1940; reprint, 1966.

_____. *The Encyclopaedia Logic*: Part 1 of the *Encyclopaedia of the Philosophical Sciences* with the *Zusätze*. Translated by T. F. Geraets, W. A. Suchting, and H. S. Harris. Indianapolis: Hackett Publishing, 1991.

_____. *Faith and Knowledge*. Translated by Walter Cerf and H. S. Harris. Albany: State University of New York Press, 1977.

_____. "Hegel's Foreword to Hinrichs's *Die Religion im inneren Verhältnisse zur Wissenschaft*." Translated by A. V. Miller. In *Beyond Epistemology*, edited by Frederick Weiss. The Hague: Martinus Nijhoff, 1974.

_____. "Hegel's Foreword to Hinrichs's *Die Religion im inneren Verhältnisse zur Wissenschaft*." Translated by Eric von der Luft. In *Hegel, Hinrichs, and Schleiermacher on Feeling and Reason in Religion*. Lewiston, New York: Edwin Mellen Press, 1978.

_____. *Hegel's Lectures on the History of Philosophy*. 3 vols. Vol. I translated by E. S. Haldane. Vols. II and III translated by E. S. Haldane and Frances Simson. London: Kegan Paul, Trench, Trübner, 1892 (vol. I), 1894 (vol. II), 1896 (vol. III); reprint, London: Routledge and Kegan Paul, 1963.

_____. *Hegel's Logic*. Part 1 of the *Encyclopaedia of the Philosophical Sciences*. Translated by William Wallace. Oxford: Clarendon Press, 1975.

_____. *Hegel's Philosophy of Mind*. Part 3 of *The Encyclopaedia of the Philosophical Sciences*. Translated by William Wallace, with *Zusätze* translated by A. V. Miller. Oxford: Clarendon Press, 1971.

_____. *Hegel's Philosophy of Nature*. Part 2 of *The Encyclopaedia of the Philosophical Sciences*. Translated by William Wallace. Oxford: Clarendon Press, 1970.

_____. *Hegel's Philosophy of Right*. Translated by T. M. Knox. Oxford: Oxford University Press, 1967.

_____. *Hegel's Science of Logic*. Translated by A. V. Miller. London: George Allen and Unwin, 1969.

———. *Introduction to the Lectures on the History of Philosophy*. Translated by T. M. Knox and A. V. Miller. Oxford: Clarendon Press, 1985.

———. *Lectures on the Philosophy of Religion*. 3 vols. Edited and translated by Peter Hodgson et al. Berkeley: University of California Press, 1984 (vol. I), 1987 (vol. II), 1985 (vol. III).

———. *The Phenomenology of Mind*. Translated by J. B. Baillie. New York: Harper and Row, Torchbooks, 1967.

———. *Phenomenology of Spirit*. Translated by A. V. Miller. Oxford: Clarendon Press, 1977.

———. *Vorlesungen: Ausgewählte Nachschriften und Manuskripte*. Vols. 3–5: *Vorlesungen über die Philosophie der Religion*. Part 1: *Einleitung. der Begriff der Religion*. Edited by Walter Jaeschke. Hamburg: Felix Meiner, 1983. Part 2: *Die bestimmte Religion*, 1985. Part 3: *Die vollendete Religion*, 1984.

———. *Werke in zwanzig Bänden*. Frankfurt am Main: Suhrkamp Verlag, 1969.

## Secondary Works

Averroës. *Averroës on the Harmony of Religion and Philosophy*. Translated by G. Hourani. London: Luzac, 1961; reprint 1976.

Barth, Karl. *Protestant Thought: From Rousseau to Ritschl*. Translated by Brian Cozens. New York: Harper and Row, 1959.

Black, Edward. "Religion and Philosophy in Hegel's Philosophy of Religion." *The Monist* 60, 2 (1977): 198–212.

Blanchette, Oliva. "The Philosophic Beginning." *Thought* 56 (September 1981): 251–62.

Bloch, Ernst. *Sujet-Objet*. Translated by Maurice de Gandillac. Paris: Gallimard, 1977.

Bruaire, Claude. *Logique et religion chrétienne dans la philosophie de Hegel*. Paris: Editions du Seuil, 1964.

Burbidge, John. *On Hegel's Logic*. Atlantic Highlands, N.J.: Humanities Press, 1981.

Clark, Malcolm. *Logic and System: A Study of the Transition from "Vorstellung" to Thought in the Philosophy of Hegel*. The Hague: Martinus Nijhoff, 1971.

Cook, Daniel. *Language in the Philosophy of Hegel*. The Hague: Mouton, 1973.

Copleston, Frederick. *Fichte to Nietzsche*. Vol. 7 of *A History of Philosophy*. Westminster: Newman Press, 1963.

———. "Hegel and the Rationalization of Mystery." In *New Studies in Hegel's Philosophy*, edited by Warren Steinkraus. New York: Holt, Rinehart and Winston, 1971.

Crites, Stephen. "The Gospel According to Hegel." *The Journal of Religion* 46 (1966): 246–63.

Desmond, William. *Art and the Absolute*. Albany: State University of New York Press, 1986.

———. "Hegel and the Problem of Religious Representation." *Philosophical Studies* 30 (1984): 9–22.

Donceel, Joseph. *The Searching Mind.* Notre Dame, Ind.: University of Notre Dame Press, 1979.

Dubarle, Dominique. "Révélation de dieu et manifestation de l'esprit dans la philosophie de Hegel." In *Manifestation et révélation.* Paris: Editions Beauchesne, 1976.

Dupré, Louis. *A Dubious Heritage.* New York: Paulist Press, 1977.

———. "Hegel's Absolute Spirit." In *Hegel: le Sens de l'Esprit Absolu/The Meaning of Absolute Spirit: Proceedings of the International Symposium on the Meaning of Absolute Spirit Held at the University of Ottawa November 6–8, 1981,* edited by Théodore Geraets, pp. 127–47. Ottawa: University of Ottawa Press, 1984.

———. *Kierkegaard as Theologian.* London: Sheed and Ward, 1963.

———. *The Other Dimension.* Garden City, N.Y.: Doubleday, 1972.

———. "Religion and Representation." In *The Legacy of Hegel: Proceedings of the Marquette Hegel Symposium Held at Marquette University June 2–5, 1970,* edited by J. J. O'Malley, K. W. Algozin, H. P. Kainz, and L. C. Rice. The Hague: Martinus Nijhoff, 1973.

Ely, Peter. *Hegel's Version of the Ontological Proof: Key to the Reconciliation of Religion and Philosophy.* Ann Arbor, Mich.: University Microfilms, 1974.

Fackenheim, Emil. *The Religious Dimension in Hegel's Thought.* Bloomington: Indiana University Press, 1967.

Findlay, J. N. Foreword to *Hegel's Logic.* Oxford: Clarendon Press, 1975.

Fitzer, Joseph. "Hegel and the Incarnation: A Response to Hans Küng." *Journal of Religion* 52 (1972): 240–67.

Gadamer, Hans-Georg. *Hegel's Dialectic; Five Hermeneutical Studies.* Translated by P. Christopher Smith. New Haven: Yale University Press, 1976.

———. *Truth and Method.* Translated by Garrett Barden and John Cumming. New York: Seabury Press, 1975.

Geraets. Théodore. "Dialectique et interrogation." *Archives de Philosophy* 39 (1976): 269–83.

———. "The End of the History of Religions 'Grasped in Thought'." *Hegel-Studien* 24 (1989): 55–77.

———. "The Impossibility of Philosophy ... and Its Realization." *The Owl of Minerva* 16, 1 (Fall 1984): 31–38.

———. "Socialité universelle et 'histoire divine' selon Hegel." *Archivio di Filosofia* 54 (1986): 637–51.

———. "La Verité entre concept et récit." *Archivio di Filosofia* 53 (1985): 409–20.

Harris, Errol. *An Interpretation of the Logic of Hegel.* Lanham, Md.: University Press of America, 1983.

Harris, H. S. "Religion as the Mythology of Reason." *Thought* 56 (September 1981): 301–15.

Haught, John. *Religion and Self-Acceptance*. Lanham, Md.: University Press of America, 1980.

Hinrichs, Herman. *Religion in Its Internal Relationship to Systematic Knowledge*. Translated by Eric von der Luft. In *Hegel, Hinrichs, and Schleiermacher on Feeling and Reason in Religion*. Lewiston, N.Y.: Edwin Mellen Press, 1987.

Hodgson, Peter. "Hegel's Christology: Shifting Nuances in the Berlin Lectures." *Journal of the American Academy of Religion* 53, 1 (1985): 23–40.

Husserl, Edmund. *Logical Investigations*. 2 vols. Translated by J. N. Findlay. New York: Humanities Press, 1970.

Hyman, Arthur and James Walsh, eds. *Philosophy in the Middle Ages*. Indianapolis: Hackett, 1973.

Jaeschke, Walter. *Reason in Religion: The Foundations of Hegel's Philosophy of Religion*. Translated by J. Michael Stewart and Peter Hodgson. Berkeley: University of California Press, 1990.

————. *Die Religionsphilosophie Hegels*. Darmstadt: Wissenschaftliche Buchgesellschaft, 1983.

————. "Speculative and Anthropological Criticism of Religion: A Theological Orientation to Hegel and Feuerbach." *Journal of the American Academy of Religion* 48 (September 1980): 345–64.

————. *Die Vernunft in der Religion: Studien zur Grundlegung der Religionsphilosophie Hegels*. Stuttgart–Bad Cannstatt: Frommann-Holzboog, 1986.

Kainz, Howard. *Paradox, Dialectic, and System*. University Park: Pennsylvania State University Press, 1988.

Kierkegaard, Søren. *Concluding Unscientific Postscript*. Translated by David Swenson. Princeton: Princeton University Press, 1968.

Klubertanz, George. *St. Thomas Aquinas on Analogy*. Chicago: Loyola University Press, 1960.

Küng, Hans. *The Incarnation of God*. Translated by J. R. Stephenson. New York: Crossroad, 1987.

Labarrière, Pierre-Jean. Recorded discussion comments. In *Hegel: le Sens de l'Esprit Absolu/The Meaning of Absolute Spirit: Proceedings of the International Symposium on the Meaning of Absolute Spirit Held at the University of Ottawa November 6–8, 1981*, edited by Théodore Geraets, pp. 138–47. Ottawa: University of Ottawa Press, 1984.

Lakeland, Paul. *The Politics of Salvation*. Albany: State University of New York Press, 1984.

Lauer, Quentin. "Hegel on Infinity." *Thought* 56 (September 1981): 287–300.

————. "Hegel on Proofs for God's Existence." *Kant-Studien* 55 (1964): 443–65.

————. "Hegel on the Identity of Content in Religion and Philosophy" and "Reply to My Commentators." In *Hegel and the Philosophy of Religion*, edited by Darrel Christensen. The Hague: Martinus Nijhoff, 1970.

————. *Hegel's Concept of God*. Albany: State University of New York Press, 1982.

―――――. "Is Absolute Spirit God?" In *Hegel: le Sens de l'Esprit Absolu/The Meaning of Absolute Spirit: Proceedings of the International Symposium on the Meaning of Absolute Spirit Held at the University of Ottawa November 6–8, 1981*, edited by Théodore Geraets, pp. 89–99. Ottawa: University of Ottawa Press, 1984.

―――――. *A Reading of Hegel's* Phenomenology of Spirit. New York: Fordham University Press, 1976.

Léonard, André. *Commentaire littéral de la logique de Hegel*. Louvain: Editions de l'Institut Supérieur de Philosophie, 1974.

Loewenberg, J. *Hegel's Phenomenology: Dialogues on The Life of Mind*. LaSalle, Ill.: Open Court, 1965.

Luft, Eric von der. *Hegel, Hinrichs, and Schleiermacher on Feeling and Reason in Religion*. Lewiston, N.Y.: Edwin Mellen Press, 1987.

Lyttkens, Hampus. *The Analogy between God and the World*. Uppsala: Almqvist and Wicksells Boktryckeri, 1952.

McCumber, John. "Hegel's Philosophical Languages." In *Hegel-Studien*, vol. 14, pp. 183–96. Bonn: Bouvier, 1979.

McRae, Robert. *Philosophy and the Absolute*. Dordrecht: Martinus Nijhoff, 1985.

McTaggart, J. M. E. *Studies in Hegelian Cosmology*. Cambridge: Cambridge University Press, 1901.

Migne, Jacques Paul, ed. *Patrologiae cursus completus* [Series latina]. Parisiis, 1844– [82].

Min, Anselm. "Hegel on the Foundation of Religion." *International Philosophical Quarterly* 14, 1 (1974): 79–99.

―――――. "Hegel's Absolute: Transcendent or Immanent?" *The Journal of Religion* 56 (1976): 61–87.

―――――. "Hegel's Retention of Mystery as a Theological Category." *Clio* 12 (1983): 333–53.

―――――. "The Trinity and the Incarnation: Hegel and Classical Approaches." *The Journal of Religion*, 66 (1986): 173–93.

Mure, G. R. G. *An Introduction to Hegel*. Oxford: Oxford University Press, 1940.

―――――. *A Study of Hegel's Logic*. Oxford: Clarendon Press, 1950.

Murray, Michael. "Time in Hegel's *Phenomenology of Spirit*." *The Review of Metaphysics* 34 (1981): 682–705.

Pannenberg, Wolfhart. *The Idea of God and Human Freedom*. Translated by R. Wilson. Philadelphia: Westminster Press, 1973.

Panofsky, Erwin. *Gothic Architecture and Scholasticism*. New York: New American Library, 1976.

Ping, Charles. *The Genius of the Christian Religion: A Study in the Religious Thought of Georg Wilhelm Friedrich Hegel*. Ann Arbor, Mich.: University Microfilms, 1961.

Pomerleau, Wayne. "The Accession and Dismissal of an Upstart Handmaid." *The Monist* 60, 2 (1977): 213–27.

Rahner, Karl and Herbert Vorgrimler. *Theological Dictionary*. Translated by Richard Strachan. New York: Herder and Herder, 1965.

Ricoeur, Paul. "The Status of *Vorstellung* in Hegel's Philosophy of Religion." In *Meaning, Truth and God*, edited by Leroy Rouner. Notre Dame, Ind.: University of Notre Dame Press, 1982.

Rohs, Peter. *Form und Grund: Interpretation eines Kapitels der Hegelschen Wissenschaft der Logik*. Bonn: Bouvier, 1969.

Rosenkranz, Karl. *Georg Wilhelm Friedrich Hegels Leben*. Berlin, 1844; reprint, Darmstadt: Wissenschaftliche Buchgesellschaft, 1963.

———. "The Report of Rosenkranz about Hegel's Philosophy of Spirit in the Early Jena Period." Translated and edited by H. S. Harris and T. M. Knox. In *Hegel's System of Ethical Life and First Philosophy of Spirit*. Albany: State University of New York Press, 1979.

Schillebeeckx, Edward. *Jesus. An Experiment in Christology*. Translated by H. Hoskins. New York: Seabury Press, 1979.

Schlitt, Dale. "Book Review of Walter Jaeschke's critical edition of Hegel's *Vorlesungen über die Philosophie der Religion*, in three parts." *The Owl of Minerva* 16, 1 (1984): 69–80; 18, 2 (1987): 179–97; 19, 1 (1987): 63–83.

———. "Feature Book Review: Hegel's Berlin Lectures: The Consummate Religion." *The Owl of Minerva* 19, 1 (1987): 70.

———. "Hegel on the Kingdom of God." *Église et Théologie* 19 (1988): 33–68.

———. *Hegel's Trinitarian Claim*. Leiden: E. J. Brill, 1984.

Schmitz, Kenneth. "The Conceptualization of Religious Mystery." In *The Legacy of Hegel: Proceedings of the Marquette Hegel Symposium Held at Marquette University June 2–5, 1970*, edited by J. J. O'Malley, K. W. Algozin, H. P. Kainz, and L. C. Rice. The Hague: Martinus Nijhoff, 1973.

Shepherd, William. "Hegel as a Theologian." *Harvard Theological Review* 61 (1968): 583–602.

Siemens, Reynold. "Hegel and the Law of Identity." *The Review of Metaphysics* 42, 1 (September 1988): 103–27.

Smith, John. "Hegel's Reinterpretation of the Doctrine of Spirit and Religious Community." In *Hegel and the Philosophy of Religion*, edited by Darrel Christensen. The Hague: Martinus Nijhoff, 1970.

———. "The Relation of Thought and Being: Some Lessons from Hegel's *Encyclopedia*." *The New Scholasticism* 38, 1 (January 1964): 22–43.

Stace, W. T. *The Philosophy of Hegel: A Systematic Exposition*. New York: Macmillan, 1924; reprint, New York: Dover, 1955.

Taylor, Charles. Recorded discussion comments. In *Hegel: le Sens de l'Esprit Absolu/The Meaning of Absolute Spirit: Proceedings of the International Symposium on the Meaning of Absolute Spirit Held at the University of Ottawa November 6–8, 1981*, edited by Théodore Geraets, pp. 138–47. Ottawa: University of Ottawa Press, 1984.

———. *Hegel*. Cambridge: Cambridge University Press, 1975.

Thomas Aquinas. *Summa Contra Gentiles*. Rome: Desclée and Herder, 1934.

———. *Summa Contra Gentiles*. Book I translated by Anton Pégis; book II translated by James Anderson; book III translated by Vernon Bourke; book IV translated by Charles O'Neil. Garden City, N.J.: Doubleday, 1955 (book I), 1956 (book II), 1956 (book III), 1957 (book IV).

———. *Summa Theologiae*. Edited by Thomas Gilbey. Cambridge: Blackfriars, 1964.

Tracy, David. *Blessed Rage for Order*. New York: Seabury Press, 1975.

Wagner, Falk. "Die Aufhebung der religiösen Vorstellung in den philosophischen Begriff." *Neue Zeitschrift für Systematische Theologie und Religionsphilosophie* 18 (1976): 44–73.

Westhelle, Vitor. *Religion and Representation: A Study of Hegel's Critical Theories of "Vorstellung" and Their Relevance for Hegelianism and Theology*. Ann Arbor, Mich.: University Microfilms, 1985.

Westphal, Merold. "Hegel and Gadamer." In *Hermeneutics and Modern Philosophy*, edited by Brice Wachterhauser. Albany: State University of New York Press, 1986.

Williamson, Raymond. *Introduction to Hegel's Philosophy of Religion*. Albany: State University of New York Press, 1984.

Yerkes, James. *The Christology of Hegel*. Missoula, Mont.: Scholars Press, 1978.

# Index

Anselm, 21
Aquinas, Thomas, 19–20, 46, 65, 89–93, 101–2, 106, 138, 183, 193 n. 1, 198 nn. 20 and 21, 199 n. 34, 203 n. 19, 204–5 n. 1, 205 n. 3, 208 n. 26
Aristotle, 19, 20, 21, 22, 143, 148
Art, 49, 77–78, 81–82, 84, 141, 176
Athenagoras, 17
Augustine, 18, 96
Averroës, 19, 31

Barth, Karl, 182, 208 n. 26
Bauer, Bruno, 167
Being, 29, 66–67, 114, 116, 193 n. 4, 197 n. 4, 200 n. 45, 202 n. 4
Böhme, Jacob, 26, 97
Burbidge, John, 51, 196 n. 15, 200 n. 46

Christ, 31–32, 41, 71, 83, 122, 127, 128
Christian religion, the, 33, 41, 43, 46, 51, 58, 59, 71, 76, 83, 84, 85, 96, 118, 121, 126–29, 151–54, 167, 169, 175, 180–83, 185, 188
Clark, Malcolm, 75–76, 104
Clement of Alexandria, 17
Concept of religion, the, 31–36, 41–43, 51, 84, 149–54, 158
Cook, Daniel, 197 n. 7, 198 n. 17, 201 n. 47
Copleston, Frederick, 65, 179, 182, 194 n. 8

Daub, Carl, 173
Descartes, René, 22
Desmond, William, 86, 92–93, 198 n. 18
Determinate religion, 42, 43

Devotion (*Andacht*), 34, 118
Dialectic, 29–30, 43, 50, 53, 59, 64, 66, 91, 94, 103–4, 108, 113–17, 123, 129, 133, 135, 137, 141, 142, 144–45, 175, 176, 202 nn. 57, 2, and 5
Dubarle, Dominique, 76, 98
Dupré, Louis, 203 nn. 23 and 24, 204 n. 30

Eternity, 30, 103–6, 108–11, 161, 177–78, 185, 202 n. 57
Ethical Life (*Sittlichkeit*), 169, 171, 173, 177

Fackenheim, Emil, 49
Fall, the, 64, 179, 181, 189
Feuerbach, Ludwig, 72
Fichte, Johann Gottlieb, 26
Findlay, J. N., 195 n. 11

Gadamer, Hans–Georg, 102–5, 109, 200 nn. 43 and 45
Geraets, Théodore, 161–62, 201 nn. 56 and 57, 206 n. 20
Göschel, Carl Friedrich, 88–89, 97–98, 199 nn. 26 and 29

Harris, Errol, 52, 55, 108, 123, 124, 125, 196 n. 20, 201 n. 51, 202 n. 58
Hinrichs, Herman, 48, 173–76, 207 n. 9
History of philosophy. *See* Philosophy, history of
History of religion. *See* Religion, history of
Hotho, Heinrich Gustav, 36, 84, 132, 164, 170 195 n. 11
Husserl, Edmund, 140

221

Identity, 42, 50–52, 54, 56–57, 59, 74, 129, 137, 149, 206 n. 1
Incarnation, the, 31, 43, 44, 64, 71, 100, 121, 179, 181–82, 189, 199 n. 34, 208 n. 23
Inclusive subjectivity, 144, 149–50, 165

Jacobi, Friedrich Heinrich, 26, 39, 47, 93, 169
Jaeschke, Walter, 96
Jesus, 31–32, 83, 94, 180, 181, 208 n. 26
Judgement (*Urteil*), 42, 141

Kant, Immanuel, 24–26, 36, 38, 52, 93, 124, 140, 148, 168, 183
Kierkegaard, Søren, 47, 113, 123, 125–29, 133, 135, 182
Klubertanz, George, 198–99 n. 21
Küng, Hans, 194 n. 7

Labarrière, Pierre–Jean, 176
Lauer, Quentin, 23, 72, 122, 134, 157, 193 n. 3, 194 n. 1, 206 n. 1
Léonard, André, 53
Loewenberg, J., 146, 205 n. 10
Luft, Eric von der, 173–75
Lyttkens, Hampus, 198 n. 19

Marheineke, Philipp, 173
McCumber, John, 200 n. 46
McRae, Robert, 201 n. 56, 203 n. 16
McTaggart, J. M. E., 9, 179–81, 182, 194 n. 8
Metaphysics, 38, 39, 66–67, 114–15, 132, 133, 139, 145, 148, 186, 204–5 n. 1
Min, Anselm, 99–100, 208 n. 23
Mure, G. R. G., 53, 54, 101–2, 103, 113, 116, 117, 123–25, 133, 140, 143, 144, 201 n. 54, 206 n. 2

Mystical, the, 65

Necessity, 118–20, 124, 150, 165, 169, 181, 193 n. 1, 199 n. 34, 206 n. 12

Ockham. *See* William of Ockham

Pascal, Blaise, 22, 35, 47
Philosophy, history of, 30, 32, 156–57, 166
Ping, Charles, 41, 127–28, 182

Religion, concept of. *See* Concept of religion
Religion, history of, 33, 188
Ricoeur, Paul, 87, 93–95, 122, 157, 160
Rohs, Peter, 54, 58, 196 nn. 20 and 25
Rosenkranz, Karl, 97 207 n. 3

Schleiermacher, Friedrich Daniel Ernst, 26, 39, 47, 93
Schlitt, Dale, 193 n. 3, 198 n. 14, 200 n. 39, 203 n. 5
Spinoza, Benedict, 22, 56, 58, 108, 110, 113, 114, 119, 129, 135
Stace, W. T., 55

Tatian, 17
Taylor, Charles, 176–77, 181, 182
Thomas à Kempis, 21
Tracy, David, 65–66, 67, 98
Trinity, 20, 31, 44, 84–85, 179, 181

Wagner, Falk, 59
Westhelle, Vitor, 199 nn. 26 and 29
Westphal, Merold, 104
William of Ockham, 21
Williamson, Raymond, 89